TOMART illustrated DISNEYANA

catalog and price guide

CONDENSED EDITION
of fastest growing values

by Tom Tumbusch

Edited by Bob and Claire Raymond

Consultant David R. Smith, Archivist
The Walt Disney Company

Judy Sikora, Copy Editor

Color Photography by Tom Schwartz

Wallace-Homestead Book Company
Radnor, Pennsylvania

Prices listed are based on the author's experience and are presented as a guide for information purposes only. No one is obligated in any way to buy, sell, or trade according to these prices. Condition, rarity, demand and the reader's desire to own determine the actual price paid. No offer to buy or sell at the prices listed is intended or made. If there are any questions as to the prices listed, please direct them in writing to the author c/o Tomart Publications, P.O. Box 292102, Dayton, OH 45429. Buying and selling is conducted at the reader's risk. Neither the author nor publisher assumes any liability for any losses suffered for use of, or any typographic errors contained in, this book. All value estimates are presented in U.S. dollars. The dollar sign is omitted to avoid needless repetition.

Tomart's illustrated DISNEYANA catalog and price guide will be updated on a regular basis. If you wish to be notified when the supplements become available, send a self-addressed stamped envelope to Tomart Publications, P.O. Box 292102, Dayton, OH 45429.

First published by Wallace-Homestead Book Company in 1990

Library of Congress Catalog Card Number: 89–51678

ISBN: 0–87069–558–4   Printed in U.S.A.

1 2 3 4 5 6 7 8 9 0

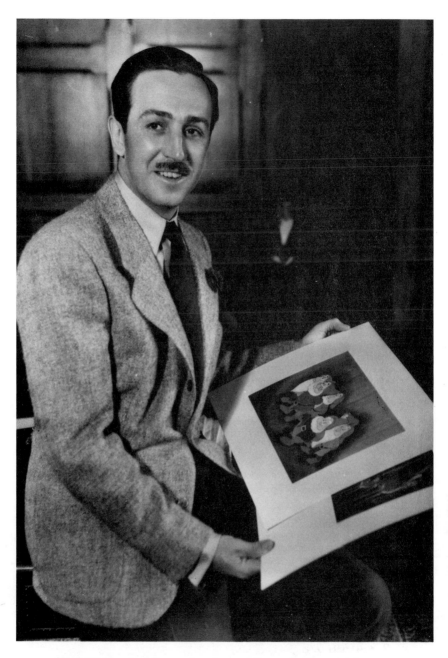

Walt Disney holding cels released through Courvoisier.

ACKNOWLEDGEMENTS

This book builds on the ones produced in the past. Many people have helped. Some made major contributions to this extensive DISNEYANA research project. Every bit of information, photocopy, or actual photo helped make the book a little better. I would like to thank these individuals plus the many collectors and dealers who permitted me to photograph their Disneyana items.

Special thanks go to Bob Lesser, Harvey and Jan Kamins, Richard Kamins, Ted Hake, Harry Hall, Jim Silva, Bob Coup, John Koukoutsakis, Joe Sarno, Bill Joppeck, Dave and Elaine Hughes, Jerry and Mona Cook, Joel Allen, Bruce and Linda Cervon, Donna and Keith Kaonis, Bernie Shine, Morris Hamasaki, Phil Ellis, Ed and Elaine Levin, Bob Molinari, Don and Dee Toms, Evie Wilson, Jean Toll, Charles Sexton, Karl Price, Stan Pawlowski, Kim and Julie McEuen, Jerry Turner, David Welsh, Jack Melcher, Ron Stark, Josha Arfer, Ron Aubry, Lee and Linda Kazee, Bill Young, Rick Koch, John Lawson, Ray Walsh, Dennis Mathiason, Roger Le Roque, Nick Farago, Keith Schneider, Greg Shelton, George McIntyre, Von Crabill, George Hagenauer, Dean Mancina, Rebecca Greason and Virginia Gann.

For their support and guidance outside the field of Disneyana I am deeply indebted to Stan Freedman, Barbara DeHays, Judy Sikora and Rebecca Trissel.

Everyone who enjoys the color photography can thank Tom Schwartz and his assistants, Fred Boomer and Terry Cavanaugh.

And to the editors -- collectors Bob and Claire Raymond, and Dave Smith, Archivist, The Walt Disney Company and Paula Sigman, Assistant Archivist -- for all the time they spent reviewing, correcting, and otherwise improving the manuscript, I extend my personal gratitude.

Lastly it's a proud father who thanks his son, Thomas N., for creating the original data base on an Atari 800 computer, taking calls and providing general backup; and daughter, Amy, for assistance in many ways, particularly in assembling and filing the thousands of bits of data. It's been a joint effort.

Tom Tumbusch
March 1989

TABLE OF CONTENTS

COLOR PLATES

ESSENTIAL GUIDELINES TO THE DATA
AND PRICES IN THIS BOOK

At each classification there is a brief overview of the material covered, followed by item listings. Included is the best information currently available on manufacturers and the years licensed. THIS INFORMATION IS NOT ALL-INCLUSIVE AND ERRORS UNDOUBTEDLY EXIST. The data is most reliable for the years 1934-50 and from 1970 to 1989, although it might not be precise. In some cases the possible error is the listing of a year licensed. More often it will be the absence of a year in which Disney products were made.

Price range estimates are based on the experience of the author as witnessed at major shows across the country. Auction results are not generally considered. (See page 18 for a more complete explanation of prices listed.) In cases where sufficient trade experience is absent, best guesstimates are provided. Where a price range refers to different size items, the high end refers to the largest size. The greater the price spread, the more valuable a strictly mint item. Also, in the case of a wide price range, "fine" grade items are worth substantially less than the average or mid-price shown. If the price range shown is 10-100, the fine value is around 40 not 50 to 55.

This sometimes flawed information is provided in the belief that available data will lead to improved scholarship in the future. Any collectors or former Disney employees having data or dated Disneyana material that clarifies this information are encouraged to send photos of items or photocopies of printed material to Tom Tumbusch c/o Tomart Publications, P.O. Box 292102, Dayton, Ohio 45429.

ABOUT THE AUTHOR

Tom Tumbusch has had a life-long interest in popular culture subjects. He is a graduate of the University of Dayton where he studied fine art, communications, and business. He became involved in dramatics in high school which led to a long association with amateur and professional musical theatre. A series of articles published in *Dramatics Magazine* was collected into his first book, a small paperback of production tips entitled *A New Look at Musical Theatre*.

He became a correspondent for *Variety* while working for a leading regional advertising agency. The paperback was expanded into the *Complete Production Guide to Modern Musical Theatre* published by Richard Rosen Press as part of their Theatre Student series in 1969. *Guide to Broadway Musicals* followed in 1972, was revised in 1978, and completely rewritten and expanded in 1983.

Concurrently in the mid-seventies an advertising campaign led Tumbusch to old radio broadcasts. Included in some programs were commercials offering premium giveaways. The search for information on these items came up blank and the *illustrated Radio Premium catalog and price guide* was the result. Tumbusch contributed to other publications including *The Nostalgia Bible* and the Time-Life *Encyclopedia of Collectibles*.

"Reconstructing history from bits of information scattered all over the nation was a welcome relief from the hectic pace of the advertising world," he said. "And I felt the system used to develop the premium information could be used for other collecting areas." His next choice was the field of Disney collectibles.

Tomart's *illustrated DISNEYANA catalog and price guide* was the resulting four volume work. This definitive series covers the entire spectrum of Disney merchandise manufactured or licensed for sale in the U.S. The books also include collectors' information plus a history of Walt Disney, his characters and The Walt Disney Company. The Condensed Edition presents the latest values from the most popular categories edited from the four volume series.

Tumbusch has been a guest at conventions featuring musical theatre, Disneyana and other popular culture subjects. He has appeared on TV and radio talk shows and been consulted on nostalgia subjects by such publications as the *Chicago Tribune, Los Angeles Times, Orlando Sentinel, USA Today, The Wall Street Journal* and *Money Magazine*.

FOREWORD

The Condensed Edition of Tomart's *illustrated DISNEYANA catalog and price guide* features the latest values on the fastest growing Disney collectible items.

This edition has been made possible by the success of the original series. The contribution of additional information has been very supportive and this book represents a more collective effort of people who share an interest in Disneyana.

Prices for the items listed reflect the current market as of publication and update prices in previously published volumes.

The index has been expanded to help the reader find a specific item of interest with greater ease. Cross references are also included to previous volumes to help owners verify a photo reference.

The goal of Tomart's DISNEYANA continues to be twofold: 1) to identify and classify, and 2) to provide an estimate of value. In regards to the latter, it should be noted that price guides are out of date the day they roll off the press. Prices go up and down -- and may vary from one area to another. The price ranges shown in this book are, however, relative to each other at the time of publication. In that context, with condition taken into account, prices can be adjusted for local demand factors and changes in market trends.

This book is a compilation of major Disneyana sources and the experience of the author. The manuscript has been reviewed by David R. Smith, Archivist, The Walt Disney Company, and by Disneyana experts, Claire and Bob Raymond. Specialized collectors have been consulted on their areas of expertise.

Disney characters and theme park graphics are, of course, copyrighted by The Walt Disney Company.

With the continued support of the collectors and sellers of Disneyana, the work of finding and publishing additional items of Disneyana will go forward. If you like Tomart's DISNEYANA series, please express your thanks to the wonderful, helpful people listed in the acknowledgements.

THE MARKET REPORT

Press agents have been reaching for adjectives to describe the collector growth and skyrocketing value of Disneyana over the past five years. In 1986 a cel and master background estimated to sell for up to $2,500 brought $20,900 at auction. In November 1988 a black and white Mickey Mouse cel and master background sold for a record $148,500.

In 1986 Robert Lesser sold his comic character collection. The *New York Times* reported the ultimate buyer paid $1.2 million for the collection. The impact on prices was immediately seen at the January 1987 All American Collectibles show at Glendale, California. Each major show since has seen escalated prices and brisk sales.

The Alexander Gallery in New York and The Shine Gallery in Los Angeles are presenting Disneyana as popular culture art and attracting a new type of buyer for museum grade collectibles.

The Disney Company expanded theme park operations and improved merchandise. Limited edition collectibles are helping to expand the collector base. Disney Stores are being opened in major shopping malls across the country and The Disney Family Catalog mail order operation makes collectible merchandise available to anyone. The Disney Gallery at Disneyland features theme park original art and limited edition prints and other art collectibles. The Animation Gallery at the Disney/MGM Studios Theme Park at Walt Disney World offers original animation art and other animation collectibles. New 10-year agreements with Sears and McDonalds are building a new grass roots base for future development. So the outlook for continued growth looks strong.

Mushrooming prices have resulted in more specialized collecting. Character watches have regained popularity after a period of slow movement. Disneyland souvenirs are big on the West Coast and perhaps signal future strength for items from Walt Disney World, EPCOT and other attractions. The prime market for ceramics is still in the West, but the trend is flowing eastward.

The number of Disneyana collectors continues to grow. Membership in both The Mouse Club and The National Fantasy Fan Club for Disneyana Collectors is increasing.

There was a time when only items produced prior to 1955, in particular those of the 30's, were considered collectible. In more recent years, attractive limited edition items have contributed to the growth of the Disneyana hobby. The amount of new "collectible" merchandise is almost staggering, but eventually it all seems to be sold. In fact, many people collect mainly newer items. Therefore, limited editions and other new items actively collected have been included in this book.

The market for animation cels and backgrounds is universally strong, with interest being primed by reports from each succeeding auction. Outstanding examples of figural items -- principally 30's celluloid toys and figures, older tin wind-ups, character dolls, and porcelain bisque figures -- are seeing values from $1,000 to $5,000 with extremely rare items in mint condition selling for over $10,000.

Along with market appreciation have come more frequent reports of fakes and misrepresented pieces. Foreign licensed merchandise is being imported in much greater quantities and being sold for much higher prices than the pieces would command in the licensed country. Often it would be less expensive to enjoy a week in Europe and buy a few items on the trip than to purchase the same items in the U.S.

WHAT IS DISNEYANA?

Any item associated with The Walt Disney Company or its affiliated operations, past or present, is considered to be Disneyana. The degree to which any item of Disneyana becomes collectible depends on many factors. What is utilitarian today will become collectible tomorrow. Certainly some segments of the total Disneyana spectrum are more popular than others. Even infringement items (those items not authorized or licensed by Disney) are also collected on a selected basis.

People who buy Disneyana can be categorized into four groups:

1) Consumers who purchase items such as a toy, game, doll, etc. to be used, and then discarded or sold in a garage sale.

2) Admirers who purchase a Disney piece because it appeals to them as a souvenir or a small piece of art they can own. It is bought with the intent to preserve and perhaps display as they would any object of art.

3) Collectors who purchase a piece of Disneyana to add it to a collection. These people may collect only plates, figures, records, or items from the 30's. They may confine their interest to several specialties or collect everything marked with a Disney copyright. Collectors buy Disneyana for their personal enjoyment and, perhaps, for investment.

4) Dealers and investors buy Disneyana with the intent of realizing a profit from their knowledge and interest.

Many who buy Disneyana as utilitarian toys know they sell well at garage sales and flea markets. And, of course, the other three types of purchasers are interdependent on each other as buyers, sellers, and traders in the secondary market.

WHAT DISNEYANA IS INCLUDED?

Identified products produced under a U.S. license and selected Canadian licenses are included. Many of these products were produced in England, Germany, Japan, Mexico, France or other countries, but were distributed in the U.S.

There are tens of thousands of items produced under licenses granted in about every country on Earth. It is known the early records of William B. Levy, Disney's first foreign licensing agent, were destroyed. Examples of foreign merchandise brought into this country by collectors and dealers suggest, however, the volume of merchandise items probably exceeded the total produced under U.S. licenses, especially for the very early years (1930-34).

15

Only a few examples of foreign licensed merchandise are included in Tomart's illustrated DISNEYANA series. There are several reasons for this sparseness, including the void of information on what was produced, the difficulties monitoring rarity and values outside the U.S. and Canada, currency fluctuations and general collecting interest in such items. Most collectors realize items never sold in this market are obviously "rare" to find, but may be commonly available and purchased at a much lower cost in the countries of origin.

WHY COLLECT DISNEYANA?

Collecting anything -- stamps, old bottles, primitive tools or baseball cards -- has many self-satisfying rewards. Finding a rare or perfect condition piece in some junk shop is exciting. Every antique shop or flea market provides the thrill of the hunt and the chance to meet others who share a collecting interest.

Each item in a collection becomes a trophy the collector has found, bought, won in an auction, or otherwise traded to obtain. To collect is to succeed at your own pace under whatever terms and goals you set for yourself. Collecting provides a comfortable niche in a highly competitive world -- one that the collector controls -- as opposed, for example, to job or other pressures they cannot. And every collector "knows" that if they lose interest, they "can get more" than they paid when the collection is sold. Unfortunately, such assumptions are not always the case.

Everything is collected by somebody. The number of what many might consider to be "odd-ball" collector's items can be confirmed in any collecting journal. However, ask any antique/collectibles dealer about the most popular collecting categories. They'll tell you that Disneyana is among the strongest -- and growing.

WHAT MAKES DISNEYANA SO COLLECTIBLE?

Disneyana items are particularly attractive as collectibles. Some of the major reasons are as follows:

1) Disneyana is art. In most cases, it is good art which often reflects the popular culture of the era in which it was produced. Older pieces are recognized as art and are exhibited in some of the world's most famous museums ... and in a growing number of toy and children's museums. Even the Smithsonian Institution is planning a popular culture museum. Yet, Disneyana is art anyone can own.

2) Disneyana has been produced in large quantities since the 20's. There are millions of Disneyana items floating around out there to keep intriguing the collecting interest. Disneyana is found worldwide.

3) Disneyana is associated with Walt Disney, one of the world's best known and respected individuals. Even though a minute portion of Disneyana was created by him, Walt Disney continues to be a major driving force behind his company's characters long after his death in

1966.

4) Disneyana is still being produced. Some items are being manufactured as limited editions. Many are marketed by mail, thus creating a larger market for Disney collectibles with each passing day. Likewise, visitors to Disney theme parks are exposed to more and more collectible merchandise and the Disney collecting interest. As older items increase in value, many collectors specialize in more modern pieces. The result -- nearly anyone can collect some type of Disneyana which is interesting as art and has a reasonable prospect of growing in value.

5) Disneyana brings high prices at major auctions. More people are learning there is a solid base for value as a result of this exposure. They also became familiar with items they would like to own and seek out dealers in Disneyana. There are full-time dealers all across the country who make a large part of their living buying and selling Disneyana. However, it takes knowledge and experience to succeed in such a venture. Speculating in Disneyana is risky. Buying Disneyana as an investment generally leads to a small bank account and a large inventory which may be difficult to liquidate for actual value.

Whatever your interest in Disneyana, be assured you are in good company. Movie personalities, industrialists, government officials, and people in all walks of life collect various forms of Disneyana. Yearly sales of old and new Disneyana items are estimated to exceed $500 million.

HOW TO USE THIS BOOK

Tomart's *illustrated DISNEYANA catalog and price guide* was designed to be an authoritative and easy to use collector's guide. It utilizes an identification and classification system designed to catalog Disneyana.

No one, including the Disney Archives, can list the hundreds of thousands, perhaps millions, of different Disneyana items produced since the 1920's. However, this system contains the framework in which they may be organized.

The format is a classification system -- one similar to the yellow pages of a telephone book. If you want to locate a book, figure, or wind-up toy, just look under those headings. In some cases, you will find a cross index reference to help locate the item of interest. Certain classifications, such as Books, are divided into smaller groups. An explanation of these groups is found, in this example, under the broad heading of "Books."

Common usage and collecting focus were the main guidelines used in establishing classifications. Cross references and special notes are used throughout to help direct the reader. A detailed index is found on page 291.

The classification format is standardized for the most part. However, if there was a better way to communicate more information in less space, a different approach was used.

Items are listed by year at each classification. Each item is assigned a reference code number consisting of one letter and four numbers. Use of these numbers in dealer and distributor ads and collector's correspondence is encouraged. Permission for such use to conduct buying, selling, and the trade of Disneyana in lists, letters or ads is hereby granted.

The identity code numbers also serve to match the correct listing to a nearby photo. In certain vast classifications, such as "Advertisements", a cross section of available material is used for illustration. No specific ads are listed. Identity code numbers in the Condensed Edition are the same as the ones in the four volume series.

THE VALUES IN THIS PRICE GUIDE

This book is a collector's and dealer's guide to average prices, in a range of conditions. The real value of any collectible is what a buyer is willing to pay. No more. No less. Prices are constantly changing -- up and down.

Many factors have a bearing on each transaction. Not the least of these are perceived value, emotional appeal, or competitive drive for ownership.

Reference to the section on "Values" provides a more detailed rationale on prices. What it all boils down to is the two ways Disneyana items are sold ... pre-priced or by auction to the highest bidder.

This book reports market prices based on items sold at leading antique shows and flea markets, as well as toy and antique advertising shows from Boston to Glendale, CA. It reflects sales on the whole rather than just auction results.

Collectors who buy at shows can generally purchase for less. Often, they have first choice of items offered for sale; sometimes at exceptional bargain prices. But they also incur substantial time and travel expenses.

Mail and gallery auctions are preferred by collectors who don't have the time or the ability to visit major shows. Money spent and current resale value also tend to be of less concern to the auction buyer. The winning bidder must outlast the others who have an emotional fix on ownership or perhaps need the specific piece to "complete" a collection.

It's difficult to say who actually spends more money in pursuit of their collecting interest ... the show goer or the auction buyer. This much is sure. There are substantial costs involved beyond the money spent on collectibles by the show goer not normally considered in the "price" ... and higher overhead costs are included in mail or gallery auction sales where the "price" includes everything.

The up-to-date values in this edition are a compilation of information received through March 1989.

RARITY

Some Disneyana items were available for years after they were first offered. Examples of this type of continuous distribution include many early porcelain bisque figures, watches, trains, popular toys, and similar items. On the other hand, some items were available once and for a brief

18

time. Paper items had less kid tolerance than sturdy metal ones -- and thus are rarer -- especially punch or cut-out items which self-destructed when used. Some were designed to be consumed or disposed of -- items such as gum and bread wrappers, candy, paper cups, plates, or napkins. A major part of the charm of collecting this type of Disneyana is the fact they have survived the intended use.

Rarity doesn't always equate to value. In Disneyana collecting, the strongest demand is often generated by people wishing to obtain items of special interest. Thus rarity is only a part of value. Character popularity, cross-overs to other collecting fields (such as pocket knives, plates, dolls, books, etc.) and the type of item (anything showing a camera, Santa Claus, or telephone, for example) may become stronger factors. Other collectors often specialize in areas which cross the Disneyana line.

Price also has some regional influences. In Los Angeles and New York, prices are substantially higher. Selling prices are lowest in the Midwest -- especially around Chicago and in Indiana, Ohio, Minnesota and Pennsylvania. Disneyana still becomes available on a regular basis in these areas, and thereby fulfills demand. Realizing these regional price situations exist, and that isolated individuals will always let emotions rule in auction bidding, the values represented in this guide are average estimates taking into account what a given item has sold for over the last two years.

Another factor which enhances value is the completeness of the original box or package. In some cases, the boxes are more attractive than the item itself. Some include instructions, catalogs, and extra parts which made the toy more fun. The actual box sometimes increases value and demand by perhaps 20 to 50 percent.

CONDITION

Condition, like beauty, is in the eye of the beholder. When money becomes involved, the eye seems to take on an added dimension of X-ray vision or rose-colored glasses -- depending on whether you are buying or selling.

However, let there be no mistake about the price spreads set down on the following pages. The top price refers to items in "Mint", like-new condition -- no scratches, never repaired, free of any defects whatsoever selling in a top market. If paper, a mint item must be free of marks, creases (other than the original folds), ragged edges or corners, and any other defect or blemish. Mint items probably were never in circulation -- original stock, or not used.

The low end price describes items in "Good" condition. That means, first and foremost, the item is complete with absolutely no parts or pages missing. Creases, dirt, marks, chips, tears, bends, scratches, minor rust or corrosion damage, repairs without original materials, and similar shortcomings are factors that depreciate value and regulate such items to the complete, but "Good" classification. Of course, some complete items with excessive wear, major rust, deep cuts, or other mistreatment are less than good; either poor or only a source for repair parts. The value of poor condition items would obviously be less than the lowest price shown.

The range in between Good and Mint is the condition in which most items will be found. Very Good, Fine, or Very Fine are the most common grades used. In general, a "Fine" condition item would be one with only minor wear, scratches, blemishes, etc. The item has been in circulation -- used, but given some care. The value would be somewhat less than the average in the price range as true "Mint" items command a premium.

Rarity, condition, and the amount of material available in the market-place all have a direct effect on value. The overriding factor, however, is the number of individuals who wish to acquire any given item of Disneyana and have the money to satisfy their desire.

All prices shown in this book are U.S. dollar values with the dollar signs removed to avoid repetition. The amount shown is for an unboxed item, except in such cases as board games where the box is an integral part of a complete item.

INFORMATION ON COLLECTING DISNEYANA

There are new Disneyana publications and the quality of the existing ones continues to hit new heights. Here is a run down on what's currently available and how to subscribe.

The Mouse Club Newsletter is mailed to members as part of annual dues. It contains information on collecting, Disney events and artists, theme parks, and club news, plus buy, sell, and trade ads. Obtain membership information from The Mouse Club, 2056 Cirone Way, San Jose, CA 95124.

Fantasy Line, published by The National Fantasy Fan Club for Disneyana Collectors, is distributed to members. The publication features articles on theme park activities, newer collectibles, collecting Disneyana, Disney artists, events and club news. Also contains collectors' ads. Get membership information by writing P. O. Box 19212, Irvine, CA 92713.

The "E" Ticket features articles on Disney and other theme parks. A good specialized publication. To obtain copies of this newsletter, contact The "E" Ticket, 20560 Alaminos Dr., Saugus, CA 91350.

Collector's Showcase, P. O. Box 6929, San Diego, CA 91350; *Antique Toy World*, 394 Belle Plaine, Chicago, IL 60618; *Antique Trader*, P. O. Box 1050, Dubuque, IA 52001; *Toy Shop*, 700 E. State St., Iola, WI 54990 and other antique publications occasionally feature articles and ads relative to Disneyana.

StoryboarD Magazine is the newest entry in the Disneyana collecting field. This color publication covers the entire spectrum of Disneyana collecting. Subscription information can be obtained by writing Bobit

Publishing, 2512 Artesia Boulevard, Redondo Beach, CA 90278.

Christie's East, 219 E. 67th St., New York, NY 10021; Sotheby's 1334 York Ave. at 72nd St., New York, NY 10021 and Phillips, 406 E. 79th St., New York, NY 10021 publish catalogs for periodic Disneyana and comic art gallery auctions.

Hake's Americana, P. O. Box 1444, York, PA 17405; The Collector's Book Store, 1708 N. Vine St., Hollywood, CA 90028; Cartoons & Comics, P.O. Box 1694, Burbank, CA 91507 and Historicana, 1642 Robert Rd, Lancaster, PA 17601 publish mail auction catalogs containing Disneyana.

WHERE TO FIND LOST DISNEYANA

Disneyana merchandise and other collectible items first came into being in the early 20's. Walt Disney had several ventures before Mickey Mouse and all the other famous Disney characters.

Mickey Mouse merchandise was produced beginning in 1929. Posters, promotional material, and a few toys were produced in conjunction with the previous ventures.

The earlier activities of Walt Disney himself centered around Paris, France; Chicago, Kansas City and then Hollywood. One would expect Disneyana from the early days would most likely surface in one of those cities (See the *Disney Time Line*). However, Disneyana from any period seems to pop up just about anywhere.

Mickey Mouse is the single most recognized graphic symbol in the world. Walt Disney was probably the most universally recognized personage ever to inhabit the earth. No political, religious, or social bounds could contain his fame and popularity.

World War II closed off the profitable European film market, and many of the early Disneyana suppliers. In response, Walt Disney developed special films to appeal to the moviegoers of South America. As a result, Disneyana items were licensed to Mexican and other Latin American manufacturers. Many of these items found their way into the western United States before Disney licensing territories were strictly policed.

New York and Burbank have always served as the centers for licensing. Merchandise catalogs and promotional flyers tend to show up more often in these areas.

Disneyland was opened in Anaheim, California in 1955 and Walt Disney World near Orlando, Florida in 1971. Tokyo Disneyland became the first theme park outside the U.S. in 1983. Merchandise connected with the parks will obviously be found in greater quantities closer to the parks.

Disney theme parks also have Disneyana shops where newer limited edition items, animation cels, and other collectible merchandise can be purchased. Some new, limited edition pieces and theme park merchandise is available by mail. Details are given at each park classification. Once found, Disneyana is traded in a variety of ways.

TOY SHOWS AND EVENTS

Collectors have many sources available to them. Each year there are two national conventions, a growing number of specialized shows and many regional toy shows where Disneyana is sold.

Often, Disneyana items are found at Antique Toy or Advertising shows. Antique shows and flea markets are other good sources. The larger the event, the better your chances of finding outstanding Disneyana. Smaller events often yield good bargains.

The following is a list of major events where Disneyana is available:

Antique Toy and Doll World Shows
Kane County Fairgrounds
St. Charles, Illinois

The All-American Collector's Show
Glendale, California

The J.F. Kennedy Toy Show
JFK Airport, New York

Indianapolis Antique Advertising
Show and Collectors Carnival

Philadelphia International Antique Toy Convention

Brimfield Associates Spring Show
Atlantic City

Midwest Collectors Toy Association
Toy and Doll Show, Dayton, Ohio

Atlanta Toy Show

San Francisco Bay Area
Antique Advertising and Toy Show

Big-D Super Collectibles Show
Dallas, Texas

More than one show may be held at these locations each year. A growing number of other toy and/or antique advertising shows where Disneyana is sold are being held regionally. Announcements publicizing these events appear regularly in antique and toy publications.

ANTIQUE SHOWS AND FLEA MARKETS

The majority of the author's collection has been obtained from local and regional antique shows, antique malls, and flea markets. It doesn't take long to spot dealers who trade in nostalgia collectibles. Get to know them and tell them about areas of special interest. They cover more ground than you do, and will pay more for items, knowing your special interest. You pay more too, but the alternative is to miss out on an important item of interest. Still, you will probably pay less than buying the same item in an auction.

Listings of antique shows, malls, and flea markets appear in newspaper classified ad sections and in collectors' publications.

OTHER PRICE GUIDES

Values for Disneyana listed in general antique price guides and auction reports are often incorrect and misleading. Rarely is condition cited or any indication given as to completeness or if the item was in the original box. Descriptions given might apply to several different items, or may be totally incorrect.

There are, however, a number of specialized price guides which offer greater detail in specific areas. Those recommended for Disney collectors with an interest in these classifications are as follows:

The Comic Book Price Guide
by Robert M. Overstreet
780 Hunt Cliff Dr. N.W.
Cleveland, TN 37311

Lowey's The Collector's Guide to Big Little Books and Similar Books
by Lawrence F. Lowey
P.O. Box 732
Danville, CA 94526

Non-Sports [Gum] Cards
by Richard and Mark Sikes
P.O. Box 3092
Springfield, MA 01101

Disneyland/Walt Disney World Postcards
A Complete Checklist and Historical Guide
by Roger Le Roque and Nick Farago
R&N Postcard Company
P.O. Box 217
Temple City, CA 91780

THE WALT DISNEY ARCHIVES

The Walt Disney Company maintains an extensive archives in the Roy

O. Disney Building at its Burbank, California Studio location. It is open daily, by appointment, to students and others doing serious research on Disney subjects. The hours are 8 to 5:30.

There is an ever changing collection of Disneyana on display, as well as an extensive reference library and card catalog. The Archives maintains collections of everything imaginable in Disney material, including the following special catalogs and files:

1. Magazine article index: Disney stories indexed by subject and author.

2. Annual reports: Complete collection of reports from 1940 to date.

3. Photographs of Walt Disney: Arranged by subject and date.

4. Biographies: Studio personnel and talent biographies arranged in alphabetical order.

5. Attractions, shops, and food facilities: An alphabetical file of historical information for Disneyland, Walt Disney World, EPCOT Center, and Tokyo Disneyland.

6. Books: Cataloged by author, title, and illustrator.

7. Phonograph records: Cataloged by title, performer, and film.

8. Merchandise licensees: An alphabetical file giving inclusive years and items licensed.

9. Employee newsletters: Complete collection of employee periodical publications from the Studio, Disneyland, Walt Disney World, EPCOT Center, Tokyo Disneyland, WDI and MAPO.

10. Stockholder reports: Proxy statements, stock and bond offerings, 10-K reports, and other related items.

11. Insignia: Photographs of all military insignia produced by Disney, with a card index and original correspondence.

A brochure on the Disney Archives is available. To obtain a copy, or to inquire about research, contact David R. Smith, Archivist, The Walt Disney Company, 500 S. Buena Vista Street, Burbank, CA 91521, Telephone (818) 560-5424. The Archives will answer telephone or mail inquiries about Disneyana merchandise, but will not appraise or authenticate.

DATING DISNEYANA --
OLD, NEW, REAL OR FAKE

Dating Disneyana is often challenging, but there are hundreds of clues to help pinpoint a more exact age. Major identifying factors include graphic style, wording of the copyright notice, the characters depicted, manufacturer's name, country where produced, release date of films, and any association with dated pieces. Secondary identifiers of significance include any incidental characters illustrated, reference to historical events, material used, background attractions appearing on theme park items, or the use of postal zone or zip code in an address appearing on the item.

In the past there have been a number of oversimplified guidelines published in general antique books and magazine articles. People have been heard to say: "If it's copyrighted by Walt Disney Enterprises, it's old and valuable" or "A Mickey Mouse with pie-cut eyes is from the 30's." Generally, these statements are true, but there have always been exceptions -- and the number is growing.

Disneyana has been a popular target for rip-off manufacturers who create unauthorized merchandise. In a similar vein, reproductions of earlier items have been authorized with minor modification. Some one-time licensees have used old molds or dies to produce authorized or unauthorized products years later.

Counterfeiting of animation art and cels has been going on for years, with authenticating seals just as good looking as the artwork. In one Disney court victory it was estimated the individual created over 18,000 phoney cels.

Secondly, there has been a new wave of the "30's Mickey." The biggest confusion may have been created by the "Pop- Art" era of the mid-60's and the decision to re-emphasize the pie-cut eyes characters. Around 1970 Mickey and Minnie with the pie-cut eyes were used once again on Colorform playsets and a wide variety of other merchandise. They were, of course, copyrighted by Walt Disney Productions. It was felt that the copyright notice would be enough to distinguish newer merchandise from that of the 30's. Those early items were copyrighted by Walt Disney Enterprises -- except for a period in 1939 when original pie-eyed characters were copyrighted by Walt Disney Productions. Certain books from the early 30's were also copyrighted by "Productions."

Exceptions to the generally accepted guidelines are many. And knowing an item is simply from the 30's isn't very illuminating anyway.

In keeping with the definitive goals of this catalog, a *Disney Time Line* has been constructed to broaden the understanding of the many factors used to accurately date Disneyana.

THE DISNEY TIME LINE

Walt Disney-related artifacts are available for approximately ten years prior to the creation of Mickey Mouse. Mainly this material would consist of letters, drawings, documents, promotional material, posters, and a sparse amount of character merchandise.

Mickey Mouse, on the other hand, sparked a tide of goods. At first some manufacturers produced unauthorized toys, and those seeking permission presented a growing diversion from the Studio's prime task of turning out cartoons.

So in late 1929, Roy Disney (the brother responsible for the Studio's business affairs) negotiated with the George Borgfeldt Company to license character toys. It was a very broad agreement the Disneys were soon to regret. There was much dissatisfaction with early merchandise and designs changed frequently. A similar deal was made for foreign rights.

25

Before the contracts were up for renewal in 1933, the Disneys met Kay Kamen, a Kansas City advertising executive who put together some attractive plans for character merchandise. He was brought aboard to do some "in-house" promotions and took over character licensing once the other contracts expired. He was Mr. Merchandise for 17 years. Kamen was killed in a plane crash in 1949. Following his death, all character merchandising activities were assumed by the company.

The majority of licenses have been granted by Disney's New York offices. These offices were originally created by Kay Kamen. O.B. Johnston continued the east coast operation when the Character Merchandise Division was formed. There were several personnel changes during the conversion years until the employment of Vincent Jefferds, Disney's long-time Director of Merchandising. He eventually moved to the Studio headquarters. Pete Smith took over the New York operation for many years. Barton K. ("Bo") Boyd succeeded Jefferds as Vice President of Character Merchandising.

The following *Disney Time Line* is a detailed chronological overview of events related to the identification and dating of Disneyana. Photos, drawings, and details are included to illustrate changes as they occurred.

1915-1919

In 1915 Walter Elias Disney, age 13, took his first art lessons. Reluctantly, his hard toiling father agreed to let him attend Saturday morning classes at the Kansas City Art Institute.

In 1917 the family moved to Chicago. There Walt enrolled in a few classes at the Chicago Academy of Fine Art and studied cartooning under *Chicago Herald* cartoonist, Leroy Gossitt. Presumably, some of Disney's first work may yet surface to become known as the very first Disneyana.

When brother Roy joined the Navy in 1917, Walt wanted to go too, but was only 15. By the time he managed to serve as an ambulance driver in Neufchateau, France the war was over. While there, he made numerous drawings on helmets, paper, and canvas during his brief tour of duty.

In 1919 Walt returned to Kansas City and was employed by the commercial art firm of Pesmen and Rubin. There he met Ubbe "Ub" Iwerks. A partnership resulted. By 1920, however, Walt was on his own again.

1920-1923

Early in 1920 Walt took a job with the Kansas City Film Ad Company doing his first animation work. On the side, he drew and filmed Newman Laugh-O-Grams for a local theater.

These films employed stop action animation to give the illusion a single frame editorial type cartoon was being magically drawn.

Soon the part-time business became Laugh-O-Gram Films, Inc. Walt hired other animators, including friend Iwerks. The film company produced six "modern version" fairy tales: *Bremen Town Musicians*, *Little Red Riding Hood*, *Puss in Boots*, *Jack and The Beanstalk*, *Goldilocks and the Three Bears* and *Cinderella*.

The distributor for these limited animation films failed, forcing the company into bankruptcy.

Then, in 1923, Walt came up with an new idea -- a reversal on Max and Dave Fleischer's "Out of the Inkwell" series in which an animated Koko the clown was featured against a real life background.

In *Alice's Wonderland*, Disney had a live-action Alice caught up in the antics of a cartoon world. Her cartoon counterpart was a cat named Julius, who shared her adventures. The first Alice film was favorably received, but Walt figured Kansas City was not the best location for his company.

Brother Roy had previously moved to Southern California and had been sending Walt money. Hollywood was rapidly being established as the capital of the movie business, so it was the logical place to move. It was to become Walt's permanent residence.

Roy and Walt's ties to Kansas City and Chicago resulted in many Disneyana items mailed to friends they knew in the earlier years.

1924-1925

Late in 1923 Walt closed a deal to produce one Alice cartoon per month for Margaret J. Winkler, a New York film distributor.

Walt joined with his brother Roy to form Disney Bros. Studio. They recruited Ub Iwerks to join them from Kansas City. The original 12 Alice films were completed in 1924.

Eighteen Alice films were done in 1925. On July 6 of the same year the Disneys bought a lot for a new studio at 2719 Hyperion Avenue. The structure, the first of many building projects, was constructed under the Disneys' watchful eyes. It was ready for occupancy early in 1926.

1926

The new Hyperion Ave. studio turned out 26 Alice titles and the film *Clara Cleans Her Teeth*. Even though Alice cartoons continued to be produced through Aug 1927, interest in them was declining and it was time to go on to something else. The Alice cartoons were all silent, but served as a major workshop for the Disney art of animation. The only remains of Alice are rare posters, promotional materials, and the films themselves.

1927

It was the year of the rabbit -- Oswald the Lucky Rabbit. Introduced in *Trolley Troubles*, the new character was the subject of 26 Disney films before Walt learned the producer owned all the rights to the character.

Oswald films continued to be produced on into the 30's by the copyright owner. The Disney Oswald had longer, floppier ears than his successor, who was known simply as Oswald the Rabbit.

In addition to movie posters and other promotional materials, there were a number of Oswald toys: Fisher-Price pop-up puppet, a stencil set, pinback buttons, candy wrappers and display signs, celluloid figures plus posters and promotional items. All the merchandise was copyrighted in the name of the distributor, Universal.

1928

Having lost several animators along with the rights to Oswald the Lucky Rabbit, Disney needed a new character. As the legend goes, Walt came up with an idea for Mortimer Mouse just as the train from New York (where he had just received the bad news about Oswald) was passing through his old Kansas City stomping grounds. As the tale continues, wife Lillian said she thought Mickey would be a better name.

Fact or press agentry, it's a good story no one would care to challenge at this point. The Mickey Mouse character, however, was first drawn by Ub Iwerks and he was so credited on the first films.

The first Mickey cartoon produced was a silent film called *Plane Crazy*, done between April and June. At this point Mickey was very rat-like in appearance, had no shoes, and lines completed full circles outlining his eyes. The second film was *Gallopin' Gaucho*, also a silent picture. Walt was still trying, unsuccessfully, to get Mickey before an audience as work proceeded on a third film. Walt decided it needed sound and used a new process introduced in *The Jazz Singer*. *Steamboat Willie*, after a tireless sales effort, premiered Nov 18, at the Colony Theater in New York City (now operating as the Broadway). Mickey was an overnight smash. The next eleven years were to be the worldwide "Golden Age of Mickey Mouse."

Sound was added to the first two films. These and others which followed were released by Disney through Celebrity Productions until 1930. Minnie Mouse and Pete (later Pegleg Pete) were also in the premiere film.

1929

Walt had completed only five Mickey Mouse films when he introduced another new idea in animation: the Silly Symphony. The original idea

The drafting style of Mickey Mouse changed as the character developed in 1928. In *Plane Crazy* he had large encircled eyes, teeth and no shoes, Midway in the production of *Gallopin' Gaucho*, the lower part of the eye circles were deleted leaving Mickey with the "widow's peak" still seen today. Shoes were added in the second film. In *Steamboat Willie* visible teeth were eliminated and Mickey appeared a little less rat-like.

Mickeys pie-cut eyes were developed in 1930 and an extra eyebrow line was added about the same time. Shaded snouts were used for a brief time in 1931. The extra eyebrow line was dropped in 1934 and his eye became solid black ovals again in 1935.

was to take an existing musical composition and create an animated story which fit. The first was *The Skeleton Dance*. No merchandise was associated with the very early Silly Symphonies, nor was there much official merchandise in 1929 -- only promotion material, school tablets and handkerchiefs. Unofficially, Mickey Mouse was the bright new star of European toy and doll makers. Some U.S. firms produced unlicensed Mickey merchandise as well.

In September the original Mickey Mouse Club was formed. It was a Saturday movie theater matinee promotion which mushroomed to over 800 clubs nationwide at its peak in 1932 (see M4500 -- Mickey Mouse Clubs).

Each film showed gradual changes from rat to mouse. Mickey's look and personality underwent major changes in 1930 and again in 1933.

The early toys developed in England, France, and Germany featured a five-finger rat-like Mickey with teeth. Few have any copyright indication.

In the beginning Walt and Roy viewed character merchandising as publicity rather than an income-producing tool. Probably the extensive contract they signed with George Borgfeldt and Company early in 1930 was a move to concentrate on film production and let someone who knew the business handle the retail merchandise.

Clarabelle Cow and Horace Horsecollar were introduced in *The Plow Boy*. The one other film of note was Mickey Mouse in *The Haunted House*. On Dec 16, the Disney Brothers converted their Walt Disney Productions partnership into four corporations: a production company, a licensing and merchandising company (Walt Disney Enterprises), a film recording company, and a real estate holding company.

1930

Ub Iwerks left the Disney Studio early in 1930, but not before he drew the first five weeks of the new Mickey Mouse comic strip for King Features. His departure resulted in a reshaping and rounding out of Mickey's character. The rat in him rapidly disappeared. An accent line above the facial features remained which helps date Disneyana from 1930 to 1934. The shoes were still too big for the stick legs.

The first character merchandise contract was signed with George Borgfeldt and Co. of New York on Feb 3. It granted them broad retail merchandise rights, including sub-licensing. A like agreement for foreign licensing was signed with William B. Levy, who represented the Disney foreign interest from London. Most items produced under their direction are Copyright Walt E. Disney, or Walter E. Disney.

Borgfeldt, principally a cheap toy and novelty company, had manufacturing offices and contacts worldwide. The merchandise they produced was generally poor in quality -- a factor contributing to the end of their

30

Roy O. Disney signed the company's first sole licensee agreement with the George Borgfeldt and Company of New York on February 3, 1930. Through a world wide network of sub-licensees the company produced most of the earliest Disney merchandise. Most notable were the porcelain bisque, wood and celluloid figures, Dean Rag Book and Steiff dolls and early tin toys.

31

sub-licensing arrangement in 1933. However, they continued as a licensee until 1950.

Borgfeldt's major contributions to Disneyana were celluloid figures and toys, wood jointed figures and bisque figures from Japan. Copyright notices originally appeared somewhere on all Borgfeldt merchandise, but often small paper labels or decals used for the purpose came off easily.

Borgfeldt and/or Levy sub-licensed the Dean's Rag Book Co. of England to make character dolls. The design used was the five-finger Mickey with teeth associated with 1929 unlicensed merchandise. Roy and Walt preferred the design of Charlotte Clark, who was employed by them to make gift dolls and to fill small retail doll orders.

In 1930 Disney films were distributed by Columbia Pictures. Major Mickey Mouse films included *The Barnyard Concert* and *Fire Fighters*. Pluto the Pup was introduced in *The Chain Gang*.

The black and white Mickey Mouse comic strip began on Jan 13. After the departure of Ub Iwerks, artist Win Smith introduced continuing stories, and the first villain, Sylvester Shyster. On May 5 Floyd Gottfredson began drawing the stories "temporarily", but continued until his retirement in 1975.

Bibo and Lang published the first Mickey Mouse book.

1931

Borgfeldt was slow to bring Disney merchandise to market in 1930, but by 1931 Mickey and Minnie merchandise was on track to meet a rapidly growing demand.

The first major Disney story book, *The Adventures of Mickey Mouse,* was published by the David McKay Company (Donald Duck is mentioned, but does not appear until 1934). Saalfield Publishing issued the first coloring book. Pluto, having appeared unnamed in early shorts and as Rover in *The Picnic*, got his permanent name in *The Moose Hunt.*The first Mickey Mouse fan card was offered May 18 and for several weeks thereafter in the daily comic strip.

Films of special note and the characters they introduced were: *Birthday Party, Mickey's Orphans* (nominated for an Academy Award), *The Ugly Duckling* (b&w version) and *Mother Goose Melodies* (in which Mother Goose characters got a Disney interpretation). A total of 22 one reel shorts were released during 1931.

1932

Mickey Mouse Sunday color comics began Jan 10. The page was shared with a Silly Symphony series until July 12, 1942. Bucky and June Bug appeared frequently in this series.

Film distribution, handled by Columbia Pictures since 1930, was switched to United Artists. All Disney films were released through them until 1937.

Disneyana got a major boost early in 1932. Herman "Kay" Kamen, a Kansas City advertising executive, made a proposal to Walt and Roy Disney regarding his ideas on character merchandising.

The Borgfeldt agreement was a sore spot. The company still wasn't meeting the quality and design standard made amply clear in Roy's letters to them. Kamen was quick to seize the opportunity and returned soon after the first meeting with a detailed plan which became the backbone of Disney character merchandising. The first contract was signed July 1. Agreements with Borgfeldt and Levy were extensive, but not all inclusive.

Kamen officially became the Disney brothers' personal representative for character licensing. When existing contracts with Borgfeldt and Levy ran out, Kay Kamen became the sole Disney licensing agent.

Kamen worked exceedingly fast in publishing Christmas promotional catalogs and eventually merchandise catalogs which promoted all licensees (see M3900 -- Merchandise Catalogs). In those days Kay Kamen arranged a license, then helped the licensee sell their products. Mickey and his gang were great characters and Kamen knew how to communicate their sales power to exhibitors, department stores, and other retailers. He traveled almost continuously to meet buyers and help close deals. The result was higher quality Disney merchandise in time for Christmas. By mid-1933 the whole character merchandise program was under Kamen's control. Disneyana items were now being produced in tremendous quantities, many in the millions.

Even though Disney lost key animators in 1928 and 1930, many people feel the Disney Studio produced its best shorts from mid-1932 thru mid-1939.

Films of note and key characters introduced were: *Mickey's Revue* (introduced Dippy Dawg -- later called Goofy), *King Neptune*, *Flowers and Trees* (first color cartoon), *Touchdown Mickey* (most exciting Mickey cartoon), *The Klondike Kid*, *Babes in the Woods*, *Santa's Workshop* and *Mickey's Good Deed*.

In all, 22 Mickey Mouse and Silly Symphony cartoons were released in 1932.

Kay Kamen produced a special campaign book for distribution by United Artists. It included promotional ideas and ads for character merchandise. The first corporate Christmas card was mailed.

1933

Kay Kamen and Mickey merchandise took charge of department store toy departments and other retailers' shelves. By Christmas approximately 50 major toy departments used Disney characters as their

Christmas promotion theme. Kamen used the Mickey Mouse Club to dispense 10 million ice cream cones. It was a year of many firsts:
Mickey Mouse Giveaway Magazines
 -- Theater and merchant version: Jan '33 thru Sept '33
 -- Dairy version: Nov '33 thru Oct '35
Mickey Mouse watches and clocks
Big Little Books
Gum cards and albums

Tanglefoot appeared as Mickey's horse in the Sunday funnies. The Academy Award-winning *Three Little Pigs* (May 27) rallied the spirit of a depression-wracked nation. This triggered a new wave of character merchandise.

Nineteen short subjects were released, including: *Building a Building*, *Mickey's Pal Pluto*, *Ye Olden Days*, *The Mail Pilot*, *Mickey's Gala Premiere* (incorporating Disney caricatures of leading movie stars), *Puppy Love* (introducing Pluto's girlfriend, Fifi), *The Pet Store* (a take-off on *King Kong*) and *Giant Land*.

1934

In 1934 $35 million worth of character merchandise was sold -- a huge increase over the previous year. General Foods purchased the rights to use Mickey and friends on *Post Toasties* cereal boxes for $1.5 million. Lionel Corporation was licensed to make trains and handcars, a move acknowledged for saving the company from bankruptcy.

The *Big Bad Wolf* reappeared in a cartoon of the same name to retell the story of Little Red Riding Hood. Peter and Polly Penguin appeared in *Peculiar Penguins* to prove walking birds were poor subjects for animation. Donald Duck, Disney's third historic creation, took his first bow on June 9 in *The Wise Little Hen*. Like Mickey, his character developed over a period of several years. Donald's drafting style changes are particularly helpful in dating Disneyana produced from late 1934 to 1938. Books, games, and other materials indicate his long bill style lasted approximately a year on most merchandise. It was modified to a medium length by mid-1935. By 1938 Donald's style was largely set. Exceptions are long billed Donald porcelain bisque and celluloid figures and toys which were made until 1939.

Other film highlights were: *The Grasshopper and the Ants*, *Mickey's Man Friday*, *Mickey's Steamroller* (introduced nephews, Morty and Ferdy), *Orphans' Benefit* (introduced Clara Cluck) and *Two-Gun Mickey*.

Kay Kamen's first merchandise catalog was sent to 25,000 motion picture exhibitors, manufacturers and retailers in the United States. Foreign language editions were circulated from 88 worldwide distribution centers.

1935

Two Silly Symphonies won Academy Awards -- *The Tortoise and The Hare* and *Three Orphan Kittens* -- and on Feb 23 *The Band Concert* featured Mickey Mouse in full color for the first time. Pie-cut eyes ended at this point, but continued on dolls and many toys thru 1939. Most books and other printed pieces switched to solid black, oval eyes on Mickey Mouse by year end.

The newsstand *Mickey Mouse Magazine* went on sale May 15 and continued until it was replaced by comic books in 1940.

Adolph Hitler declared Mickey an enemy of the Third Reich. Disney films were banned in Germany. The production of German Disneyana was halted. A major source of ceramics, tin and wood toys, and other character items was cut off.

It was a zenith year for shorts. Standouts included: *Mickey's Service Station, Water Babies, The Cookie Carnival, The Robber Kitten, Who Killed Cock Robin?, Mickey's Fire Brigade, Pluto's Judgement Day, On Ice* and *Music Land.*

By year end over 2.5 million original design Mickey Mouse watches were sold. On the whole, if Kay Kamen's merchandise catalogs are a valid yardstick, 1935 was the peak year for golden age Mickey Disneyana.

1936

FDR's "New Deal" programs were getting people back to work. The long years of the Great Depression were behind for most folks. Mickey did his part for the nation's morale, the art of animation, and the fortunes of character merchandise licensees. Walt Disney realized there was a limited future in shorts and had started work on his first animated feature.

The Three Pigs appeared in the Silly Symphony newspaper strip from Jan 19 - Aug 23; Donald Duck Aug 30, 1936 to Dec 5, 1937. The quality of cartoons remained high and produced a large quantity of merchandise. Pluto got his first starring role in *Mother Pluto*. Bobo was the co-star in *Mickey's Elephant*. The Silly Symphony *Elmer Elephant* introduced Elmer and his girlfriend, Tillie Tiger. The term "Mouseketeers" was coined in *Three Blind Mouseketeers*. Other key works of the year were: *Orphans' Picnic, Three Little Wolves, Thru The Mirror, Moving Day, Mickey's Rival* and *Donald and Pluto.*

The Disney organization recruited artists from art schools nationwide. These recruitment mailings are an interesting form of Disneyana.

Kay Kamen's merchandise catalog combined a two year period for the first time in the 1936-37 edition.

1937

With so much of the Studio's energy going into the production of *Snow White and the Seven Dwarfs*, it is difficult to understand how so many Disney classic shorts could be produced in the same year. Donna Duck (later Daisy) made her debut in *Don Donald*. *Magician Mickey, Moose Hunters, Hawaiian Holiday, Clock Cleaners* and *Lonesome Ghosts* were released in a steady stream.

The Old Mill tested out multiplane camera technology and won an Academy Award. Another Silly Symphony, *Little Hiawatha*, interpreted the classic poem in a fashion which delighted moviegoers of all ages. The little Indian boy proved to be a popular character and appeared for many years in Disneyana. Little Minnehaha joined him in a 1940 Sunday comic strip.

Donald Duck got his name above the title for the first time in *Donald's Ostrich*. The name of the ostrich was Hortense.

Snow White and the Seven Dwarfs premiered at the Carthay Circle Theater in Hollywood on December 21. The film introduced the world to Bashful, Doc, Dopey, Grumpy, Happy, Sleepy, Sneezy, The Wicked Queen, an Old Witch, a Charming Prince, the beautiful Snow White and a mysterious Magic Mirror. A skeptical public was enchanted and a new wellspring of character merchandise poured forth. A Snow White Sunday comic strip began as pre-release publicity on Dec 12, and ended Apr 24, 1938. The series, based on feature films, continued through *Alice In Wonderland*, concluding on Dec 16, 1951. It was soon continued under the title *Treasury of Classics*.

Upon the release of *Snow White*, RKO Pictures took over distribution of all Disney theatrical films until 1953; except *Victory Through Air Power* (United Artists, 1943).

1938

Snow White went into national release on Feb 4 and eventually received a special Academy Award. On Feb 7 the daily Donald Duck newspaper comic strip began. Donald was receiving greater prominence in the movies as well. In *Donald's Nephews* he acquired Huey, Dewey and Louie; and starred in *Donald's Better Self, Good Scouts, Polar Trappers, The Fox Hunt* and *Donald's Golf Game*. This rapidly rising duck also had a role in three of the five new Mickey cartoons: *Boat Builders, Mickey's Trailer* and *The Whalers*. Also produced this year were five new Silly Symphonies: *Wynken, Blynken and Nod, The Moth and the Flame, Farmyard Symphony, Merbabies* and *Mother Goose Goes Hollywood*, plus the highly merchandised Academy Award-winning short, *Ferdinand the Bull*.

Character merchandise accelerated on the wave of new characters.

Mickey, Donald and the Seven Dwarfs provided new impact for boy-oriented products; while Snow White generated the first real strong appeal to the femininity of girls and women. The Kay Kamen catalog for 1938-39, for example, included corsets, premium cookbook pamphlets, dresses, bonnets, pure silk printed fabrics and the biggest array of dolls ever.

1939

The profits from *Snow White* were invested in a new Burbank studio and the company underwent a major reorganization to prepare for Walt's expanding dreams. In the process Walt Disney Enterprises, the special company set up for non-film activities, was eliminated. The copyright notice appearing on merchandise items produced after this date reads © Walt Disney Productions or © W.D.P. Items produced for the following Christmas are often puzzling to Disneyana collectors, for it is possible to find pie-cut eye character items with the new copyright notice. Some characters underwent major design changes in 1940 and the new notice was used on old style characters for only a few months. It is important to add this caution. The vast majority of pie-cut eye items with a © Walt Disney Productions notice were produced from the late 60's to the present. This "mod" Mickey design is similar to the original 1931-35 version, but zip codes on boxes, labels listing man-made fabrics, glazes on ceramics and other clues can be used to identify modern merchandise.

Donald Duck color Sunday funnies began Dec 10. The Mickey strip introduced Chief O'Hara and The Phantom Blot.

The color remake of *The Ugly Duckling* was the final Silly Symphony produced. Fittingly, it won an Academy Award to add a crowning touch to this revolutionary series of animated films. Goofy became a star performer for the first time in *Goofy and Wilbur*. There were only two Mickey cartoons: *Society Dog Show* and *The Pointer*. *The Practical Pig* was the lone special for the year, but Donald screened eight new cartoons including: *Donald's Lucky Day*, *Donald's Cousin Gus*, *Sea Scouts* and *The Autograph Hound*.

1940

Only one time in the company's history were two fully animated features released in a single year. *Pinocchio* premiered Feb 7 and *Fantasia* on Nov 13. Artistically, it was the studio's finest year. Both films made extensive use of the multiplane camera. One can only wonder what would have happened had the public received *Fantasia* as well as *Pinocchio*. Where might have the Disney genius led us then?

The year was busy in many other respects as well. *Walt Disney's*

Donald Duck first appeared in *The Wise Little Hen* in 1934. He had a long bill until it was shortened a bit in 1937. The bill was reduced still more in 1938 to the way Donald looks today. Mickey Mouse was re-designed with pupil eyes for his appearance in *Fantasia* in late 1940 and had dimensional ears for a brief time in 1941. The Studio underwent major changes after the release of *Snow White and the Seven Dwarfs* in 1938.

Donald Duck -- Dell Color Comic No. 4 -- was issued in Feb, to be followed by the first issue of *Walt Disney's Comics and Stories* in Oct. Some characters were redesigned with more human-like qualities and the company went public with its first stock offering on Apr 2.

Pinocchio introduced The Blue Fairy, Cleo, Figaro, Geppetto, "Honest John" (J. Worthington Foulfellow), Gideon (the silent cat), Jiminy Cricket, Lampwick, Monstro the Whale, Stromboli and the title character. In *Mr. Duck Steps Out* Donald's girlfriend officially became Daisy, and Pluto's nemesis, Butch the Bulldog, was first seen in *Bone Trouble*. Notable characters in *Fantasia* included Apollo, Bacchus, Ben Ali Gator, the centaurs and centaurettes, Chernabog, Diana, Elephanchine, Heloise, Hop Low, Hyacinth Hippo, Iris, Mademoiselle Upanova, Morpheus, The Sorcerer Yen Sid, Zeus and, of course, Mickey Mouse.

Fourteen cartoons were produced: eight Donalds, three Plutos, two Mickeys and *Goofy's Glider*.

The 1940-41 Kay Kamen merchandise catalog featured *Pinocchio* merchandise, but none from *Fantasia*. It would be the last catalog until 1947.

1941

Even though there were some live takes of Leopold Stokowski in *Fantasia, The Reluctant Dragon* (June 20) is considered Disney's first film to rely on live action to carry most of the story. The production is a tour of the Disney Studio. Walt and many other Studio regulars took part. In the course of seeing the Studio at work, Robert Benchley sees four animated shorts unreeled: *Casey Jr., Baby Weems, How to Ride a Horse* (Goofy) and *The Reluctant Dragon*.

Release of the low budget *Reluctant Dragon* wasn't enough to recover the losses *Fantasia* posted. So *Dumbo* (Oct 23) was designed to bolster Studio finances. It is one of the shortest Disney animated features and the only one to cost less than $1 million to produce. Characters of note included: Dumbo, Mr. Stork, Timothy Mouse, Casey Jr. and the Crows who first taught an elephant to fly.

Eighteen cartoons were released. A Pluto cartoon won an Academy Award -- *Lend a Paw*, while Mickey and Minnie shined in *The Nifty Nineties* and a color remake of the *Orphans' Benefit*. Mickey appeared with dimensional ears for a brief time during this period -- in cartoons and on a very few Disneyana items. *Truant Officer Donald* led the slate of eight Duck cartoons. Pluto did a total of four, Mickey and Goofy each did three.

The bombing of Pearl Harbor on Dec 7 had an immediate impact on the Studio and Disneyana. The military took over the sound stage for several months for use as a repair facility. Material shortages developed and, of course, Japanese-produced Disneyana came to an abrupt halt.

39

1942

The Disney Studio supported the war effort, savings bond drives and USO entertainment activities. Disney artists designed over a thousand military insignias and made scores of animated training films. *Bambi* premiered Aug 13 and went into general release on the 21st. The main characters were Aunt Ena, Bambi's Mother, Bambi, Faline, Friend Owl, Ronno, Flower and Thumper. Merchandising on the film was restrained due to the war. Still, Bambi has endured as a popular Disneyana character ever since.

Dell Full Color Comic No. 9 featured "Donald Duck Finds Pirate Gold", the first to feature the unique comic art talent of Carl Barks. Barks' mastery of simple black lines communicated greater character depth and expression than most other comic artists. Donald's explosive character was a perfect foil for Barks, who often wrote the stories as well. In future years he created new characters, including Gladstone Gander, Grandma Duck and Uncle Scrooge. Most Barks art has a distinctive eye treatment used to quickly identify his work.

Several of the 19 cartoons released had war themes: *Donald Gets Drafted*, *The Army Mascot* (Pluto), *Donald's Garden* and *The Vanishing Private*. Mickey's fifteenth birthday was celebrated in *Mickey's Birthday Party*. The cartoon breakdown was Donald (8), Pluto (5), Goofy (4) and Mickey (2). Mickey had become "Mr. Nice Guy" in response to his respected worldwide reputation. Any hint of bad behavior would bring a flood of letters to the Studio.

1943

It must have been an interesting year at the Studio. Disney's appeal to South American countries to replace lost revenues from war torn Europe was a great success. Major films and cartoons continued to support the war effort. It also seemed to be a period of philosophical questioning and some interesting films were the result.

Saludos Amigos (Hello Friends) used footage of Walt's tour of South America to patch together four animated shorts: *Lake Titicaca* (with Donald Duck), *Pedro* (a young airmail plane on his first solo flight through treacherous, but beautiful mountains), *El Gaucho Goofy* and *Aquarela do Brasil* (Watercolor of Brazil). The Feb 6 release introduced Pedro and Joe (or Jose) Carioca.

Training film production exposed Walt to many military concepts and theories. He became convinced the U.S. needed to develop long range strategic bombing capability (not a popular idea at the Pentagon) and produced *Victory Through Air Power* (Aug 13) to factually state the case.

Donald starred in the Academy Award-winning *Der Fuehrer's Face*, *Fall Out-Fall In* and *The Old Army Game*. Chip an' Dale made their debut in *Private Pluto*, but weren't named until 1947. Goofy did *Victory Vehicles*. Two characters from an animated feature tried a solo act in *Figaro and Cleo* and for the first time since 1928, there wasn't a new Mickey Mouse cartoon. There were, however, three rather heavy shorts -- *Education for Death* featuring Germania, Hans and Hitler; *Reason and Emotion* and *Chicken Little* with Cocky Locky, Ducky Lucky, Foxey Loxey, Goosey Loosey, Henny Penny and
Turkey Lurkey all worrying about the sky falling.

The Gremlins, curious little characters (Gremlins, Fifinellas, and Widgets) which plague aviators, were the subject of an abandoned 1943 project. The film is known to Disneyana collectors due to a Random House book licensed for publicity.

Postal zones first came into effect this year. Any original Disneyana on which a postal zone appears (i.e., New York 1, N.Y.) was produced between 1943 and 1964.

1944

The Studio was deeply involved in the war effort. Only twelve shorts were released. There were no features of note. On June 6 "Mickey Mouse" was used as the code word when Allied Forces landed on the occupied French coast in the battle which eventually led to victory in Europe. *Donald's Trombone Trouble* and Goofy's *How to Play Football* represented the better films ... and for the second straight year there were no new Mickey cartoons.

On the surface it didn't appear much was happening. However, a 1944 Simon and Schuster edition revealed several projects were already in development. Titled *"Surprise Package"* it provided the first look at Disney's Brer Rabbit, *Alice in Wonderland*, *Peter Pan*, *Adventures of Mr. Toad*, *Lady and the Tramp* and several characters seen in later feature films.

1945

The Three Caballeros (Feb 3) provided signs the Disney Studio was alive and well. This time it was Donald visiting the lower Americas publicizing their natural beauty. Animated segments were *The Cold-Blooded Penguin*, *The Flying Gauchito* and the brilliantly combined live action/animation of Donald and Joe Carioca's tour of various countries and their meeting Panchito -- culminating in the razzle dazzle *The Three Caballeros* animated sequence.

There were 15 shorts -- one headlined Donald and Goofy, while Donald did six others and Goofy four. *The Legend of Coyote Rock* paced Pluto's four films. *Donald's Crime* was nominated for an Oscar and *Tiger Trouble* was possibly Goofy's best for the year.

The *Uncle Remus* color Sunday strip began Oct 14, and ran through Dec 31, 1972. Character merchandise income had declined throughout the war years due to shortages that restricted the production of typical licensed products. Food products, while rationed, still competed in an open market. Earlier efforts to develop this sort of revenue started to pay off. Donald Duck, due to his popularity, was almost always the endorsing character. A large variety of food and drink companies became licensees. When Disney became involved in television, new food licensing was discouraged to avoid conflicts with advertisers. A few licensees (such as Donald Duck Orange Juice) continue to the present.

1946

The return to peace time paved the way for lighter, happy films and a resurgence of Disneyana merchandise. *Make Mine Music* (Aug 15) was planned as a popular music counterpart to *Fantasia*. The ten animated shorts were: *A Rustic Ballad* with the Martins and the Coys; Tone Poem ("Blue Bayou"); A Jazz Interlude ("All the Cats Join In"); A Ballad In Blue ("Without You"); A Musical Recitation ("Casey at The Bat"); Ballade Ballet ("Two Silhouettes"); A Fairy Tale With Music ("Peter and the Wolf"); *After You've Gone*, a surrealistic jazz sequence; A Love Story ("Johnny Fedora and Alice Blue Bonnet"); and *Opera Pathetique* with Willie the Whale doing several arias while realizing his fantasy on stage at the Met.

Brer Rabbit, Brer Fox and Brer Bear came to life in *Song of the South* (Nov 12). "Zip-A-Dee-Doo-Dah" won an Oscar for best song, but the sheet music art ranks among the poorest designs. There were twelve cartoons along the same pattern of previous years.

Disneyana from Japan began to reappear. Items produced from 1946 to 1951 are often marked "Made in Occupied Japan."

1947

A new Kay Kamen merchandise catalog was issued, indicating character licensing had regained much of its pre-war strength.

Fun and Fancy Free (Sept 27) included two featurettes: *Bongo* and *Mickey and the Beanstalk*, along with live action sequences of Edgar Bergen, Charlie McCarthy and Mortimer Snerd. *Mickey's Delayed Date* was the first Mickey cartoon since 1942. *Chip an' Dale* formally named the chipmunks. *Pluto's Blue Note* was another outstanding short of the 15 new ones released. Cartoons from the Disney library were also re-released for the first time.

1948

Melody Time (May 27), often acclaimed the best of the postwar musical short composites, featured *Little Toot*, *Johnny Appleseed*, *Once Upon A Wintertime*, *Bumble Boogie*, *Trees*, *Blame it on the Samba* (reuniting Donald Duck, Joe Carioca and the Aracuan bird) and *Pecos Bill* (featuring the cowboy star, Roy Rogers).

Three for Breakfast, *Mickey and the Seal* and *Tea for Two Hundred* were the most notable of the 16 shorts released. Gladstone Gander first appeared in *Walt Disney Comics and Stories* #88 -- another product of Carl Barks.

The 1948-49 edition of Ice Capades introduced arena audiences to Disney costumed characters similar to the ones which would later inhabit Disneyland.

1949

So Dear To My Heart (Jan 19) introduced Danny, the little black lamb. *Seal Island* (May 4) was the first True Life Adventure, a series of naturalist films designed to both educate and entertain. Films in the True Life Adventure series were originally two-reel shorts. Later titles were made feature length.

Toy Tinkers was nominated for an Academy Award over the other 14 cartoons released. The major film of the year was *The Adventures of Ichabod and Mr. Toad* (Oct 5). Once again Disney characters showed depth -- the animation, real class. Respectively based on *The Legend of Sleepy Hollow* and *The Wind in the Willows*, the film produced little character merchandise -- a puzzling situation in view of such grand characters as Ichabod Crane, Katrina Van Tassel, Brom Bones and the Headless Horseman astride Gunpowder. Fun-loving J. Thaddeus Toad, Winky and Cyril, along with Mole, Rat, and Mac Badger (the sensible keepers of Toad Hall) also seemed to offer some great merchandise opportunities.

Perhaps those opportunities were lost due to the untimely death of Kay Kamen, who, together with his wife, was killed in a European plane crash on Oct 29. Soon after his death the company established the Character Merchandising Division. The last Kay Kamen Merchandise Catalog (1949-50) had already been printed. Since that time merchandise has been promoted in smaller mailers and catalogs and in film press books.

1950

Cinderella, the first animated feature since *Bambi* to relate a single story, arrived on Feb 15. In addition to the age old characters of

Pinocchio and *Fantasia* followed *Snow White and the Seven Dwarfs* before the outbreak of World War II. *Bambi*, already well into production, was released in 1942. The Studio was very active in supporting the war effort and there were no more single subject animated feature films released until *Cinderella* in 1950.

Cinderella, the Prince, stepmother and stepsisters, Disney added Gus, Jaq, a handful of neatly dressed mice, Bruno the dog and an obese, aptly named cat called Lucifer. The King and Grand Duke were also new characters. The Fairy Godmother was a delightful departure from the stock version. *Cinderella* was the most merchandised film since *Pinocchio.Treasure Island* (July 19), one of several live action films made in England to use cash restricted to the country, was a limited source of Disneyana.

Eighteen cartoons and the Oscar-winning *Beaver Valley* True Life Adventure were released. Pluto was the major star with eight films headed by *Pluto's Heart Throb.* Donald appeared in six. Cartoons, at one time the total basis for character merchandise, were having less and less influence. The characters were no longer merchandised in relation to any particular film. Their personalities were established and the handwriting on the wall numbered the days for theatrical cartoon shorts.

TV was introduced in the U.S. the same year as Mickey in 1928 -- color TV in 1929. The Depression slowed development, but the one-eyed marvel was impressively demonstrated at the 1939 New York World's Fair. World War II prevented production. Post-war sets were few and expensive. Programming sparse. By 1948 there was a scramble for VHF broadcasting licences. Lower cost TV sets were in mass production by 1949. The new medium had a major impact on network radio and movie theaters by 1950. Movie theaters were being forced to cut expenses by eliminating newsreels and short subjects. Walt was cautious about TV, but got a deal on his own terms.

The first Disney TV special -- "One Hour In Wonderland" -- aired Christmas Day at 4:00 pm to a huge audience -- the largest ever at that time.

1951

The animated *Alice In Wonderland* (July 28) was a disappointment at the box office and thus produced a smaller amount of character merchandise. *Nature's Half Acre* became the third True Life Adventure to win an Oscar and 18 new cartoons were released. "Occupied Japan" marks were revised to "Made in Japan." Walt Disney hosted his second Christmas TV special entitled "The Walt Disney Christmas Show."

1952

The Story of Robin Hood (June 26) was the second live action feature made in England ... one that inspired a good variety of books and merchandise. Walt fell short of his goal of one new animated feature each year, but some memorable cartoons resulted: *Donald Applecore*; *Lambert, The Sheepish Lion*; *Trick or Treat* and *Pluto's Christmas*

Tree. Water Birds was an Academy Award winner, the fourth year running a True Life Adventure won the honor.

Walt continued to resist tempting TV offers as plans for a "theme park" were taking shape.

1953

Peter Pan, Disney's best sight gag feature, premiered Feb 5, generating more merchandise than *Cinderella*. *Bear Country* continued the string of True Life Academy Award winners. There were more winners as well -- *The Alaskan Eskimo*, the first "People and Places" film, and *Toot, Whistle,*
Plunk, and Boom, Disney's first Cinemascope cartoon. *The Simple Things* was the last Mickey Mouse theatrical cartoon short. *Melody (Adventures in Music)* was the first 3-D cartoon, followed by another later in the year with Donald in *Working for Peanuts. Ben and Me* was the year's best animated featurette.

The Sword and the Rose (July 23) and another British product, *Rob Roy the Highland Rogue*, were the last features released by RKO. *The Living Desert* (Nov 10) was the first film released by Disney's new Buena Vista Distribution Company, and it too won an Academy Award.

1954

Features of note were *Rob Roy the Highland Rogue* (Feb 4); *The Vanishing Prairie* (Aug 17) and *20,000 Leagues Under the Sea* (Dec 23), the first Disney film use of elaborate special effects. Cartoons and animated segments of 40's composite movies were being re-released to supply a large portion of the declining cartoon market. *Pigs Is Pigs* and Donald in *Grand Canyonscope* led the sparse list of new entries.

The big event of the year was the first weekly TV contract. All three networks had been after Walt to air his cartoon classics on TV. Disney finally agreed to a different idea. He and Roy were risking everything they had to build Disneyland. Walt wanted to do a TV show for promotional purposes. The program was initially called "Disneyland" and the first show "The Disneyland Story". This and subsequent "progress reports" took the viewer behind the scenes and made them feel part of Disneyland's planning and construction process. Millions became involved and Disneyland was a global phenomenon before opening day. Opening day (7/17/55) was the occasion for a live spectacular on ABC-TV.

The first season was a smash in every respect. A great deal of the programming came from Disney's existing library. The made for TV "Davy Crockett, Indian Fighter" (Dec 15), starring Fess Parker and Buddy Ebsen, triggered a gigantic fad. The next two shows in the trilogy

46

-- "Davy Crockett Goes to Congress" (1/26/55) and "Davy Crockett at the Alamo" (2/23/55) -- are classic examples of Disney's storytelling genius. His family programming truly entertained everyone in the family -- not just the kids.

1955

The year proved to be a major milestone for Walt Disney Productions and an important one in the history of Disneyana. Once it was the generally accepted dividing year between items deemed collectible and those which were not. Today events of 1955 are the subject of some specialized areas of collecting.

Lady and the Tramp premiered in June and the Disneyland theme park opened in July. Davy Crockett had become the biggest hero since Hopalong Cassidy. The TV "Mickey Mouse Club" began as an hour show on Oct 3, airing each Monday thru Friday in most parts of the country from 5:00 to 6:00 pm.

During the 30's and 40's merchandise wasn't normally available until 5 or 6 months after a film's release. O.B. Johnston, the head of the Character Merchandising Division since it was formed, instituted a new policy. Manufacturers were pre-licensed in time to have merchandise available for the film's release date. Since the late 40's Kay Kamen representatives visited the Studio a year or so in advance of a filming release, but licensees didn't realized the full value of this policy until *Lady and the Tramp*. Publicity was enhanced, more manufacturers participated and products were available when most filmgoers wanted them -- soon after seeing the film. *Lady* animation cels are more widely distributed than those of other features. Great quantities were mounted, priced under $5 and sold at Disneyland's Art Corner so anyone could own Disney original art.

Disneyland opened July 17, representing an initial investment of $17 million. Originally there were 22 major attractions, divided in five themed lands -- Main Street USA, Adventureland, Frontierland, Fantasyland and Tomorrowland. The pre-sell job on TV, plus spectacular fulfillment on the promise of a special "Magic Kingdom" made Disneyland a "must" for worker and world leader alike. The constantly changing maps, postcards, guidebooks, buttons and souvenirs have become popular Disneyana. Disneyland never stops growing and there is always some special event being commemorated throughout the park and on merchandise.

The "Mickey Mouse Club" pumped new life into the title character as he reached a new generation of children. They found him just as delightful as their parents had in the 30's. The result was a new wave of Mickey merchandise hallmarked by the club emblem. This time around there were also Mouseketeers -- a cast of talented kids and two adult leaders. Monday was "Fun With Music Day." Tuesday: "Guest Star

47

Day." Wednesday: "Anything Can Happen Day." Thursday: "Circus Day." Friday: "Talent Roundup Day." The format also included cartoons, science, a variety of educational and "what I want to be" sequences, plus teen adventure serials such as "The Hardy Boys" and "Spin and Marty." Thousands of merchandise items, many untraditionally Disney, were connected with the club. There were 38 licensed manufacturers the first year. The program was reduced to a half-hour in the fourth year and went into off-network syndication in 1962.

There were more re-released cartoons than new ones, most of which were being made in Cinemascope in an attempt to save a dying market. *Men Against the Arctic*, a People and Places short, won an Academy Award. Donald's *No Hunting* was nominated. *The African Lion* was released in Oct, *The Littlest Outlaw* in Dec.

1956

The last series of theatrical cartoon shorts made by Walt Disney ended with: *Chips Ahoy, Hooked Bear* and *In the Bag.* That part of the business was dead. It was the age of TV and Disneyland.

Davy Crockett and the River Pirates (July 18) was the most popular release of the year even though it had already appeared on TV. *Secrets of Life* (Nov 20), likely the most inventive of the True Life Adventure feature documentaries, opened the viewer's eyes to natural phenomena impossible to see without the advances in camera technology developed in conjunction with the film.

Disneyland's expansion included the addition of Tom Sawyer's Island, Storybook Land, Rainbow Caverns and the Skyway between Tomorrowland and Fantasyland.

1957

Our Friend The Atom appeared Jan 23 on the Disneyland TV show and was released theatrically in Europe. It explained atomic energy in laymen's terms.

The "Andy Burnett" series began Oct 2 and was the subject of six adventures in the 57-58 TV season. The TV smash of the year was "Zorro", a weekly half hour series which ran two years.

Disneyland opened the Sleeping Beauty Castle exhibit, Midget Autopia and the Viewliner (since replaced by the Monorail system).

Perri (Aug 28) was a popular True Life Fantasy theatrical feature. *Old Yeller* was released in Dec. Non-animated shorts: *The Wetback Hound* and *Niok*, as well as the animated *Mars and Beyond*, received acclaim.

Walt Disney was presented with the 25th million Mickey Mouse watch produced.

1958

The Disneyland TV series was retitled "Walt Disney Presents." "The Nine Lives of Elfego Baca" and "Tales of Texas John Slaughter" first appeared. Each was the subject of many TV episodes into the early 60's. *The White Wilderness* True Life Adventure feature was released in Aug. *Tonka* followed in Dec.

Big things were taking shape at Disneyland. The sailing ship *Columbia*, the Grand Canyon Diorama, Alice in Wonderland and the excursion train were added.

1959

The long awaited $6 million animated feature, *Sleeping Beauty*, arrived Jan 29, the first to be made in 70mm Technirama. Public response was disappointing and the film only barely covered its production cost. Fortunately, *The Shaggy Dog* (Mar 19), produced for just over a million, grossed over $10 million in film rentals. *Darby O'Gill and the Little People* was released in June.

The weekly TV series generated "The Birth of the Swamp Fox" (Oct 23), and the Revolutionary War hero became the subject of many TV episodes and appeared on some merchandise. *Grand Canyon* won an Oscar and *Mysteries of the Deep* was the year's nature film candidate.

The biggest expansion since Disneyland's opening included the addition of the Submarine Voyage, the Disneyland-Alweg Monorail system, the 14 story high Matterhorn Mountain bobsled run, two replacement Autopia Freeways, the enlargement of the Motorboat Cruise and Super Autopias in Tomorrowland.

1960

Notable feature films of the year were *Toby Tyler* (Jan), *Kidnapped* (Feb), *The Sign of Zorro* (June), *Pollyanna* (May) and *Swiss Family Robinson* (Dec). Zorro also returned to appear on the weekly TV show. "El Bandito" (Oct 30) was the first such special.

Disneyland added Nature's Wonderland, inspired by the True Life Adventures series. Over 200 animals, birds, and reptiles were viewed, in a re-creation of wilderness and desert regions, as seen from Western mine trains (since replaced by Big Thunder Mountain Railroad).

The demand for Mickey Mouse watches reached a new low. No new watches with Mickey's picture were produced until 1967, only ones with the words "Mickey Mouse."

1961

101 Dalmatians (Jan 25) was the first animated feature to fully utilize a special Xerox camera developed by Ub Iwerks. It eliminated the need for inking the animator's line drawing onto the cel by substituting an electrostatic transfer from the animation art. This gave the characters a "sketcher" look.

The Absent Minded Professor (Mar 16) introduced the world to "flubber." The huge success of the film resulted in take-offs and sequels produced in later years. *The Parent Trap* was released in June and *Babes In Toyland* was the Christmas film.

The weekly TV program moved to the NBC network in the fall. The program was re-named "Walt Disney's Wonderful World of Color." Ludwig Von Drake, a new animated character, was introduced and went on to host many Disney network TV shows. "Hans Brinker, or, The Silver Skates", "The Prince and the Pauper" and "Disneyland After Dark" were standouts in the first season of color programs.

Additions to Disneyland included expansion of the Monorail system to the Disneyland Hotel and the Flying Saucer ride in Tomorrowland (since removed). The first Grad Night was held.

1962

The major films were: *Moon Pilot, Bon Voyage, Big Red, Almost Angels, The Legend of Lobo* and *In Search of the Castaways*. A telltale pattern was setting in at the Studio. The emphasis was being put on production rather than the unique quality that made the Studio world renowned. Formula, for a large part, had replaced experimentation and risk-taking. Few features during this period produced Disneyana other than pressbooks and film promotional material. Since this is of little interest to collectors, only live action features featured on merchandise will continue to be mentioned. One test for future stories under consideration might be "how can it be merchandised?" Merchandise potential can provide a good indication on how involved a viewer could get in the story.

The focus of the company was on Disneyland. *The Golden Horseshoe Revue*, a film built around the theme park attraction, premiered the fall TV season -- and was released theatrically in Europe. It was also the year when too many programs featured animals as heroes. Each was well done, but still there was a feeling you saw it all before.

The Jungle Cruise was enlarged at Disneyland. The Swiss Family Treehouse, the Plaza Pavilion Restaurant and Tahitian Terrace were added.

50

1963

Mechanical robotics were used in the original Jungle Cruise back in the 50's. However, the Lincoln exhibit being prepared for the New York World's Fair required something more. The result was "Audio-Animatronics", a sophisticated system which created life-like movements in robot animals and humans -- down to the blink of an eye. The technique was also the basis of the Enchanted Tiki Room, Disneyland's major addition for the year.

Son of Flubber (Jan), *Savage Sam* (Aug) and *Sword in the Stone* (Dec) were reflected in character merchandise.

1964

Disney was a big participant in the 1964-65 New York World's Fair. The company had developed several exhibits: "It's a Small World" for Pepsi Cola/UNICEF, "Great Moments with Mr. Lincoln" for the State of Illinois, the "Carousel of Progress" for GE and "Primeval World" for Ford.

The Misadventures of Merlin Jones (Jan) and *Emil and the Detectives* (Dec) resulted in books, but *Mary Poppins* (Aug 29) was the subject of the biggest merchandise bonanza since *Lady and the Tramp*. "The Scarecrow of Romney Marsh" (Feb 9) and several episodes of "Gallegher", a teenage detective, highlighted TV events of the year.

The zip code became totally effective on July 1. Announced the previous year, zip codes appear in the manufacturers' addresses found on original boxes of items produced circa 1964 or later.

Major construction was underway at Disneyland, but the only new offering was Below Decks, the living and working quarters on the *Columbia*, a replica of the first ship to sail around the world.

1965

Disneyland marked its 10th anniversary and "Great Moments with Mr. Lincoln" became the first World's Fair exhibit to be transplanted to the park. Slightly over 43 square miles of land in central Florida had been secretly pieced together in preparation of the announcement of Walt Disney World in Nov.

The Sunday night TV show had developed a regular mix of theatrical live-action films, animal as hero episodes, made for TV adventure shows and cartoon anthologies. *That Darn Cat* (Dec), a live-action feature, resulted in books and a few promotional items.

1966

Winnie the Pooh and the Honey Tree (Feb) was released as a featurette. Walt Disney World planning was a genuine news event whenever new ideas surfaced or there was a hint when construction might begin. Disneyland opened New Orleans Square, It's A Small World and Primeval World.

The impact of the death of Walt Disney on Dec 15 was one of world leader magnitude. His passing was noted in virtually every major newspaper in the world. It was a fitting tribute to a man who entertained in the universal communication of animated cartoons. Walt was driven by projects he wanted to bring to reality. The money and prestige which resulted were viewed as a means to attempt bigger undertakings. Each one was a chance to do things differently and better than before. Excellence was the only acceptable option. Disney's fertile imagination could envision dreams in great detail. His greatest assets were storytelling and his ability to extend himself through others who complemented his ideas and did much of the actual work. His real reward was seeing his dreams come true. Disney's sense of history and public relations were exceeded only by his knack of knowing what to do when things went wrong.

1967

Work on Walt Disney World, soon the largest private construction project in America, began on May 30.

Feature films included *The Adventures of Bullwhip Griffin* (Mar), *The Gnome-Mobile* (July) and *The Happiest Millionaire* (June). *The Jungle Book*, Disney's 19th animated feature, premiered Oct 18.

Pirates of the Caribbean and a completely new Tomorrowland opened at Disneyland. Included were the People-Mover, G.E. Carousel of Progress (since moved to Walt Disney World), Adventures thru Inner Space, Flight to the Moon, Rocket Jets, Tomorrowland Terrace and the Circle-Vision 360 version of America the Beautiful.

Character watches with Mickey's picture resumed production for the first time since 1960.

1968

A nostalgia boom had been building since 1966. Classic pie-eyed Mickeys and Minnies were appearing on a growing variety of unauthorized merchandise. Joining the trend, the company agreed to license old style characters. They have appeared on new merchandise ever since.

Winnie the Pooh and the Blustery Day was released Dec 20.

1969

The Love Bug (Mar) introduced Herbie the VW and was a surprise box office winner.

The engineering masterpiece of Disneyland, The Haunted Mansion, began operation. The name of the Sunday TV program was changed again: from "Walt Disney's Wonderful World of Color" to "The Wonderful World of Disney."

1970

The Walt Disney Archives was established June 22.

The Aristocats, the last animated feature in which Walt Disney was involved, premiered on Dec 24.

1971

Walt Disney World opened on Oct 1 at an initial cost of $400 million. Roy O. Disney was on hand to dedicate the "Vacation Kingdom", but died soon after on Dec 20. He was president of Walt Disney Productions from 1945 to 1968, chairman and CEO until his death. He was a quiet man largely responsible for making Walt's dreams come true.

Bob Hope hosted a TV special opening "The Florida Project." In addition to the theme park, there were hotels, golfing, swimming, tennis, horseback riding, boating and convention facilities. Not all the attractions from Disneyland were duplicated at Walt Disney World, but the Florida park opened with some new ones: The Country Bear Jamboree and The Mickey Mouse Revue (since removed to Tokyo Disneyland). The centerpiece was Cinderella Castle.

The Walt Disney Distributing Company was formed and operated from Lake Buena Vista on the Walt Disney World property. The company sold Disney character merchandise of its own design and an extensive catalog of giftware. Items sold outside the theme parks were marketed under the label of "Disney Gifts." The company published merchandise catalogs from 1971 to 1977 when the operation was dissolved.

Bedknobs and Broomsticks was released Dec 13.

© W.D.P., a copyright form widely used in the 40's and 50's, was specifically eliminated from the company's official copyright practices.

1972-1980

The first known attempt to organize a Disneyana Collectors Club was made by Stephen Horn in 1972. Members received a membership card, homemade button and a ditto newsletter.

Walt Disney Productions celebrated its 50th anniversary in 1973 with a series of events that concluded with the Nov release of the animated version of *Robin Hood.*

DISNEYANA, by Cecil Munsey, was published by Hawthorn Books in 1974. Pirates of the Caribbean was the first major attraction added to Walt Disney World. America Sings (since removed) was added to Disneyland, replacing the Carousel of Progress, which was moved to Walt Disney World.

The Space Mountain attraction opened Jan 1975 at Walt Disney World. Disneyland got the simulated space ride in 1977. In June 1975 "America on Parade", commemorating the 200th birthday of the United States, began in both theme parks. It was the broadest merchandised event the theme parks had ever produced. The elaborate show parade continued until Sept 1976.

The Disneyana Shop in the Disneyland Emporium complex opened in Jan 1976. Originally the shop sold antique Disneyana items purchased at toy shows and from private dealers. Each item was authenticated and sold with a description card. Maintaining a steady supply of merchandise, however, was impossible. Within three years the shop converted completely to limited edition collectibles, cels, and other items of a collectible nature.

In Jan 1977 a new "TV Mickey Mouse Club" went on the air. It failed to attract interest equal to the old black and white episodes being syndicated at the time. It didn't last two full seasons. *The Rescuers* (Jun) and *Pete's Dragon* (Nov) were 1977's best merchandised features.

The big event of 1978 was Mickey Mouse's 50th birthday, celebrated the year long at Disneyland, Walt Disney World and in a special release of *Mickey's Birthday Party* at theaters across the nation. Big Thunder Mountain Railroad opened Sept 1978 at Disneyland and two years later at Walt Disney World. *The Black Hole* was released Dec 21, 1979.

The Mouse Club, a group of Disneyana collectors, was organized and issued its first newsletter in Jan 1980. Disneyland was 25 years old in 1980. After 20 years on NBC "The Wonderful World of Disney" was cancelled. CBS picked up the program, but the arrangement concluded with the 1982 season, ending a 29-year institution.

1981-1983

Walt Disney World had its Tencennial in 1981. EPCOT Center opened Oct 1, 1982 at an initial cost exceeding $1 billion. *The Fox and the Hound* premiered in July 1981.

The first Mouse Club convention was held in Anaheim, CA in Aug 1982. The second, a year later. The annual convention was skipped in '84 due to the Olympics, but resumed in '85. *TRON* (July '82) was designed in tune with the electronic game craze.

Apr 15, 1983 was the official opening day of Tokyo Disneyland. The Disney Channel, a pay-TV service, began broadcasting Apr 18. "Horizons" was added to EPCOT and a new Fantasyland greeted June visitors to the original Disneyland (The Pirate Ship, Skull Rock and a movie theater were removed to make room). The year ended with the release of *Mickey's Christmas Carol*, the first new Mickey film in 30 years.

1984

Donald's 50th birthday was the major event of 1984 until the Olympics took over in July and Aug. Back in 1980 Disney artist Bob Moore designed Sam the Eagle, the mascot for the Olympics, and Walt Disney Productions donated him to the Los Angeles Olympic Committee. Sam appeared on thousands of items and promotional material in the four year period. Sport Goofy, the official mascot of the French Olympic team, was also widely merchandised.

Disney's feature films had been going downhill for several years. The film business and audiences changed while Disney continued to turn out "G" rated family entertainment. Older teens and young adults (the majority of movie audiences) preferred "PG" and "R" rated films. Even top Disney animated features caused problems for exhibitors. The films would do well in day and evening showings -- the child and family market -- but did poorly for showings after 8:45 pm. The Disney name on a film, long an asset, became a liability to the movie house and a turn-off to many filmgoers. Thus Touchstone Films was formed. *Splash* was the first release in Mar 1984.

The company survived two takeover attempts in 1984 and attracted new management. Michael Eisner and Frank Wells joined the company in September as Chairman and President respectively.

1985

Disneyland marked its 30th year in 1985 with a prize awarded to every 30th, 300th, 3000th, 300,000th and 3 millionth visitor. An estimated $12 million dollars worth of gifts and GM automotibles were awared to attract visitors -- over two-thirds the amount needed to construct the original Disneyland 30 years previous.

The Black Cauldron (July) was the first animated feature in which the Xerox camera was replaced by a new photo transfer process that restored the hand-inked look of earlier animation. The process has since been abandoned because of cost and artistic problems.

New management raised prices at the theme parks and to return Disney to network TV with two Saturday morning kid shows: "The Wuzzles" and "Disney's Adventures of The Gummi Bears."

1986

An expanded management team, led by Michael Eisner, Frank Wells and Jeffery Katzenberg, stepped up marketing and development. The name was changed to The Walt Disney Company on Feb 6. The gift-giver machines introduced for Disneyland's 30th anniversary worked overtime making every park guest a winner. Some won new GM cars. Most got a pin or free popcorn. The live action success, *Down and Out in Beverly Hills* (Jan 31), was quickly followed by *Ruthless People* (June 27). *The Great Mouse Detective* (July 2), based on *Basil of Baker Street*, was the 26th animated feature produced, and the last begun by previous management. Captain EO finally opened at EPCOT and Disneyland after several delays (Sept 18). Walt Disney World began celebrating its 15th birthday on Oct 1 with a car/prize giveaway promotion similar to the one used at Disneyland the previous two seasons.

The studio underwent major remodeling. The once inconspicuous location was marked with a sign and Mickey was painted on the water tower.

The Living Seas opened Jan 15 at EPCOT Center.

The Disney Sunday Movie premiered on the ABC network Feb 2.

The Disney characters were also invited to EPCOT Center and merchandise produced under foreign licenses is now sold at World Showcase shops, a practice instituted by the new management.

The Cinderella Castle Mystery Tour, Alice's Tea Party and American Journeys in Circle-Vision 360 opened in Tokyo Disneyland.

1987

The year began with the 60 hour "interplanetary launch" of Star Tours at Disneyland. A special free watch and 3 to 5 hour lines awaited visitors. The attraction was the first using the Lucas film *Star Wars* characters. A new copyright form -- © Disney -- began showing up on merchandise.

The Euro Disneyland agreement was signed March 24 for a location near Paris, France. A 1992 opening was planned.

The 50th Anniversary of Snow White was the year-long theme park and merchandise promotion. Disney Dollars were issued at Disneyland. Nearly $2 million worth of $1 Mickey and $5 Goofy bills were printed.

Disney Dollars went on sale at Walt Disney World Oct 2. Disney Stores opened in Glendale and San Francisco malls.

"Duck Tales", an animated series of 65 original episodes produced for the TV syndication market, began airing on Sept 18.

Tokyo Disneyland premiered Captain EO and Big Thunder Mountain Railroad.

1988

Mickey Mouse celebrated his 60th birthday in style in a year-long promotion centered around Mickey's Birthday Land at Walt Disney World. The Norway Pavilion opened in EPCOT's World Showcase. The Grand Floridian Resort Hotel officially began operation at Walt Disney World, to be joined by the Caribbean Beach Resort. Construction was begun on the Dolphin and Swan luxury hotels connecting to EPCOT.
Tokyo Disneyland celebrated its 5th anniversary.
Who Framed Roger Rabbit (Jun 22), produced in association with AMBLIN Entertainment, was the top grossing film of the year and the animated feature *Oliver and Company* (Nov 18) introduced the latest Disney characters -- Dodger, Oliver, Georgette, Tito, Fagin, Sykes, Einstein, Francis, Rita, Jenny, Roscoe and Desoto.
The first Pleasure Island building at Lake Buena Vista, a 10 screen theatre complex, opened Dec 11.

1989

Hollywood Pictures, the third motion picture producing division, was created by The Walt Disney Company (Feb 1). Major focus was on Walt Disney World where the third gated attraction, the Disney/MGM Studio Tour, opened May 1. Pleasure Island, a complex of nightclub and shops geared to young adults, and Typhoon Lagoon, the latest in water parks, were to open later in the summer. The first of several Roger Rabbit cartoons scheduled premiered with *Honey, I Shrunk the Kids*.
Splash Mountain, the new log flume attraction at Disneyland, was to open at Disneyland by late summer while Star Tours was added to Tokyo Disneyland and site development began at Euro Disneyland near Paris.

A5000 AMERICAN POTTERY COMPANY

The American Pottery Company was the marketing name used from 1943 to 1945 by what became the Evan K. Shaw Company of Los Angeles. The ceramic figures, planters and chinaware produced in the American Pottery name and style are included here. They were sold with identifying paper foil labels, but most were removed like price tags. Some figures are stamped under the glaze in a place not visible when displayed. Markings varied on identical pieces by year. American Pottery pieces are normally characterized by the large, outlined eye treatment. American designs were continued by Evan K. Shaw, some under the American name.

Vernon Kilns, another California pottery, ceased production of Disney figures in 1942. Selected pieces produced from the Vernon Kilns molds were produced and sold by American, but do not appear in ads after 1945. American operated independently, or as an isolated Shaw division, for 2 years. Identical pieces were produced by Shaw until 1955, some still identified as American Pottery. (see S3000 EVAN K. SHAW COMPANY)

A5001	Bambi w/butterfly, large	50 - 135
A5002	Bambi w/o butterfly, large	50 - 120
A5003	Bambi w/o butterfly, small A	50 - 125
A5004	Bambi w/o butterfly, small B	50 - 115
A5005	Faline, large	45 - 90
A5006	Thumper	20 - 65
A5007	Thumper's Girlfriend	20 - 65
A5008	Flower	20 - 65
A5010	Wise Owl	35 - 125
A5015	Mickey	55 - 175
A5016	Minnie	55 - 185
A5017	Donald	50 - 160
A5025	Dumbo	20 - 60
A5026	Pinocchio	50 - 200
A5027	Jiminy Cricket	60 - 225
A5028	Figaro, walking	40 - 145
A5030	Brer Rabbit Planter	200 - 350
A5035	Snow White	50 - 200
A5036	Seven Dwarfs, each	30 - 80
A5040	Bambi Dinnerware Cup	15 - 45
A5041	Bambi Pitcher	35 - 125
A5042	Bambi Bowl	25 - 80
A5043	Bambi Plate	25 - 80
A5045	Donald, from nephews baseball set	45 - 175
A5046	Huey, Louie or Dewey, baseball set, each	25 - 65
A5050	Thumper Planter	45 - 175
A5055	Playful Pluto w/ball	25 - 90
A5056	Playful Pluto, crouched	25 - 90

A5057 Playful Pluto, sniffing	25 - 90
A5058 Playful Pluto, alert	25 - 90
A5060 Donald Cookie Jar	80 - 240

A7000 ANIMATION CELS & BACKGROUNDS

A cel, short for celluloid, represents the action of usually one character in one frame of an animated film. It takes 24 cels, photographed one at a time against a painted background, for each second of screen time, or 1440 per minute. Except for some recently produced serigraphed (screen printed) cels, limited edition "gallery" cels and souvenir cels from the Animation Studio Tour in Florida, each is a one-of-a-kind piece of art. Collecting them demands a certain amount of knowledge and expertise.

Originally, cels were traced onto the front of clear celluloid sheets using pen or brush and ink then painted on the reverse with specially prepared gum-based paints. Cels were intended to last long enough to meet production needs. The paints and inks were designed for easy removal, as early cels were washed and reused from film to film. Thus, it is a gift of fortune when old cels remain intact today. The paint dehydrates and flakes easily, especially on older cels. So care is recommended during handling and framing. Prior to 1940 cels were made of nitrocellulose, an unstable and flammable material. The change to safety cels, made of cellulose acetate, began with Disney's *Fantasia*.

Cels continue to lead Disneyana to new value heights at auctions nationwide. The highest value realized at press deadline exceeded $148,500 for a prominent B&W cel and matching background from the 1934 production of *The Orphans' Benefit*. Competition for choice set-ups -- cels and their matching backgrounds -- has been nothing short of mercuric since 1985 when around $2,000 would have bought a set-up now selling for over $10,000. Nonetheless, excellent examples of Disney animation art are still available for $150 and up.

Cels first became commercially available in 1937 as a result of a licensing agreement between San Francisco art dealer Guthrie Courvoisier and the Disney brothers. Art first offered through the Courvoisier Gallery was from *Snow White*. Special set-ups were prepared by a 20 artist unit at the Disney Studios using original and stenciled backgrounds on a variety of art boards and wood veneer. Characters in studio-prepared set-ups were usually cut out of the original cel and adhered directly to the background. Set-ups usually had two small labels: a copyright/"handle with care" notice and a label noting the title of the film. Backs were sealed using a special colored paper and a white label was added stating the art's provenance. Because Courvoisier distributed animation art to many other galleries it is not unusual to see labels from local framers and sellers in addition to those placed by the Studio. *Pinocchio* was the last film prepared by the Studio unit for Courvoisier.

59

By 1938-39 cels from other Disney films were offered through Courvoisier, but the cost of preparing the art at the Studio was getting out of balance with the revenue the program was yielding. Roy Disney suggested Courvoisier begin preparing the set-ups themselves. Working out of a warehouse in San Francisco, Courvoisier hired artists from nearby colleges to put together the Disney art. The elaborate wood veneer and stenciled backgrounds were no longer produced. In their place were chalk and pencil concepts of what a background might look like. The Courvoisier artists, in most cases, never saw the films. The Courvoisier-prepared backgrounds may be distinguished from those prepared at the Disney Studios by a tiny "WDP" symbol placed in the lower right corner of the art. It seems ironic Courvoisier would place a studio-like symbol on their own art in order to make it seem as though it came from the Disney Studios. There were no paints to repair the cels in Courvoisier's warehouse so they began laminating the cels in a rigid high-heat plastic envelope. As America entered World War II sales of animation art began to decrease and Courvoisier ceased the sale of Disney cels in 1942. The company remained a licensee until 1946 by selling prints and imitation multiplane camera set-ups screen printed on glass and cardboard. These multiplane decorative units sell for $100 to $300. About 15 different ones were produced.

The Studio continued to prepare cel set-ups as decorative items for internal use and as gifts for special visitors. Most are identifiable by a Walt Disney Productions label with copy very much like the one used by Courvoisier. No animation art marketing effort was in effect from 1943 to 1954. Set-ups from films produced during those years were scare and now command high prices.

Beginning in 1955 cels were sold at Disneyland as souvenirs at the Art Corner in Tomorrowland. Featured were cels from *Lady and the Tramp* and later *Sleeping Beauty* as well as other current features and television shows. Prices began at $1.25. A distinctive metallic gold label authenticates the art as having been sold at Disneyland. Over the years five different versions of the label were used. The cels sold in the theme park had inexpensive paperboard mats and no backgrounds. As the program continued, the Studio mass produced litho backgrounds from *Sleeping Beauty*, *101 Dalmatians*, *The Sword in the Stone* and *Mary Poppins* for use in these souvenir set-ups. In addition, for a limited time, the Studio produced *Disney Classics*, high grade photographic prints of special cel set-ups especially made for this purpose. An embossed mat was used for the Classics and a gold metallic label with green ink noted the "art's" authenticity.

101 Dalmatians, released in 1961, was Disney's first feature-length film using the xerographic process. The animation drawings were "copied" onto the cel by machine instead of by hand, giving the characters a softer, sketchier look. Gone was the intricate colored hand inking. And in 1966 the Art corner was gone as well to make way for a new Tomorrowland. The remaining Art Corner cels were sold at the Emporium on Main Street until the supply ran out. Cels were not offered again at Disneyland until 1973 when the Disney Original Art Program was organized under the Consumer Products Division.

Instead of offering cels in trimmed sizes as before, the Disney Original Art Program offered the art in full size with better mats and featuring the special embossed seal. Later the seal would be changed to a hot stamp version about the size of a silver dollar, and in 1988 the seal was again changed to dime size.

In recent years the Studio has begun to issue Limited Edition cels along with cels from current film releases. For a list of dealers offering original Disney art you may write to: The Disney Original Art Program, Consumer Products Division, The Walt Disney Company, 500 S. Buena Vista Street, Burbank, CA 91521.

Because of their age and fragility it is not unusual to find damaged cels and backgrounds. S/R Laboratories animation art conservation center in Agoura, CA is the recognized authority on Disney animation art and they are glad to answer the needs of collectors, galleries, museums and dealers. Call the lab at 818-991-9955 for further information and assistance.

Many outstanding cels were never sold commercially and have no labels or seals. Animator Ward Kimball recalls giving out cels and drawings to the children in his neighborhood. Very often a cel or original drawing was sent to a young would-be animator just for writing a letter to Walt and many pieces were sent to relatives or friends of employees as examples of the Studio's work. These cels of virtually every Disney film still exist somewhere.

Now that animation art has entered the fine art arena and values have begun to climb, counterfeit cels and backgrounds are more common. It requires a trained eye to recognize a fake. In a single case in 1982, Walt Disney Productions prosecuted an artist for the creation of over 18,000 bogus cels. A supply of equally fake labels was confiscated as well. So collectors should be aware it is possible to get an education the hard way. Any questions regarding authenticity should be directed to S/R Labs.

Each cel should be appraised individually for the best estimate of value, but some general guidelines are provided for value comparison. Cel set-ups sold through the Courvoisier Galleries are usually priced from $1,200 up, but sales or trades of less desirable cels are more often in the $600 to $900 range. Higher demand cels from the early Disney classics can command $1,500 to $3,000 or more. Cels with matching back-grounds usually start at around $5,000 with $10,000 to $30,000 buying all but the record setters. Trimmed cels with Disneyland seals can command $50 to $500 depending on subject matter. Full cels released through the Disney Original Art Program are sold at the parks in the $100 to $500 range. *Oliver & Company* and *Who Framed Roger Rabbit?* cels were available with printed and photographic backgrounds.

Record Setting Cels and Background Setups (at the time sold)
- Mickey Mouse swatting flies, *Brave Little Tailor*, December 8, 1984 - $20,900
- Cel from *The Band Concert*, December 4, 1985 - $24,000
- Old Hag preparing the poison apple for Snow White, *Snow White and the Seven Dwarfs*, November 1986 - $30,800
- Pinocchio searching for Monstro underwater, *Pinocchio*, June 8, 1988 - $39,600
- Wicked Queen seated on the peacock throne, *Snow White and the Seven Dwarfs*, June 8, 1988 - $52,800
- Set-up from *The Mad Doctor*, June 8, 1988 - $63,800
- Background of the organ from the Seven Dwarfs cottage, *Snow White and the Seven Dwarfs*, November 10, 1988 - $28,600
- Background of the scary woods, *Snow White and the Seven Dwarfs*, November 10, 1988 - $37,400
- Mickey Mouse, *Lonesome Ghosts*, November 10, 1988 - $49,500
- Set-up of Mickey Mouse prompting from the wings, *Orphans' Benefit*, November 10, 1988 - $121,000
- Set-up of the orphans enjoying the performance, *Orphans' Benefit*, November 10, 1988 - $148,500

The totals above include a 10% buyer's premium.

A7500 ANIMATION ART

There are many kinds of animation art. Character sketches, model sheets, story board panels, camera movement layouts and painted backgrounds are various types of art required in addition to actual character animation pencil drawings. Animators do key drawings for character movement required for a scene. Assistant animators and "inbetweeners" do all the other necessary drawings to make the action flow smoothly. Once checked and "pencil tested" these final drawings are transferred to cels.

Over the years many examples of this type of art have reached the public. Each piece must be evaluated individually. Major factors affecting collector desirability include the artist, type of drawing, character, the film and artistic nature of the work.

B1350 BANKS

The first Mickey banks were produced before licenses were granted. There has been a steady supply of new designs ever since. They are sought by both bank and Disneyana collectors -- a "cross collectible." No polyethylene banks are included in this edition.

B1354 Five Fingered Tin Litho Mechanical Bank 1,800 - 10,000
B1358 Mickey, ceramic head, pie-cut eyes   100 - 350

Zell Products Corp. produced a variety of Mickey Mouse and Three Little Pigs banks in the years 1933 and 1934.

B1360	Leatherette Covered Mickey Book Bank, 1933-34	25 - 80
B1361	Same as B1410 -- World's Fair version	60 - 125
B1362	Leatherette Covered Treasure Chest, 1933-34	25 - 80
B1363	Same as B1412 -- World's Fair version	60 - 125
B1364	Telephone, candlestick or cradle type, N.N. Hill Brass	75 - 260
B1368	First Step Book Bank, 1935-37	35 - 125
B1369	Suitcase Bank, 1935-37	90 - 275
B1372	Glaser Crandell Jam Jar w/label, 1935	100 - 250
B1372	Same w/no label	20 - 85
B1374	Post Office, litho tin	40 - 90
B1375	Mickey Dime Register, 1939	25 - 85
B1376	Donald Dime Register, 1939	25 - 85
B1377	Dopey Dime Register, 1939	20 - 75
B1378	Snow White Dime Register, 1938	20 - 65
B1382	Mickey, figural, 1938	35 - 225
B1383	Donald, figural, 1938	50 - 250
B1384	Dopey, figural, 1938	25 - 125
B1386	Pinocchio or Jiminy Cricket, figural, 1940, Crown	25 - 75
B1387	Hyacinth Hippo, leaping, ceramic	200 - 700
B1391	Ferdinand the Bull, Crown	25 - 75
B1392	Dumbo, figural, Crown	70 - 150
	Nash Mustard (see D8000 DONALD DUCK PRODUCTS)	
B1399	Pluto, Leeds	8 - 25
B1400	Dumbo, Leeds	10 - 35
B1401	Mickey, Leeds	10 - 35
B1402	Donald, standing, Leeds	10 - 35
B1403	Donald, sitting, Leeds	10 - 35
B1405	Dopey, Leeds	9 - 30
B1410	Alice In Wonderland, Leeds	10 - 35
B1415	Marx 5¢, 10¢ and 25¢ Register, tin litho	50 - 175
B1416	2nd National Duck Bank	50 - 175
B1420	Mickey Mouse Club, figural, ceramic	18 - 45
B1425	Mickey Mouse, band leader, plastic	10 - 35
B1428	Western Donald, plastic	10 - 35
B1430	Donald Book, plastic, 1964, Ideal	8 - 20
B1435	Sitting Minnie Mouse, ceramic	8 - 24

Enesco Imports, Inc. (Chicago) 1968-71 (B1440-B1443)

B1440	Uncle Scrooge, in bed	20 - 65
B1441	Clock, available in red, blue and yellow	10 - 35
B1442	Snow White at Wishing Well	7 - 20
B1443	Winnie the Pooh and Honey Jar	6 - 18
B1444	Mickey's Head	8 - 30
B1445	Donald's Head	8 - 30

he major escalation in the value placed on Disney animation cels began December 984 when this Mickey Mouse swatting flies from the *Brave Little Tailor,* estimated ing up to $2,500, sold for $20,900. The following December 4, 1985 this cel from *Th and Concert,* the first Mickey Mouse cartoon in color, went to the high bidder for $24,00 hotos courtesy of Christie's East, New York.

In November 1986 the Old Hag preparing the poison apple for Snow White realized $30,800. Two backgrounds from *Snow White and the Seven Dwarfs* have since joined the ranks of animation art record breakers. The organ from the Seven Dwarfs cottage was sold for $28,600 and the scary woods went for $37,400 at the November 10, 1988 auction. Photo courtesy of Christie's East, New York.

Pinocchio searching for Monstro underwater holds the current record for a cel and background setup from Walt Disney's second animated feature. It fetched $39,600 in the June 8, 1988 auction at Christie's East. Mickey Mouse from *Lonesome Ghosts*, a popular 1937 cartoon, sold for $49,500 at the November 10, 1988 Animation Art sale. Photos courtesy of Christie's East, New York.

The Wicked Queen seated on the peacock throne, easily one of the most beautiful Disney multi-cel and background setups from *Snow White and the Seven Dwarfs,* went to the highest bidder for $52,800 on June 8, 1988. The same day a setup from *The Mad Doctor,* a 1933 Mickey cartoon, set a new record of $63,800. Photos courtesy of Christie's East, New York.

SCENE	FIELD	N.S.	E.W.	ANIMATOR		SCENE	FIELD	N.S.	E.W.	ANIMATOR			
10				LUNDY	UMR 5	6	3¾			LUNDY		14	LUNDY 9

Two more black and white cel and background setups were in the November 10, 1988 auction at Christie's. There were two pieces from the original 1934 version of the *Orphans' Benefit.* Mickey prompting from the wings was expected to set a new record, but few foresaw a selling price of $121,000. The biggest surprise was yet to come. A setup of the orphans enjoying the performance, void of any major character, sold for $148,500. Four other cels from the *Orphans' Benefit* were found with these two. They have been described as the superior pieces from the lot. What price will they bring? Photos courtesy of Christie's East, New York.

PICTURE
SOUVENIR
BOOK of **Disneyland** IN NATURAL COLOR
© 1955 WALT DISNEY PRODUCTIONS

Know All Ye By These Presents:

that _____

has rocketed round trip to the moon from the Disneyland Spaceport via TWA Rocket Ship and is hereby awarded this Lunar Flight Certificate.

The distance to the moon, 238,857 miles, is exceeded daily by TWA on its regular Earth flights across the U.S.A., Europe, Africa & Asia.

Disneyland, California

Date _____ TWA Rocket Ship Captain _____

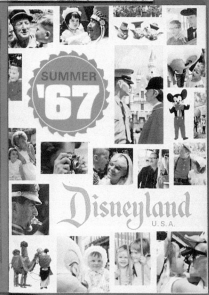

SUMMER '67

Disneyland U.S.A.

MONSANTO

Hall of Chemistry

in Disneyland
ANAHEIM, CALIFORNIA

It's time you discovered

STORYBOARD

YOUR DISNEYANA MAGAZINE

The best source for information written for, by, and about collectors of Disneyana.

Not only will you read about collectibles in this slick, full-color magazine...there's news about the artists, collectors, products, cels, buying, selling, shows, studios, theme parks...**EVERYTHING** Disneyana!

Don't miss another issue. Subscribe today!

1 year (6 issues) for $18

2 years (12 issues) for $32

Send a check or money order today. We also accept Visa or MasterCard.

StoryboarD Magazine
Bobit Publishing Company
2512 Artesia Boulevard
Redondo Beach, CA 90278
(213) 376-8788

Call us for details about advertising too!

The items shown above are just a sample of Disneyana collectibles featured in each issue.

B1448	Mouseclubhouse Treasury Bank, w/Mouse-key, Mattel	25 - 90
B1450	Mickey, on stool	8 - 20
B1451	Minnie, on stool	8 - 20
B1452	Uncle Scrooge, w/money bag	8 - 20
B1455	Uncle Scrooge, plastic premium made in Finland, but given to children opening accounts. Name of the U.S. bank often appears on reverse of chest	10 - 35
B1460	Character house & vehicle banks, 6 different, each	5 - 15

B2500 BOOKS

The first Disney book was published by Bibo and Lang (NYC) in 1930. David McKay Publishing Co. (Philadelphia, PA) published story books from 1931-39. Whitman Publishing Company (Racine, WI) began in 1933 and remains the largest producer of Disney books. Simon & Schuster initiated the Golden Book series in 1944. Both Whitman and the Simon & Schuster line of Disney books have since been acquired by Western Printing & Lithographing and operate as Western Publishing Company, Inc.

Many other publishers have produced Disney titles over the years. These are noted throughout the listings.

This major classification is broken down into 15 subsections. Titles are chronological by copyright date in each section. Characters and book series are grouped whenever possible. All Golden Books, for example, appear together rather than in copyright order under B5200 BOOKS -- STORY.

B2501 BOOKS -- ART AND ANIMATION

Books in this section deal with the work of the Disney studio as art -- not merely drawings required to produce a film. Most provide some history and identify artists involved. They are virtually all of the coffee table variety -- large, colorful, and attractively produced. Dust jackets increase value. B2531 also came in a collector's edition with serigraph inserts. The collector's edition of B2538 included a strip of original motion picture film.

B2503	Snow White Sketch Book, 1938, Collins	100 - 850
B2505	Fantasia, 1940, w/dust jacket, Simon & Schuster	85 - 400
B2507	The Art of Walt Disney, 1942, Macmillan	60 - 200
B2510	He Drew As He Pleased, 1948, Simon & Schuster	12 - 100
B2515	The Art of Animation, 1958, Golden Press	25 - 100
	(A copy was given to every Disney employee at the time.)	
B2518	The Disney Films, 1973, Crown	4 - 15

B2519	Magic Moments, 1973, Mondadori	8 - 35
B2520	The Art of Walt Disney, 1973, Abrams, 1st Ed	
	w/mylar dust jacket	30 - 100
B2521	The Art of Walt Disney, 1975, Abrams, 8-1/2"	
	by 11", hard	1 - 12
B2522	The Art of Walt Disney, 1975, Abrams, 8-1/2"	
	by 11", paper	1 - 10
B2523	The Art of Walt Disney, 1984, Abrams, 2nd E	8 - 35
B2525	Building a Better Mouse, 1976, Library of	
	Congress	5 - 25
B2527	Walt Disney's America, 1978, Abbeville	5 - 20
B2528	Walt Disney's Treasury of Children's Classics,	
	1978, Abrams	5 - 18
B2529	Walt Disney's Christmas Treasury, 1978, Abbeville	5 - 15
B2530	Great Moments from the Films of Walt Disney,	
	1981, Rutledge	5 - 25
B2531	Walt Disney's Snow White and the Seven Dwarfs,	
	1979, Viking	5 - 20
B2532	Treasury of Stories from Silly Symphonies, 1981,	
	Abrams	5 - 15
B2535	The Fine Art of Walt Disney's Donald Duck,	
	1981, Another Rainbow, bound folio of paint-	
	ings by Carl Barks	100 - 350
B2536	Walt Disney's Uncle Scrooge McDuck:	
	His Life and Times, 1981, Celestial Arts	75 - 150
B2538	Disney Animation -- The Illusion of Life, 1981,	
	Abbeville	20 - 75
B2539	Treasures of Disney Animation Art, 1982,	
	Abbeville	15 - 75
B2540	Walt Disney's World of Fantasy, 1982, Everest	
	House	5 - 15
B2541	Walt Disney's Fantasia, 1983, Abrams	5 - 25
B2544	Snow White and the Seven Dwarfs & the Making	
	of the Classic Film, 50th Anniversary, 1987, Simon	
	& Schuster	5 - 15
B2545	The Complete Story of Walt Disney's Snow White	
	and the Seven Dwarfs, 50th Anniversary reprint	
	of B5285, Abrams	5 - 15

B2600 BOOKS -- BIG LITTLE BOOKS, BIG BIG BOOKS, BETTER LITTLE BOOKS, WEE LITTLE BOOKS AND PENNY BOOKS

Whitman began publishing a "Big Little Book" series in 1932. The books featured comic, radio, and movie heroes and sold for 10¢. The first Disney title appeared in 1933. There have been more Mickey Mouse titles (29) than any other character. There have also been 20

Donald Duck BLB's and numerous other Disney titles as listed.

In 1938 the series name was changed to "A Better Little Book." This logo was used until 1949 when a short series of tall format "New Better Little Books" appeared. TV knocked this popular childhood series of comic character books out-of-print until 1967, when it once again appeared under the Big Little Book logo. At first the new books had a thinner, hard cover, since replaced by a simple cover weight printing stock. Many of the modern BLB's, however, have appeared in color vs. the historical black and white. All Disney titles are simply credited to the Disney Studio.

There were six Wee Little Books sold as a boxed set. The series is a single story of BLB length divided into six paper bound books. Perhaps it was a test.

The words "Walt Disney's" precede many titles. Whitman stock numbers are shown following the copyright date.

Penny Books were printed on a very cheap paper and are rarely found in fine or better condition. The market for BLB's has been sluggish for several years. Values given are for books with complete covers and no missing pages.

Big Little Books

B2600	Mickey Mouse, 1933, #717	10 - 120
B2601	Mickey Mouse , 1933, new cover, #717	10 - 90
B2602	Mickey Mouse in Blaggard Castle, 1934, #726	8 - 35
B2603	Mickey Mouse the Mail Pilot, 1933, #731	8 - 30
B2604	Same as B2603 except soft cover & larger size, 1933	8 - 30
B2605	Same as B2603 except soft cover American Gas giveaway, 1933	10 - 50
B2610	Mickey Mouse Sails For Treasure Island, 1933, #750	8 - 40
B2612	Mickey Mouse Presents a Walt Disney Silly Symphony, 1934, #756	8 - 35
B2614	Mickey Mouse Sails For Treasure Island, 1935, Kolynos giveaway, two versions, no #	10 - 50
B2615	Mickey Mouse the Detective, 1934, #1139	8 - 30
B2616	Same as B2615 except soft cover	10 - 40
B2617	Mickey Mouse and the Bat Bandit, 1935, #1153	5 - 25
B2618	Same as B2617, 1935, different soft cover, no #	10 - 45
B2620	Mickey Mouse and Bobo the Elephant, 1935, #1160	8 - 30
B2621	Mickey Mouse and the Sacred Jewel, 1936, #1187	8 - 30
B2622	Mickey Mouse Presents Walt Disney's Silly Symphonies Stories, 1936, #1111	10 - 45
B2623	Mickey Mouse and Pluto the Racer, 1936, #1128	8 - 30
B2624	Silly Symphony Featuring Donald Duck, 1937, #1169	10 - 45

NOT only is Mickey Mouse the most popular motion picture and comic strip character, but he is the most beloved personality in modern children's fiction. He has proved himself to be the super book salesman of today. The BIG BIG BOOK is our latest. Be sure you have a "big" stock of this number as it is one of the "biggest" sellers we have ever presented.

Write for full particulars

WHITMAN PUBLISHING COMPANY

Licensee

Racine, Wisconsin

New York Office: 200 Fifth Avenue · Chicago Office: 209 So. State Street

Bibo & Lang published the first Mickey Mouse book in 1930. The David McKay Company was Mickey's major publisher from 1931 to 1934 and continued to do a few titles until 1939. Whitman produced its first titles in 1933 and by 1935 became the leading publisher of Disney books. The Big Little Book and Big Big Book lines were some of the most widely sold.

B2626	Mickey Mouse Runs His Own Newspaper, 1937, #1409	5 - 55
B2628	Silly Symphony Featuring Donald Duck and His Misadventures, 1937, #1441	8 - 30
B2629	Snow White and the Seven Dwarfs, 1938, #1460	5 - 25
B2630	Pluto the Pup, 1938, #1467	5 - 20
B2631	Mickey Mouse in the Race for Riches, 1938, #1476	5 - 25
B2632	Donald Duck Hunting for Trouble, 1938, #1478	5 - 20

Better Little Books

B2635	Such A Life! Says: Donald Duck, 1939, #1404	5 - 20
B2636	Mickey Mouse in the Foreign Legion, 1940, #1428	5 - 20
B2637	Donald Forgets to Duck, 1939, #1434	5 - 20
B2638	Pinocchio and Jiminy Cricket, 1940, #1435	8 - 35
B2639	Mickey Mouse and the Pirate Submarine,1939, #1463	5 - 25
B2642	Mickey Mouse On Sky Island, 1941, #1417	4 - 22
B2643	Donald Duck Says: Such Luck! , 1941, #1424	4 - 22
B2644	Donald Duck Gets Fed Up, 1940, #1462	4 - 22
B2645	Mickey Mouse and the Seven Ghosts, 1940, #1475	4 - 22

New Better Little Book Series With Flip Movies

B2648	Dumbo: Only His Ears Grew!, 1941, #1400	5 - 30
B2649	Mickey Mouse in the Treasure Hunt, 1941, #1401	4 - 15
B2650	Donald Duck Sees Stars, 1941, #1422	4 - 15
B2651	Mickey Mouse and the Magic Lamp, 1942, #1429	4 - 15
B2652	Donald Duck Headed For Trouble, 1942, #1430	4 - 15
B2653	Donald Duck Off the Beam!, 1943, #1438	4 - 15
B2654	Walt Disney's Bambi, 1942, #1469	5 - 25
B2655	Mickey Mouse and the Dude Ranch Bandit, 1943, #1471	4 - 15
B2656	Bambi's Children, 1943, #1497 (no flip movie)	8 - 35

New Whitman Numbering Series Begins -- Some Disney titles in the previous 1400 series reappear with fewer pages. Flip movies were dropped in new titles.

B2660	Thumper and the Seven Dwarfs, 1944, #1409	10 - 45
B2661	Mickey Mouse Bellboy Detective, 1945, #1483	4 - 15
B2662	Donald Duck Is Here Again, 1944, #1484	4 - 15
B2663	Donald Duck Up In the Air, 1945, #1486 (Barks)	5 - 35
B2664	Mickey Mouse on the Cave-Man Island, 1944, #1499	4 - 18
B2665	Donald Duck and Ghost Morgan's Treasure, 1946, #1411	5 - 30
B2666	Mickey Mouse and the 'Lectro Box, 1946, #1413	4 - 18
B2667	Brer Rabbit, 1947, #1426	5 - 22
B2668	Donald Duck and the Green Serpent, 1947, #1432	5 - 25
B2669	Mickey Mouse and the Lazy Daisy Mystery, 1947, #1433	4 - 15
B2670	Mickey Mouse in the World of Tomorrow, 1948, #1444	4 - 15

B2671	Donald Duck Lays Down the Law, 1948, #1449	5-30
B2672	Mickey Mouse and the Desert Palace, 1948, #1451	4-18
B2673	Donald Duck in Volcano Valley, 1949, #1457	5-27
B2674	Mickey Mouse and the Stolen Jewels, 1949, #1464	5-20

New Better Little Book Series

B2675	Brer Rabbit, 1949, #704	2-12
B2676	Donald Duck and the Mystery of the Double X, 1949, #705	5-25
B2677	Mickey Mouse on the Haunted Island, 1950, #708	2-18
B2678	Cinderella and the Magic Wand, 1950, #711	2-12

Tall Book Series

| B2679 | Mickey's Dog Pluto, 1937 - 1943, #532 | 5-22 |

Big Big Books

| B2680 | The Story of Mickey Mouse and the Smugglers, 1935, #4062, two cover versions available | 15 - 90 |

Wee Little Books

B2681	Mickey Mouse at the Carnival	5-20
B2682	Mickey Mouse and Tanglefoot	5-20
B2683	Mickey Mouse's Up Hill Fight	5-20
B2684	Mickey Mouse's Misfortune	5-20
B2685	Mickey Mouse Will Not Quit	5-20
B2686	Mickey Mouse Wins the Race	5-20
B2687	Boxed set of 6 books, 1934, #512	40 - 140

Penny Book Series 1938-39

B2687	Brave Little Tailor	5-25
B2688	Donald Duck's Cousin Gus	5-25
B2689	Donald's Better Self	5-25
B2690	Donald's Lucky Day	5-25
B2691	Farmyard Symphony	5-25
B2692	Goofy and Wilbur	5-25
B2693	Mickey's Gold Rush	5-25
B2694	The Practical Pig	5-25
B2695	Pluto at the Society Dog Show	5-25
B2696	The Ugly Duckling	5-25

Big Little Books -- Hardcover 1967-69 Series

B2700	Donald Duck - The Fabulous Diamond Fountain, 1967, #2009	3 - 8
B2701	Mickey Mouse Adventure in Outer Space, 1968, #2020	3 - 8
B2702	Goofy in Giant Trouble, 1968, #2021	2 - 6
B2703	Donald Duck Luck of the Ducks, 1969, #2033	3 - 6

Big Little Books -- Reissue and new paperback titles

(Different versions have printed prices ranging from 39¢ to 79¢)

B2710	Mickey Mouse Adventure in Outer Space, 1973, reissue, #5750	2 - 4
B2711	Goofy in Giant Trouble, 1973 reissue, #5751	2 - 4
B2712	Donald Duck The Fabulous Diamond Fountain,	

	1973 reissue, #5756-1		2 - 4
B2713	Donald Duck in Volcano Valley, 1973 rework of B2673, #5760		2 - 4
B2714	Donald Duck Luck of the Ducks, 1974 reissue, #5764		2 - 4
B2715	Mickey Mouse Mystery at Disneyland, 1975, #5770-1		3 - 5
B2716	Donald Duck The Lost Jungle City, 1975, #5773-1		2 - 4
B2717	Mickey Mouse Mystery at Dead Man's Cove, 1980, #5781 - 2		2 - 4

Golden Star Library

In 1967, Golden Press published BLB's with hard covers. There were four Disney titles in the series of twelve books.

B2750	Pinocchio, 1967, #6071	5-18
B2751	Sleeping Beauty and Cinderella, 1967, #6072	5-18
B2752	Snow White, 1967, #6076	5-18
B2753	Peter Pan, 1967, #6082	5-18

B2775 BOOKS -- COLORING, PAINTING AND ACTIVITY

There have been hundreds of titles in this class. Titles through 1955 are listed. Selected representative books are included thereafter. Several story books were printed on pulp stock and were intended for coloring. These titles are listed at BOOKS -- STORY. Whitman "reproduced" six titles in 1975. They are not faithful repros and each has a violet burst identifying them as "special edition from the 1930's original publication."

Saalfield Publishing Co. of Akron issued the first coloring/paint book in 1931 and remained a licensee until 1937. Whitman issued a Silly Symphony coloring book in 1934 and boxes of pictures to color soon after. They took over publication of coloring books in 1937.

Saalfield 1931-37

B2776	Mickey Mouse Pictures to Paint, 1931, #210	15 - 150
B2777	Mickey Mouse Coloring Book, 1931, #871	5-85
B2778	Mickey and Minnie Mouse Coloring Book, 1933, #979	5-55
B2779	Another Mickey Mouse Coloring Book, 1935, Ye Olden Days #2110	5-75
B2780	Mickey Mouse Book for Coloring, 1936, #2121	5-60
B2781 70	New Mickey Mouse Book to Color, 1937, #2165	5 -

Whitman

B2800	Silly Symphony Book to Color, 1932, #660	10 - 60
B2802	Draw and Paint Donald Duck, 1936, #670	5-50
B2803	The Walt Disney Paint Book, 1937, #2080	5-45

B2804	Walt Disney Paint Book, 1937, #677	5-45
B2808	Mickey Mouse Paint Book, 1937, #1069	5-45
B2810	Snow White & the Seven Dwarfs Paint Book, 1938, #621	2-25
B2811	Snow White & the Seven Dwarfs Paint Book, 1938, #696	4-40
B2812	Snow White & the Seven Dwarfs Paint Book, 1938, no #	4-40
B2813	Paint Book Animals from Snow White, 1938, #606	5-40
B2814	Walt Disney's Brave Little Tailor Paint and Crayon Book, 1938, #616	10 - 80
B2815	Farmyard Symphony Paintless Paint Book, 1939, #652	10 - 50
B2820	Ferdinand the Bull Paint Book, 1938, #645	5-35
B2823	Pinocchio Paint Book, 1939, #573	5-40
B2826	Fantasia Paint Book, 1939, #689	20 - 100
B2835	Bambi Paint Book, 1942, #664	5-25
B2837	Donald Duck Army Paint Book, 1942, #688	4-20
B2840	Walt Disney's Paint Book, 1943, #674	4-20
B2842	Walt Disney's Paint Book, 1944, #677	3-18
B2848	Walt Disney's Paint Book, 1946, #646	4-22
B2850	Walt Disney's Paint Book, 1946, #1150	3-18
B2860	Mickey and the Beanstalk Paint Book, 1948, #2072	4-20
B2862	Walt Disney's Paint Book, 1949, #1159	4-20
B2864	Cinderella Paint Book, 1950, #2092	4-20
B2866	Alice in Wonderland Paint Book, 1951, #2167	4-18
B2868	Peter Pan Coloring Book, 1952, #2186	3-15
B2869	Peter Pan Fun Book, 1952, #2185	3-15
B2871	Christmas Coloring Book, 1953, Dell no #	2-10
B2874	Lady and the Tramp Coloring Book, 1954, #1183	2-10
B2875	Pinocchio Coloring Book, 1954, #2031	2-12
B2878	Sketch A Graph Paint Book, 1955, Ohio Art , no #	1 - 6
B2879	Davy Crockett Coloring Book, 1955, #1190	2-10
B2880	Uncle Scrooge Coloring Book, 1955, Dell #130	10 - 50
B2883	Let's Go to Disneyland Coloring Book, 1956, Dell #140	3-20
B2884	Goofy Dots, 1956, #1413	1 - 8
B2885	True Life Adventures Coloring Book, 1957, #1656	3-15
B2886	Dutch Boy Disneyland Coloring Book, 1957, #F-39-57	3-15
B2887	Jimmie Dodd Magic Carpet Coloring Book, 1957, #1170	2-10
B2889	Zorro Coloring Book, 1958, #1190	2-10
B2890	Sleeping Beauty, 1959, Whitman #1759	8-35

Whitman reproduction coloring and story books from the 30's -- Mickey Mouse, Donald Duck and All Their Pals (#2057), A Walt Disney Paint Book (#2053), The Walt Disney Paint Book (#2055), Silly Symphony Book to Color (#2056), Mickey Mouse and Donald Duck Gag Book (#2052), and Draw and Paint Donald Duck (#2054), 1975, each .... 1 - 2

B2891	Other coloring or activity books 50's or 60's	2 - 10
B2892	Andy Burnett, 1958, #1185	2 - 10
B2893	Walt Disney Presents Disneyland Coloring Book, 1958, #1127	5 - 25
B2895	Walt Disney's Big Big Coloring Book, 1959, Watkins-Strathmore #1871	2 - 10
B2896	Donald Duck Trace and Color Book, 1960, #1661	2 - 20
B2900	Donald Duck Coloring Book, 1963, Watkins-Strathmore #1861-3	2 - 10
B2915	Winnie the Pooh, 1965, #1116	1 - 7
B2916	Bambi, w/fuzzy cover, 1966, #1180	1 - 9
B2918	The Love Bug, 1969, Hunts Catsup give-away	2 - 8
B2921	Other coloring or activity books 70's or 80's	1 - 6
B2922	Disneyland Coloring Book, 1970, #1050	2 - 10
B2925	A Visit to Walt Disney World Coloring Book, 1971, #1078	2 - 8

B3100 BOOKS -- CUT OR PUNCH OUT

There are two types -- paper doll books (see D7800 DOLLS - PAPER) and the punch or cut-out movie scenes or playsets found in this section. Prices are for complete, unpunched books. Complete sets of the punched figures and backgrounds have a value of 25%-30% of a complete book.

B3102	The Three Little Pigs, 1933, #989	80 - 350
B3104	Donald Duck and Clara Cluck, 1937, #969	190 - 450
B3106	Snow White and the Seven Dwarfs, 1938, #974	25 - 140
B3107	Snow White & Seven Dwarfs Masks, #990	15 - 55
B3108	Ferdinand the Bull, 1938, #925	25 - 90
B3110	Pinocchio, 1939, #974	20 - 180
B3111	Fantasia, 1940, #950	150 - 400
B3114	Bambi, 1942, #966	10 - 125
B3118	Alice In Wonderland, 1951, #2194	20 - 110
B3119	Peter Pan, 1952, #2112	25 - 120
B3122	Davy Crockett, 1955, #1943	8 - 80
B3125	Let's Build Disneyland, 1957, #1986	40 - 250
B3127	Zorro, 1957, Golden Funtime	5 - 45
B3130	Plastic Cut-Out Standups -- boxed sets, 1958-59	5 - 25
B3131	Individual -- Alice In Wonderland	5 - 15

B3132	Individual -- Peter Pan	5 - 15
B3133	Mickey Mouse Club	6 - 18
B3134	Donald and Daisy	5 - 15
B3135	Zorro	5 - 15
B3136	Sleeping Beauty Cut-Out Standups, 1959	10 - 35
B3145	Sleeping Beauty, 1959, Golden #GF155	6 - 25
B3146	Sleeping Beauty, 1959, Whitman #1987	6 - 25
B3149	Toby Tyler Circus Playbook, 1959, #1936	4 - 15
B3150	Dell Disneyland Park, 1960	8 - 35
B3152	101 Dalmatians, 1960	5 - 20
B3155	Babes in Toyland, 1961, Golden Giant	5 - 20
B3156	Babes in Toyland, 1961, Whitman Great Big	5 - 20
B3157	The Toymaker, 1961	4 - 15
B3160	Pinocchio, 1961, Golden	4 - 15
B3161	Pinocchio, 1961, Golden Giant	5 - 20
B3162	Pinocchio, 1961, YWP	4 - 15
B3165	Donald Duck and His Friends, 1961, Great Big	8 - 45
B3170	The Sword in the Stone, 1963, #1940	5 - 20
B3172	Winnie the Pooh, 1965, press-out	4 - 12
B3173	Winnie the Pooh, 1965, punch-out	4 - 12
B3180	Snow White, 1967	4 - 12
B3182	The Happiest Millionaire Play Money, 1967	2 - 8
B3185	Disneyland, 1963	8 - 45
B3190	Disneyland Press-out Book, 1970	5 - 30
B3193	Bedknobs and Broomsticks, 1971	3 - 10
B3194	Bedknobs and Broomsticks Soccer Game, 1971	3 - 10
B3195	A Visit to Walt Disney World, 1971	3 - 10
B3196	Country Bear Band, 1971	3 - 10
B3197	A Visit to Walt Disney World, 1971	4 - 20
B3198	Mickey Mouse Revue, 1971	5 - 25
B3200	Snow White and the Seven Dwarfs, 1973	2 - 8
B3202	Robin Hood Finger Puppets, 1973	1 - 6
B3210	Cinderella's Castle	2 - 10

Also see D7800 DOLLS -- PAPER

B3290 BOOKS -- DELL FAST ACTION

Whitman first tested four titles for distribution through Dell Publishing in 1936 -- none Disney. In 1938, 16 new titles, including 3 Disney were produced. Another 17, including 5 more Disney titles were released from 1939 through 1943. Several used BLB art.

B3291	Mickey Mouse in the Sheriff of Nugget Gulch, 1938	10 - 50
B3292	Donald Duck and the Ducklings, 1938	10 - 50
B3293	Mickey Mouse with Goofy and Mickey's Nephews, 1938	10 - 50

B3294	Donald Duck Out of Luck, 1940	5-25
B3295	Pinocchio and Jiminy Cricket, 1940	8-40
B3296	Donald Duck Takes It on the Chin, 1941	8-40
B3297	Dumbo the Flying Elephant, 1941, #10	9-45
B3298	Mickey Mouse and Pluto, 1942, #16	9-45

B3300 BOOKS -- LINEN LIKE

Linen Like picture story books get their name from the thicker, more durable paper stock used. These picture story books are oversized and extremely colorful. The words "linen-like" appear on most books, but not all the titles of similar production. Whitman was the publisher.

B3301	Donald Duck, first Donald Duck book, 1935, #978	40 - 200
B3302	Mickey Mouse and his Friends, 1936, #904	20 - 125
B3305	Mickey Mouse, 1937 (reprints Good House-keeping pages), #973	25 - 75
B3308	Pluto the Pup, 1937, #894	25 - 55
B3310	The Wise Little Hen, 1937, #888	25 - 65
B3311	Three Little Wolves, 1937, #895	10 - 45
B3312	Toby Tortoise and the Hare, 1938, #928	10 - 45
B3313	Elmer Elephant, 1938, #948	10 - 40
B3315	Hiawatha, 1938, #924	10 - 35
B3317	Mickey Mouse Alphabet, 1938, #889	25 - 65
B3319	Snow White and the Seven Dwarfs, 1938, #925	10 - 45
B3320	Snow White and the Seven Dwarfs, 1938, #927	10 - 45
B3321	Dopey -- He Don't Talk None, 1938, #955	25 - 70
B3323	Famous Seven Dwarfs, 1938, #933	30 - 150
B3324	Animals from Snow White and the Seven Dwarfs, #922	25 - 65
B3325	Clock Cleaners, 1938, #947	25 - 95
B3326	Ferdinand the Bull, 1938, #903	10 - 35
B3328	Pinocchio, 1940, #1061	12 - 40
B3329	Pinocchio, 1940, #1039	10 - 32
B3330	Pinocchio, 1940, #6881	10 - 32
B3335	Bambi Picture Book, 1942, #930	10 - 32

B3400 BOOKS -- GOLDEN BOOKS -- LITTLE, BIG, GIANT AND TINY

Little Library books, published by Simon and Schuster, began around 1942. Each was numbered and had a distinctive golden art border on the dust jacket spine and a rear panel title list. Disney titles were numbered separately from the original series. Approximately the first twenty regular series and the first three Disney titles had dust jackets. These early editions had blue binding tape spines. The name was changed to Little

Golden Books by the mid-40's, soon after D1, *Through the Picture Frame*, was issued in 1944. There are many cover and internal revisions of the more popular titles. Some original 42 page books were cut to 28, and then again to 24 pages. There were no books issued for D60 and D69. Several other small formats were tested. First editions are identified by the letter "A" on the last page in the lower right corner near the spine. Subsequent editions have progressive letters. A "G", for example, indicates the book is a 7th Edition printing.

Big and Giant Golden Books also began to appear in 1944, although the first several titles weren't called Golden Books. Again, there have been a large variety of covers, binding techniques, and editions. Popular titles are also available in library bindings. S & S sold the Golden Press line to the Western Publishing Co. in the 60's.

In 1978, the chronological "D" numbers were replaced by stocking code numbers and Disney titles mixed with the rest of the line. There have also been many special Golden Books over the years. These are listed at other classifications.

Tomart's code numbers have been adapted to include the Little Golden Books ID numbers.

Little Golden Books

B34D1	Through the Picture Frame	18 - 40
B34D2	Cold-Blooded Penguin	18 - 40
B34D3	Dumbo	12 - 25
B34D4	Snow White and the Seven Dwarfs	8 - 15
B34D5	Peter and the Wolf	6 - 12
B34D6	Uncle Remus	5 - 9
B34D7	Bambi	5 - 9
B34D8	Pinocchio	5 - 9
B34D9	Bongo	5 - 9
B3D10	Three Little Pigs	5 - 9
B3D11	Johnny Appleseed	5 - 9
B3D12	Once Upon a Wintertime	6 - 10
B3D13	Cinderella	5 - 9
B3D14	Donald Duck's Adventure	5 - 9
B3D15	Mickey Mouse's Picnic	4 - 8
B3D16	Santa's Toy Shop	4 - 8
B3D17	Cinderella's Friends	5 - 10
B3D18	Donald Duck's Toy Train	5 - 9
B3D19	Alice In Wonderland Meets the White Rabbit	5 - 9
B3D20	Alice in Wonderland finds the Garden of Live Flowers	5 - 10
B3D21	Grandpa Bunny	5 - 10
B3D22	Ugly Duckling	6 - 12
B3D23	Mad Hatter's Tea Party	6 - 12
B3D24	Peter Pan and Wendy	5 - 10
B3D25	Peter Pan and the Pirates	5 - 10

B3D26	Peter Pan and the Indians	6 - 12
B3D27	Donald Duck and Santa Claus	5 - 10
B3D28	Noah's Ark	5 - 9
B3D29	Mickey Mouse and his Space Ship	5 - 10
B3D30	Pluto Pup Goes to Sea	4 - 8
B3D31	Hiawatha	5 - 10
B3D32	Mickey Mouse and Pluto Pup	5 - 9
B3D33	Mickey Mouse Goes Christmas Shopping	4 - 8
B3D34	Donald Duck and the Witch	4 - 8
B3D35	Seven Dwarfs Find A House	5 - 10
B3D36	Mother Goose	6 - 12
B3D37	Ben and Me	4 - 8
B3D38	Chip 'n Dale at the Zoo	5 - 9
B3D39	Donald Duck's Christmas Tree	4 - 7
B3D40	Donald Duck's Toy Sailboat	3 - 6
B3D41	Donald Duck's Safety Book	6 - 11
B3D42	Lady	4 - 8
B3D43	Disneyland on the Air	4 - 7
B3D44	Donald Duck in Disneyland	4 - 8
B3D45	Davy Crockett; King of the Wild Frontier	4 - 7
B3D46	Little Man of Disneyland	5 - 10
B3D47	Davy Crockett's Keelboat Race	5 - 9
B3D48	Robin Hood	4 - 8
B3D49	Donald Duck, Prize Driver	5 - 10
B3D50	Jiminy Cricket, Fire Fighter	5 - 10
B3D51	Mother Goose	6 - 12
B3D52	Goofy, Movie Star	5 - 9
B3D53	Mickey Flies the Christmas Mail	2 - 6
B3D54	Perri	5 - 10
B3D55	Donald Duck and the Mouseketeers	4 - 8
B3D56	Peter and the Wolf	5 - 10
B3D57	Mickey Mouse and the Missing Mouseketeers	2 - 5
B3D58	Cinderella's Friends	4 - 8
B3D59	Cinderella	2 - 5
B3D60	(No book issued)	
B3D61	Sleeping Beauty	5 - 10
B3D62	Bongo	4 - 8
B3D63	Scamp	4 - 8
B3D64	Paul Revere	4 - 8
B3D65	Old Yeller	5 - 9
B3D66	Snow White and the Seven Dwarfs	2 - 6
B3D67	Seven Dwarfs Find A House	5 - 10
B3D68	Zorro	4 - 8
B3D69	(No book issued)	
B3D70	Scamp's Adventure	4 - 8
B3D71	Sleeping Beauty and the Good Fairies	5 - 10
B3D72	Peter Pan and Wendy	2 - 6

Simon and Schuster began what became the Little Golden Book series of children's books in 1942. The first Disney title appeared in 1944 and continue to date. There have been around 170 different Disney titles with countless art changes and different editions.

B3D73	Peter Pan and the Pirates	2 - 6
B3D74	Peter Pan and the Indians	3 - 7
B3D75	Manni the Donkey in the Forest World	5 - 10
B3D76	Mickey Mouse and Pluto Pup	1 - 5
B3D77	Zorro and the Secret Plan	4 - 8
B3D78	The Three Little Pigs	1 - 5
B3D79	Mother Goose	2 - 6
B3D80	Tonka	5 - 10
B3D81	Darby O' Gill and the Little People	5 - 10
B3D82	The Shaggy Dog	5 - 10
B3D83	Goliath II	5 - 10
B3D84	Donald Duck and the Christmas Carol	6 - 12
B3D85	Uncle Remus	1 - 5
B3D86	Donald Duck, Lost and Found	4 - 8
B3D87	Toby Tyler	1 - 5
B3D88	Scamp's Adventure	1 - 5
B3D89	Lucky Puppy	4 - 8
B3D90	Bambi	1 - 5
B3D91	Pollyanna	6 - 12
B3D92	Donald Duck in Disneyland	4 - 8
B3D93	Bedknobs and Broomsticks	1 - 5
B3D94	Donald Duck Private Eye	6 - 12
B3D95	Swiss Family Robinson	5 - 10
B3D96	The Flying Car	5 - 10
B3D97	Babes in Toyland	5 - 10
B3D98	Ludwig Von Drake	6 - 12
B3D99	The Toy Soldiers	4 - 9
BD100	Pinocchio	2 - 6
BD101	Pinocchio and the Whale	7 - 15
BD102	Big Red	3 - 7
BD103	Lady	3 - 6
BD104	Savage Sam	4 - 8
BD105	Surprise for Mickey Mouse	5 - 10
BD106	The Sword in the Stone	4 - 8
BD107	The Wizard's Duel	4 - 9
BD108	Mickey Mouse and his Space Ship	4 - 9
BD109	Donald Duck in Disneyland	5 - 10
BD110	Peter Pan and Wendy	3 - 7
BD111	Bunny Book	4 - 9
BD112	Mary Poppins A Jolly Holiday	4 - 8
BD113	Mary Poppins	4 - 8
BD114	Cinderella	1 - 4
BD115	Cinderella's Friends	1 - 5
BD116	Winnie the Pooh; the Honey Tree	1 - 4
BD117	Winnie the Pooh Meets Gopher	1 - 4
BD118	The Ugly Dachshund	7 - 15
BD119	Thumper	2 - 6

BD120	The Jungle Book	2 - 6
BD121	Winnie the Pooh and Tigger	1 - 5
BD122	The Aristocats	2 - 6
BD123	Disneyland Parade with Donald Duck	2 - 6
BD124	Pluto and the Adventure of the Golden Sceptre	4 - 8
BD125	Favorite Nursery Tales	1 - 5
BD126	Robin Hood	2 - 6
BD127	Donald Duck and the Witch Next Door	1 - 5
BD128	Robin Hood and the Daring Mouse	2 - 6
BD129	Mickey Mouse and the Great Lot Plot	1 - 5
BD130	The Love Bug; Herbie's Special Friend	2 - 6
BD131	Donald Duck in America On Parade	4 - 8
BD132	Bambi, Friends of the Forest	1 - 4
BD133	Mickey Mouse The Kitten-Sitters	1 - 4
BD134	Mickey Mouse and the Best Neighbor Contest	1 - 4
BD135	Mickey Mouse and the Mouseketeers, Ghost Town Adventure	1 - 4
BD136	The Rescuers	1 - 5
BD137	Pete's Dragon	1 - 5
BD138	Mickey Mouse and Goofy; the Great Bear Scare	1 - 3
BD139	Donald Duck and the One Bear	1 - 3
BD140	Donald Duck; Instant Millionaire	1 - 3
BD145	Return to OZ Escape From the Witch's Castle	2 - 6
BD146	Return to OZ - Dorothy Saves the Emerald City	2 - 6
BD147	The Black Cauldron - Taran Finds a Friend	2 - 6
BD148	Pinocchio	1 - 2
BD149	The Jungle Book	1 - 2
BD150	101 Dalmatians	1 - 2
B3A33	Sleeping Beauty Story and Paper Doll Book, uncut w/dolls unpunched	15 - 50

Golden Story Books

B3650	Mystery in Disneyville, 1949, #7	2 - 10
B3651	So Dear to my Heart, 1950, #12	2 - 10

1950 Tiny Golden Books Series (The last 12 numbers of the Tiny Golden Library boxed set). Also Walt Disney's Tiny Movie Series (with no #s).

B3660	Bambi Plays Follow the Leader	2 - 5
B3661	Bongo Stars Again	2 - 5
B3662	Bootle Beetle's Adventures	2 - 5
B3663	Brer Rabbit Plays a Trick	2 - 5
B3664	Cinderella's Ball Gown	2 - 5
B3665	Donald Duck's Wild Goose Chase	2 - 5
B3666	Dopey and the Wicked Witch	2 - 5
B3667	Dumbo's Magic Feather	2 - 5
B3668	Mickey's New Car	2 - 5
B3669	Pablo the Penguin Takes a Trip	2 - 5
B3670	Pinocchio's Surprise	2 - 5

B3671	Three Little Pigs Fool a Wolf	2 - 5
B3672	Cinderella - A Golden Open-Door Book	4 - 25

Golden Story Books

B3675	Favorite Stories, 1957	6 - 12
B3676	Donald Duck Treasury, 1957	7 - 15
B3677	Storytime Book, 1958	6 - 13

True Life Adventure (Golden Library of Knowledge)

B3680	Wildlife of the West, 1958	3 - 8
B3681	White Wilderness, 1958	3 - 8

Big Golden Books

B3700	Bambi, 1941	10 - 35
B3701	Walt Disney's Surprise Package, 1944	15 - 55
B3702	Walt Disney's Circus, 1944	10 - 35
B3702A	Walt Disney's Circus, 1944, marked "A Big Golden Book"	10 - 30
B3703	Uncle Remus Stories, 1947	10 - 35
B3705	Bongo, 1947	8 - 25
B3707	Treasure Chest, 1948	8 - 25
B3708	The Adventures of Mr. Toad, 1949	13 - 40
B3709	Bambi, fuzzy Golden Book #443	6 - 20
B3710	Bambi, 1949	4 - 12
B3711	Mother Goose, 1949	8 - 25
B3715	Cinderella, 1950	3 - 15
B3720	Alice in Wonderland, 1951	3 - 15
B3723	Peter Pan, 1952	4 - 15
B3724	Snow White and the Seven Dwarfs, 1952	4 - 15
B3725	Mickey Mouse Birthday Book, 1953	4 - 15
B3727	Pinocchio, 1953	4 - 12
B3728	Mickey Mouse, 1953	4 - 12
B3730	20,000 Leagues Under the Sea, 1954	4 - 12
B3735	Dumbo, 1955	4 - 12
B3736	Davy Crockett, 1955	4 - 15
B3737	Lady and the Tramp, 1955	4 - 12
B3738	The Great Locomotive Chase, 1956	4 - 15
B3739	Treasury of 21 Best Loved Stories, c.1956	8 - 25
B3740	Perri, 1957	4 - 12
B3741	Favorite Stories, 1957	4 - 12
B3745	Zorro, 1958, paper	4 - 15
B3750	Sleeping Beauty, 1958	4 - 15
B3760	Babes in Toyland, 1961	4 - 15
B3761	Babes in Toyland, 1961, paper	4 - 12
B3762	Wonderful World of Ducks, 1961	4 - 15
B3768	Savage Sam, 1963	4 - 15
B3769	Bunny Book, 1971	6 - 18
B3770	Winnie the Pooh and Eeyore's Birthday, 1963	2 - 8
B3771	The Sword in the Stone, 1963	2 - 8
B3773	Mary Poppins, 1964	2 - 7

B3774	Mary Poppins, 1964, paper	2 - 7
B3778	The Jungle Book, 1967	2 - 8
B3780	Mother Goose, 1970	2 - 7
B3783	Bedknobs and Broomsticks, 1971	2 - 6
B3790	Lt. Robinson Crusoe U.S.N., 1966	4 - 12

B3800 BOOKS -- PAPERBACK, POCKET SIZE

The original pocket size paperback format is more adult than child oriented. A few titles from the 40's and 50's were issued. Activity picked up as movie paperbacks became popular merchandising tools. Often they are the original book on which the movie is based. In addition, Ballantine was licensed to produce pocket paperbacks in 1979.

B3801	Pinocchio, 1939, Whitman #556	6 - 30
B3808	So Dear to My Heart, 1949, Dell	3 - 15
B3815	Our Friend the Atom, 1956, Dell	1 - 8
B3820	The Story of Walt Disney, 1959, Dell	3 - 12
B3825	Bullwhip Griffin, 1963, Avon	1 - 3
B3826	The Moon-Spinners, 1964, Crest	1 - 2
B3833	That Darn Cat, 1965, Bantam	1 - 3
B3840	101 Dalmatians, 1967, Avon	1 - 3
B3850	The Wonderful World of Disney series, 1975, Pyramid -- Dr. Syn Alias the Scarecrow	1 - 3
B3854	Of Mice and Mickey, 1975, Manor	1 - 2
B3855	Mickey Mouse Club Scrapbook, 1976, Tempo	1 - 2
B3857	Walt, Mickey, and Me, 1977, Dell	1 - 3
B3860	The Black Hole, 1979, Del Rey	1 - 4

B3900 BOOKS -- POP-UP AND MECHANICAL

These prize collectible books are valued for art, paper engineering, and the test of anxious readers. The Blue Ribbon books all came with dust jackets. The Victory March is the only printed propaganda use of Disney characters known to the author. Musical books are included in this section.

B3901	Pop-up Mickey Mouse, 1933	45 - 175
B3902	Pop-up Minnie Mouse, 1933	30 - 150
B3903	Mickey Mouse in King Arthur's Court, 1933	70 - 300
B3904	Silly Symphonies Pop-up, 1933	70 - 300
B3905	Pop-up Mickey Mouse in Ye Olden Days, 1934	80 - 325
B3906	Mickey Mouse Waddle Book, 1934, complete, unpunched	500 - 1800
B3906	Mickey Mouse Waddle Book, 1934, complete, w/punched Waddles	200 - 900
B3906	Mickey Mouse Waddle Book, 1934, punched	40 - 100

B3910	The Victory March, 1942, Random House	25 - 85
B3920	Cinderella Puppet Show, 1949, Golden	4 - 40
B3925	Fun-filled Visit to Walt Disney World, 1972,	
	Hallmark	5 - 15
B3940	Bambi's Big Day, 1976	3 - 10
B3950	Mickey's Lucky Day, 1980	3 - 10
B3951	Bambi Gets Lost, 1979	3 - 10
B3952	Donald Duck and the Chipmunks, 1980	3 - 10
B3953	Goofy and the Chimp, 1979	3 - 10
B3954	Snow White's Party, 1976	3 - 10
B3955	Pinocchio and the Puppet Theater, 1976	3 - 10
B3960	Mickey Mouse and the Martian Mix-up, 1978	3 - 10
B3964	The Black Hole, 1979	3 - 10
B3965	The Fox and the Hound, 1981	3 - 10
B3966	TRON	3 - 10
B3970	It's A Small World, 1984, Golden Melody Book	2 - 12
B3971	Snow White and the Seven Dwarfs, 1984,	
	Golden Melody Book	2 - 12
B3972	Mickey's Christmas Carol Golden Melody Book	3 - 15

B4000 BOOKS AND MAGAZINES -- SPONSORED

Books in this class are largely soft cover, magazine, and/or premium giveaway type publications. Several are connected with training or PR films produced by the studio.

B4010	A Handful of Fun, 1934, Eisendrath	25 - 150
B4025	What Causes Motor Knocks?, 1938, Sunoco	4 - 28
B4026	How's Your "I-Q", 1941, Sunoco	4 - 28
B4028	ABC's of Hand Tools, 1945, General Motors	2 - 12
B4050	Electrical Living, 1945, Westinghouse	3 - 15
B4060	The Litterbug, 1963, American Can	3 - 15
B4065	Donald Duck -- Synthetic Rubber, 1943, Goodyear	3 - 20
B4200	Wonderful World of Disney, Gulf Oil Company,	
	6 issues, 1969-70, each	1 - 5
B4300	Disney Magazine, Procter & Gamble. Two tests	
	were conducted in various cities -- 11 issues in the	
	first test and 8 in the second. Issue #1 was the same	
	in both, but dated with different month. At least one	
	other issue was a duplication. each	1 - 3
B4380	The Jungle Book Fun Book, Baskin-Robbins	1 - 5
B4382	101 Dalmatians Funny Bone Book, Smucker's	1 - 3

Also see B2600 BOOKS -- BIG LITTLE BOOKS; C6335 CHRIST-MAS PREMIUMS; C8000 COMIC BOOKS -- PREMIUM AND GIVE-AWAY and M5400 MICKEY MOUSE MAGAZINES

B4500 BOOKS – REFERENCE

This classification includes a potpourri of books dealing with Walt Disney the man; character books covering a cross section of films, comics, newspaper strips, toys, etc.; books on collecting Disneyana; and non-Disney reference sources that include Disneyana.

B4501	Christmas toy catalogs 1930 to present, especially ones from 1933-39 depict Disneyana	10 - 60
B4502	Manufacturer catalogs and sales sheets	4 - 20
B4503	Mail order catalogs 1930 to present	3 - 15
B4547	The Story of Walt Disney, 1957, Holt	8 - 35
B4550	Wisdom -- Vol 32, 1959	3 - 15
B4553	Walt Disney Magician of the Movies, 1966, Grosset & Dunlap	5 - 20
B4555	American Heritage -- Vol 14, No 3, Apr 1968	5 - 20
B4578	The Disney Version, 1968, Simon & Schuster	2 - 10
B4579	Mickey Mouse Club Scrapbook, 1975, Grosset & Dunlap	2 - 8
B4580	Walt Disney - An American Original, 1976, S & S	5 - 25
B4590	The New Mickey Mouse Club Book, 1977, G & D	2 - 8
B4600	Mickey Mouse - Fifty Happy Years, 1977, Harmony	5 - 25
B4601	Donald Duck, 1979, Harmony	5 - 25
B4610	Mickey Mouse, 1978, Abbeville	4 - 15
B4611	Donald Duck, 1978, Abbeville	4 - 15
B4612	Goofy, 1979, Abbeville	4 - 15
B4613	Uncle Scrooge, 1979, Abbeville	10 - 50
B4614	Animated Features, 1980, Abbeville	4 - 12
B4650	Disneyana, 1974, Hawthorn	25 - 100
B4651	A Celebration of Comic Art and Memorabilia, 1975, Hawthorn	10 - 65
B4658	Donald Duck and His Nephews, 1983, Abbeville	3 - 10
B4660	Cartoon Collectibles, 1984, Doubleday	4 - 15
B4661	Character Toys and Collectibles, 1984, Collectors Book	5 - 18
B4662	Donald Duck - 50 Years of Happy Frustration, 1984, HP	4 - 15
B4666	The Disney Studio Story, 1988, Crown Publishers Inc.	20 - 40
B4663	Disney's World, 1985, Stein & Day	3 - 12
B4665	Mickey Mouse Memorabilia, 1986, Abrams	8 - 30
B4670	Official Overstreet Comic Book Price Guide, 1987, Ballantine. Each annual volume is valuable to Disneyana collectors. The '87 edition has feature articles on Disneyana.	4 - 12

B4700 BOOKS -- STAMPS & STICKERS

Registered Poster Stamps were an offshoot of the stamp collecting rage of the 30's. There is a set of 8 Snow White stamps and a Pinocchio album containing stamps from this series. Golden Books did a series of stamp albums in the 50's following the introduction of Whitman sticker books.

B4701	Packages of Poster Stamps, for IGA Pinocchio album, each	6-15
B4702	Pinocchio Album & Poster Stamps, 1940, IGA	50 - 250
B4703	Combat Insignia Stamps & Album, Vol 1, 1942	5-20
B4704	War Insignia Stamp Album, Vol 2, 1942	5-20
B4705	War Insignia Stamp Album, Vol 3, 1942	5-20
B4706	War Insignia Stamp Album, Vol 4, 1942	6-24
B4714	Sticker Fun Book, 1951, #2190	8-30
B4715	Alice in Wonderland, 1951, #2193	10 - 50
B4717	Peter Pan, 1952, #2181	10 - 50
B4719	Merry Menagerie, 1953, #2160	8-30
B4720	Match and Patch Sticker Fun, 1953, #2163	8-30
B4730	Davy Crockett, Golden WD-1, 1955	3-15
B4731	The Littlest Outlaw, Golden WD-2, 1955	3-12
B4732	Robin Hood, Golden WD-3, 1955	3-12
B4733	Davy Crockett and Mike Fink, Golden WD-5, 1955	3-12
B4734	Time-Life Adventures, Golden WD-4, 1955	3-12
B4735	Disneyland, Golden WD-6	6-35
B4736	Animals of Africa, Golden WD-7, 1956	2-10
B4737	Snow White, Golden WD-8	2-10
B4738	Secrets of Life, Golden WD-9	2-10
B4739	Sleeping Beauty Stamp Book, Golden WD-10, 1958	5-20
B4740	White Wilderness, Golden WD-11	2-10
B4751	Sleeping Beauty Sticker Fun, 1959, #2175	5-25
B4755	Donald Duck Sticker Fun, 1960, #2183	2-10
B4760	Mary Poppins Sticker Fun, 1964, #1684	3-15
B4765	The Jungle Book Sticker Fun, 1971, #1680	2 - 8
B4766	Disneyland Sticker Fun, 1967, #2183	10 - 45
B4770	Bedknobs and Broomsticks, 1971, #1675	3-10
B4775	Sticker books, 60's, 70's or 80's	3 - 9

B5200 BOOKS -- STORY

This section includes shorter run series and one shot titles. They are all children's books merchandising a film scenario or an original story, or collection of stories, about Disney characters. A few include activities. Bibo and Lang issued their only Mickey Mouse Book, written by the publisher's daughter, in 1930. David McKay was the major Disney publisher from 1931 to 1937. Whitman published Disney titles in 1933 and continues as the largest book licensee to this day (1985). Blue

Ribbon (1933-34); Grossett and Dunlap (abbreviated G & D in listings) (1936-43, 1947-50), Random House (1939-44, 1979), Simon & Schuster (1944 until sold); and Heath (1939-48) were the major Disney story book publishers. The key to this section is the copyright date found in every book.

B5201	Mickey Mouse Book ("Hello Everybody"),	
	Bibo & Lang, 1930	75 - 600
B5201	2nd version has slight changes	60 - 550

1931 (McKay)

B5202	The Adventures of Mickey Mouse - Book 1,	
	hard or soft cover	15 - 135
B5204	Mickey Mouse Story Book, hard or soft cover	10 - 70
B5205	Mickey Mouse Illustrated Movie Stories	50 - 250
B5206	Mickey Mouse - Series No. 1	30 - 150
B5207	Mickey Mouse Illustrated Movie Stories, Canadian	15 - 100

1932 (McKay)

B5210	The Adventures of Mickey Mouse - Book 2	15 - 135
B5211	Mickey Mouse - Book No. 2	20 - 150

1933 (McKay unless otherwise noted)

B5215	Mickey Mouse - Book No. 3	40 - 180
B5216	Mickey Mouse, Whitman #948	15 - 75
B5218	The Three Little Pigs, Blue Ribbon	20 - 80
B5219	Who's Afraid of the Big Bad Wolf?	4 - 25

1934 (McKay unless otherwise noted)

B5221	The Big Bad Wolf and Little Red Riding Hood,	
	Blue Ribbon	30 - 100
B5222	Little Red Riding Hood and the Big Bad Wolf	20 - 50
B5223	Mickey Mouse - Book No. 4	30 - 150
B5224	Mickey Mouse in Giantland	22 - 75
B5225	Mickey Mouse Movie Stories - Book 2	65 - 400
B5226	Mickey Mouse Stories - Book 2, hard or soft	
	cover	12 - 60
B5228	Peculiar Penguins	10 - 45
B5229	The Wise Little Hen	20 - 80
B5230	Boxed - Mickey Mouse Library & Toy	80 - 450

1935 (McKay unless otherwise noted. McKay version has titles on spine.)

B5235	The Robber Kitten	15 - 65
B5236	The Robber Kitten, Whitman, no #	10 - 50
B5237	The Three Orphan Kittens	15 - 65
B5238	The Three Orphan Kittens, Whitman, no #	10 - 50
B5239	The Tortoise and the Hare	15 - 65
B5240	The Tortoise and the Hare, Whitman, no #	10 - 45
B5241	The Wise Little Hen	15 - 85
B5242	The Wise Little Hen, Whitman, no #	15 - 75

1936 (Whitman unless otherwise noted)

B5250	A Mickey Mouse Alphabet Book, #936	15 - 75
B5251	Donald Duck, G & D	15 - 60
B5252	Elmer Elephant, McKay	12 - 55
B5253	Forty Big Pages of Mickey Mouse, #945	10 - 100
B5254	Mickey Mouse (Stand Out Book), #841	15 - 85
B5255	A Mickey Mouse ABC Story, #921	15 - 65
B5256	Mickey Mouse Crusoe, #711	10 - 55
B5257	The Mickey Mouse Fire Brigade, #2029	12 - 65
B5260	Mickey Mouse and His Horse Tanglefoot, McKay	15 - 75
B5261	Mickey Mouse in Pigmyland, #711	10 - 50
B5262	Mickey Mouse and Pluto the Pup, #2028	12 - 60

1937 (Whitman unless otherwise noted)

B5265	The Country Cousin, McKay	15 - 60
B5267	Donald Duck Has His Ups and Downs, #1077	10 - 45
B5269	Donald Duck and His Friends, #507	10 - 45
B5270	Hiawatha, McKay	10 - 55
B5271	Mickey Mouse, Donald Duck and All Their Pals, #887	10 - 60
B5272	Mickey Mouse and Donald Duck Gag Book, #886	10 - 60
B5273	Mickey Mouse Has a Busy Day, #1077	10 - 60
B5276	Mickey Mouse and His Friends, Nelson	10 - 50
B5277	Mickey Mouse and His Friends Wait for the County Fair, #883	10 - 50
B5279	Mickey Mouse and Mother Goose, #411	10 - 50
B5280	Mickey's Magic Hat Cookie Carnival, #1077	10 - 50
B5282	Mickey Mouse Presents Walt Disney's Nursery Stories	10 - 45
B5283	The Golden Touch	10 - 45
B5284	Pluto and the Puppy, G & D	15 - 75
B5285	Snow White and the Seven Dwarfs, Harper	18 - 95
B5286	Snow White and the Seven Dwarfs, G & D	18 - 95
B5286A	Reprinted as an art book for 50th anniversary of Snow White, Abrams (see B2545)	
B5287	Snow White and the Seven Dwarfs, McKay	20 - 85
B5290	Walt Disney Annual, #4001	25 - 150
B5291	The Wise Little Hen, #888	25 - 65

1938 (Whitman unless otherwise noted)

B5301	Brave Little Tailor, #972	15 - 75
B5302	Edgar Bergen's Charlie McCarthy Meets Walt Disney's Snow White, #986	15 - 55
B5303	The Famous Movie Story of Walt Disney's Snow White and the Seven Dwarfs, K.K. Publications	8 - 30
B5304	Famous Seven Dwarfs, #944 (also see B3300 Books -- Linen Like #933)	8 - 30
B5305	Snow White and the Seven Dwarfs from the Famous Movie Story, no #	10 - 50

Some of the story and other books published by Whitman in 1936.

B5310	Ferdinand the Bull, #842 (also see B3300	
	Books -- Linen Like)	5 - 25
B5311	Ferdinand the Bull, Dell	5 - 30
B5312	Forest Friends from Snow White, G & D	10 - 50
B5314	Mickey Mouse the Boat Builder, G & D	25 - 65
B5315	Mickey Mouse Has a Party, #798	10 - 50
B5317	Mickey Mouse in Numberland, #745	15 - 60
B5325	Snow White and the Seven Dwarfs, G & D	12 - 55
B5326	Snow White and the Seven Dwarfs, #714	8 - 30
B5327	Snow White and the Seven Dwarfs, #927	8 - 30
B5328	Snow White and the Seven Dwarfs, #777	8 - 30
B5330	The Story of Bashful, #1044	8 - 20
B5331	The Story of Doc, #1044	8 - 20
B5332	The Story of Dopey, #1044	8 - 20
B5333	The Story of Grumpy, #1044	8 - 20
B5334	The Story of Happy, #1044	8 - 20
B5335	The Story of Sleepy, #1044	8 - 20
B5336	The Story of Sneezy, #1044	8 - 20
B5337	The Story of Snow White, #1044	8 - 20
B5340	Story of Clarabelle Cow, #1066	5 - 18
B5341	Story of Dippy the Goof, #1066	5 - 18
B5342	Story of Donald Duck,' #1066	5 - 18
B5343	Story of Mickey Mouse, #1066	5 - 18
B5344	Story of Minnie Mouse, #1066	5 - 18
B5345	Story of Pluto the Pup, #1066	5 - 18

1939 (Whitman unless otherwise noted)

B5350	Brave Little Tailor, #1058	5 - 25
B5351	Donald Duck and His Friends, Heath	5 - 25
B5353	Donald's Lucky Day, #897	5 - 35
B5354	The Farmyard Symphony, #1058	5 - 25
B5355	Little Pig's Picnic and Other Stories, Heath	5 - 25
B5356	Mickey Never Fails, Heath	5 - 25
B5358	Mother Pluto, #1058	5 - 25
B5359	The Mickey Mouse Box #2146, includes Brave	
	Little Tailor, Mother Pluto, The Practical Pig,	
	Timid Elmer, and The Ugly Duckling, set	50 - 250
B5360	Pinocchio, Dell	15 - 35
B5361	The Practical Pig, #1058	15 - 25
B5362	School Days in Disneyville, Heath	6 - 25
B5363	Timid Elmer, #1058	5 - 25
B5365	The Ugly Duckling, Lippincott	20 - 60
B5366	The Ugly Duckling, #1058	5 - 25
B5367	Walt Disney Tells the Story of Pinocchio, #556	10 - 30
B5368	Walt Disney's Version of Pinocchio, G & D	8 - 35
B5370	Walt Disney's Version of Pinocchio, Random	
	House	12 - 45
B5371	Walt Disney's Version of Pinocchio, Cocomalt	2 - 12

B5372	Walt Disney's Version of Pinocchio, #709	8 - 25
B5373	Walt Disney's Version of Pinocchio, #6880	15 - 60

1940 (Whitman unless otherwise noted)

B5375	Ave Maria, Random House	5 - 25
B5377	Dance of the Hours, Harper	12 - 50
B5378	Donald Duck and His Nephews, Heath	6 - 25
B5380	Donald's Penguin, Garden City	15 - 65
	Fantasia, Simon & Schuster (see B2505)	

Story Paint Book Series, #2035 (6, all have #1059), set in box   18 - 150

B5383	The Blue Fairy*, #1059	4 - 20
B5384	Figaro and Cleo*, #1059	4 - 20
B5385	Geppetto*, #1059	4 - 20
B5386	J. Worthington Foulfellow and Gideon*, #1059	4 - 20
B5387	Jiminy Cricket*, #1059	4 - 20
B5388	Pinocchio*, #1059	4 - 20
B5389	Figaro and Cleo, Random House	8 - 35
B5390	Honest John and Giddy, Random House	8 - 35
B5391	Jiminy Cricket, Random House	8 - 35
B5392	Here They Are, Heath	6 - 25
B5395	The Nutcracker Suite from WD Fantasia, Little, Brown	18 - 65
B5396	Pastoral from Walt Disney's Fantasia, Harper	18 - 65
B5397	Pinocchio, #846	14 - 60
B5400	Pinocchio, Heath	8 - 30
B5401	Pinocchio Picture Book, G & D	15 - 60
B5402	Pinocchio Picture Book, #849	14 - 45
B5405	The Practical Pig, Garden City	15 - 75
B5408	The Sorcerer's Apprentice, G & D	15 - 85
B5409	Stories from Walt Disney's Fantasia, Random House	15 - 75
B5410	The Walt Disney Parade, Garden City	25 - 120
B5412	Walt Disney's Version of Pinocchio, 24 pages	5 - 25
B5414	Water Babies Circus and Other Stories, Heath	5 - 25
B5415	Heath Teachers Guide	5 - 35

1941 (Whitman unless otherwise noted)

B5420	Baby Weems, Doubleday	12 - 75
B5421	Bambi, Simon & Schuster	4 - 20
B5422	Dumbo of the Circus, Garden City	10 - 50
B5423	Dumbo of the Circus, K.K. Publications	5 - 25
B5425	Dumbo, the Flying Elephant	5 - 25
B5426	Dumbo - The Story of the Little Elephant with Big Ears, Disney, distributed by Winkler & Ramen	5 - 35
B5428	The Life of Donald Duck, Random House	15 - 85
B5429	The Story of Casey, Jr., Garden City	12 - 60
B5430	Story of the Reluctant Dragon, Garden City	15 - 75
B5431	The Story of Timothy's House, Garden City	15 - 65

1942 (Whitman unless otherwise noted)
B5435	Bambi, G & D	4 - 20
B5436	Bambi Story Book, #725	4 - 25
B5438	Dumbo - The Story of the Flying Elephant, #710	4 - 25
B5439	Thumper, G & D	2 - 10

1943
B5445	Donald Duck in the High Andes, G & D	15 - 60
B5446	The Gremlins, Random House	10 - 80
B5447	Pedro - The Story of a Little Airplane, G & D	8 - 45

1944
B5450	Bambi, Heath	5 - 25
B5451	Mickey Sees the U.S.A., Heath	5 - 25
B5455	The Three Caballeros, Random House	12 - 65

1945
B5460	Donald Duck Sees South America, Heath	5 - 25
B5462	Funny Stories About Donald and Mickey, Whitman #714	2 - 16

1946
B5475	Brer Rabbit Rides the Fox, G & D	5 - 45
B5477	The Wonderful Tar Baby, G & D	5 - 45

1947
B5485	Mickey and the Beanstalk, G & D	4 - 25

1948 (Whitman unless otherwise noted.) Story Hour (SH) series published in both hardback and paper versions.
B5490	Bongo, SH, #803	5 - 20
B5492	Come Play with Donald Duck, G & D	8 - 35
B5493	Come Play with Mickey Mouse, G & D	8 - 35
B5494	Come Play with Pluto Pup, G & D	8 - 35
B5495	Come Play with the Seven Dwarfs, G & D	8 - 35
B5500	Donald Duck and the Boys, Carl Barks, #845	5 - 50
B5501	Donald Duck in Bringing Up the Boys, SH, #800	3 - 15
B5502	Donald Duck and His Cat Troubles, #845	3 - 15
B5503	Dumbo of the Circus, Heath	20 - 80
B5505	Mickey and the Beanstalk, SH, #804	3 - 15
B5507	Mickey Mouse and the Boy Thursday, #845	3 - 15
B5508	Mickey Mouse and the Miracle Maker, #845	3 - 15
B5509	Mickey Mouse's Summer Vacation, SH, #801	2 - 10
B5511	Minnie Mouse and the Antique Chair, #845	3 - 15
B5512	Poor Pluto, #845	3 - 15

1949 (Whitman unless otherwise noted.) Story Hour (SH) Tiny Tales Books (TT)
B5515	Danny, the Little Black Lamb, SH, #807	4 - 12
B5517	Donald Duck in the Great Kite Maker, TT, #2952 or #1030	4 - 12
B5518	Johnny Appleseed, SH, #808	4 - 12
B5519	Magnificent Mr. Toad, G & D	5 - 45

B5522	Mickey Mouse, Goofy and the Night Prowlers, TT, #2952 or #1030	4-12
B5525	The Runaway Lamb at the County Fair, G & D	5-45
B5526	Three Orphan Kittens, SH, #809	4-12
B5528	Bambi, Simon & Schuster w/"Touch Me Materials	3-15

Beginning in 1950, Whitman and Golden Books accounted for nearly all Disney children's story books. (see B3400 Little Golden Books) Whitman's approach included several different series -- Cozy Corner (CC), Tell-A-Tale (TAT) and Story Hour (SH) being the most prominent. The few books of other publishers are so noted. All other books are Whitman and are identified by the above abbreviations. Like Golden Books there have been many printings including price, cover number, and internal changes.

1950

B5530	Cinderella, CC, #2037	3-20
B5531	Donald and Mickey Cub Scouts, CC, #2031	3- 20

1951

B5540	Alice In Wonderland, CC, #2074	3-20
B5545	Donald Duck's Lucky Day, TAT, #2419 and #2589	1 - 6
B5546	Donald Duck and the Hidden Gold, Sandpiper	3 - 8
B5546	w/dust jacket	5-25
B5547	Alice In Wonderland, Sandpiper	3-10
B5547	w/dust jacket	7-22

1952

B5550	Peter Pan, CC, #2415	3-20
B5551	Donald Duck and the Wishing Star, CC, #2097	
B5555	Mother Goose, Simon & Schuster	3-15
B5556	Seven Dwarfs Find a House, Simon & Schuster	3-15

1953

B5565	Donald Duck Full Speed Ahead, TAT, #900	2- 6

1954

B5575	Goofy and the Tiger Hunt, TAT, #2555	2- 6
B5576	Lady, TAT, #2552	2- 6
B5580	Lady, no series, #2218	2-10
B5581	Ben and Me, CC, #2403	3-15
B5582	Stormy, CC, #2404	2 - 4
B5583	Beaver Valley, TAT, #2553	1 - 3
B5584	Cinderella, TAT	1 - 2

1955

B5585	Living Desert, S & S, dust jacket	2 - 5
B5590	Donald Duck in Help Wanted, CC, #2406	1 - 8
B5591	Davy Crockett and Mike Fink, S & S, #439	2-10
B5595	Donald Duck Goes to Disneyland, TAT, #2589	1 - 4
B5596	Water Birds, TAT, #2564	1 - 4
B5597	Bear Country, TAT	1 - 4

1956

B5600	American Folklore, no #, came boxed	5-25

B5610	The Mouseketeers Tryout Time, TAT, #2649	1 - 2
B5611	Bambi, TAT	1 - 2
B5615	Mickey Mouse Club Treasure Mine, #2918 Boxed set of 8 soft back titles -- 7 reprints of 1949-50 Tiny Tales book, plus a new MMC title -- Bongo, Mickey and the Beanstalk, The Three Orphan Kittens, Danny, Johnny Appleseed, Mickey Mouse's Summer Vacation, plus Corky and White Shadow, in box	25 - 75

1957

B5624	Snow White and the Seven Dwarfs, TAT, #2578	1 - 3
B5625	Donald Duck in Frontierland, TAT, #2589 or #2445	2 - 5
B5628	Pluto, TAT, #2590	1 - 3
B5629	Worlds of Nature, S & S	2 - 10
B5630	Snow White and the Seven Dwarfs, TAT, #2533	1 - 2

1958

| B5640 | Big Book, #7196 | 2 - 15 |

1959

| B5655 | Sleeping Beauty, SH, #2219 | 4 - 10 |
| B5656 | Sleeping Beauty, TAT, #2456, #2512 and #2649 | 2 - 5 |

1960

B5665	One Hundred and One Dalmatians, SH, #2209	3 - 6
B5666	One Hundred and One Dalmatians, TAT, #2456 and #2649	2 - 6
B5667	Donald Duck on Tom Sawyer's Island, TAT, #2409	4 - 10
B5668	Uncle Scrooge the Lemonade King, Tip-Top, Carl Barks	5 - 25
B5669	Donald Duck Treasury, S & S, #12517	2 - 4

1961

| B5674 | Babes In Toyland, Tip-Top, #2490 | 2 - 6 |
| B5675 | Pinocchio, TAT, #2520 | 1 - 2 |

1962-1977 -- Numbers change on these books

B5678	The Sword in the Stone, Whitman Tip-Top, 1963, #2459	2 - 5
B5679	Huey, Louie and Dewey's Christmas Wish, Tip-Top, 1962, #2497	2 - 5
B5680	Mickey Mouse and the Second Wish, TAT, 1963, #2418	2 - 5
B5681	Ludwig Von Drake Dog Expert, Tip-Top, #2482	2 - 5
B5683	Goofy and His Wonderful Comet, 1964, #2516	2 - 5
B5685	Mary Poppins -- She's Supercalifragilisticexpiali-docious, Tip-Top, 1964, #2450	3 - 18
B5686	Mary Poppins -- She's Supercalifragilisticexpiali-docious, TAT, 1964, #2442 or #2606	3 - 18
B5687	The Magic of Mary Poppins, 1964, no #	3 - 20
B5690	Uncle Scrooge Rainbow Runaway, Big TAT, 1965, #2422	4 - 12

B5691	Winnie-the-Pooh, Big TAT, 1965, #2443	2 - 5
B5692	A Visit to Disneyland, Big TAT, 1970, #2421	5 - 25
B5698	Donald Duck Buried Treasure, Tiny Tot Tale, 1968, #2942	2 - 6
B5710	The Aristocats - A Counting Book, TAT, 1970, #2516	2 - 5
B5711	Mickey Mouse and the Really Neat Robot, TAT, 1970, #2509	2 - 4
B5715	Big Albert Moves in - Walt Disney World, TAT, 1971, #2567	2 - 6
B5718	Cinderella, TAT, 1972, #2456	1 - 4
B5725	Winnie-the-Pooh - The Blustery Day, TAT, 1975, #2577	1 - 4
B5727	Winnie-the-Pooh and Eeyore's House, TAT, 1976, #2426	1 - 4
B5728	Peter Pan and the Tiger, TAT, 1976, #2429	2 - 6
B5730	Mickey Mouse and the Mouseketeers, TAT, 1977, #2454	1 - 4
B5731	Pete's Dragon, TAT, 1977, #2637	1 - 5
B5732	The Rescuers, TAT, 1977, #2633	1 - 4

B6150 BOOKS – WHITMAN NOVELS

This adventure series is designed to appeal to pre-teen and young teenage readers. There are some line illustrations, but the emphasis is on the text to create images.

B6155	Treasure Island, Disney dust jacket only, #2125	2 - 8
B6158	Peter Pan, 1952, #2132	3 - 15
B6166	Spin and Marty, 1956, #1535	2 - 8
B6170	Zorro, 1958, #1586	2 - 8
B6175	Annette - Sierra Summer, 1960, #1585	1 - 6
B6177	The Swiss Family Robinson	1 - 6
B6178	Toby Tyler, 1960, #1545	1 - 6
B6180	Annette - The Desert Inn Mystery, 1961, #1546	1 - 5
B6182	Annette and the Mystery at Moonstone Bay, 1962, #1537	1 - 5
B6184	Annette and the Mystery at Smugglers Cove, 1963, #1574	1 - 5
B6186	Donald Duck and the Lost Mesa Ranch, 1966, #1758	1 - 6
B6189	The Jungle Book, 1967, #2726	1 - 6
B6190	Blackbeards Ghost, 1968, #1575	1 - 5

B6200 BOOKS -- OTHERS

This classification includes cloth books, autograph books, telephone

The 1935 Bubble Buster was one of the unique toys which was sold
on the coattails of Mickey Mouse's tremendous success.

books, and others of different configuration or made of unusual material. Foreign language publications are also included in this section.

B6201	Cloth books	1-10
B6220	Panorama books	2-20
B6230	Colorform books, complete	2-20
B6250	Mix and Match books	1-10
B6300	Autograph books	1-8
B6320	Personal telephone books	1-8
B6350	Lake Buena Vista telephone books, each	1-5
B6370	Telephone books -- Disney Intercompany	2-10
B6400	Autograph books, each	1-10

B6500 Foreign Language Publications. Most collectors enjoy having samples of Disney books from around the world. They have been published since 1930 and exceed the number of volumes published in the U.S. Older books are naturally more valuable. Many are merely translations of domestic books. Books from English speaking countries, Europe, Scandinavia and Mexico are most often found. Mickey Mouse is known in various countries as Topolino (Italy), Miky Maoye (Greece), Mikke Mus (Norway), Miki Maus (Yugoslavia), and Musse Pigg (Sweden).

B6501	England version of pop-up books	10 - 250
B6550	Early story books in English	5-70
B6600	Early French, Italian or German	3-60
B6700	Other languages	2-50
B6750	Foreign book last 25 years	1-10

B8300 BUBBLE BUSTER, BUBBLE PIPES, AND BUBBLE MAKERS

B8301	Bubble Buster, 1935-37	15 - 75
B8302	Box of Bubble Buster Rubber Bubblets	4-18
B8330	Lido Bubble Pipes, Mickey, Donald or Goofy, each	4-12
B8340	Donald the Bubble Duck	5-20

C5000 CASTING SETS AND FIGURES

The earliest character statue sets produced figures of lead. Plaster was the popular medium from the 40's to 60's when new "child safe" compounds were introduced. Model-Craft was the major plaster casting set producer in the 40's or 50's. Figures from these sets are sometimes confused with porcelain bisque figures made in Japan

Yankee Homecraft Corp. made individual mold sets for 24 different figures -- including a set of 6 from *The Jungle Book*. These were also packaged in boxed sets. A sizeable find of Yankee Homecraft molds was discovered in 1986.

C5005	Home Foundry Basic Set w/Mickey, Minnie & Pluto molds	65 - 375
C5006	Lead Figures from C5005, each	2 - 10
C5007	Extra Mold, Donald & Mickey	20 - 100
C5008	Lead Figures from C5007, each	3 - 15
C5009	Extra Mold, Big Bad Wolf & Horace	40 - 250
C5010	Lead Figures from C5009, each	5 - 25
C5011	Extra Mold, Three Little Pigs	25 - 130
C5012	Lead Figures from C5011, each	2 - 10

Plaster casting sets -- J.L. Wright (Chicago) 1938-39 appears to have been succeeded by Model-Craft, Inc. (Chicago) a licensee from 1944-55.

C5015	Snow White -- Set A, w/names, 4" dwarfs	15 - 85
C5016	Figures from C5015, each	1 - 6
C5017	Snow White -- Set B, no names	10 - 75
C5018	Figures from C5017, each	1 - 6
C5019	Snow White -- Set C, larger, 5" dwarfs	18 - 95
C5020	Figures from C5019, each	2 - 10
C5100	Model-Craft Set #9 produced Mickey, Minnie, Donald, Pluto, Mickey's nephew & Donald's nephew	10 - 55
C5101	Figures from C5100, each	1 - 8
C5102	Model-Craft Set #15 produced Bambi, Joe Carioca, Goofy, Flower, Thumper & Dumbo	12 - 60
C5103	Figures from C5102, each	2 - 10

Yankee Homecraft Corp. 1968

C5120	Snow White and the Seven Dwarfs, mini-mold set	10 - 35
C5121	Snow White and the Seven Dwarfs, mini-plaques moulding & color set	12 - 40
C5122	Character Mini-mold Set	10 - 35
C5123	Individual molds for Mickey, Donald, Goofy, Huey, Pluto, Winnie the Pooh, Snow White and the Seven Dwarfs, Pinocchio, Jiminy Cricket, Bambi, Dumbo, Mowgli, Girl Cub, King Louie, Baloo, Sonny & Shere Khan, each	4 - 12
C5150	Walt Disney World Mickey Dough, 1971	6 - 20

C6100 CHINAWARE

Chinaware in this classification includes regular dinnerware and children's tea sets. China figures and collector's plates are listed elsewhere. Borgfeldt probably sold crude tea sets as early as 1930 or 31. Schumann Brothers imported a line of Bavarian China in 1932 and Salem China (also labeled Patriot China), identified by a single color line of trim on each piece, produced attractive sets of juvenile chinaware in 1934. Vernon Kilns, American Pottery and Evan K. Shaw did exceptional dinnerware in the 40's (listed at their classifications). Welborn did ceramic dinnerware in 1955 and Royal Orleans a Mickey and the

The Schumann China Company sold juvenile chinaware imported
from Bavaria from 1932 through 1934. (In 1935 Hitler banned the
manufacture of Mickey Mouse merchandise and the showing of his
films in Germany.) The Salem China Co. took over the license the
same year and produced "Patriot China" through 1939.

Beanstalk set in 1981.

The Bavarian China pieces were imported by Schumann Brothers under a sub-license from George Borgfeldt from 1932-34.

C6103	Crude Hand Painted Tea Set for 8, Japan	25 - 100
C6105	Schumann Child's Tea Set, 1932	50 - 150
C6106	Schumann Cereal Bowl, 1932	10 - 50
C6107	Schumann Alphabet Cereal Bowl, 1932	80 - 350
C6108	Schumann Cup, Saucer, Cup or Dinner Plate, each	40 - 140
C6112	Schumann Flower Vases	30 - 110
C6113	Schumann Candy Dishes	25 - 100
C6115	Borgfeldt Tea Sets, tan or blue	70 - 240
C6117	Krueger Enamel Ware Plate, Cup & Saucer, pink or blue, set	200 - 400
C6120	Figural Three Little Pigs Mugs, Salem, each	10 - 55
C6121	Three Little Pigs Mug, Bowl & Plate Set, Salem	35 - 140
C6125	Mickey, Minnie or Pluto Mugs, Salem, each	18 - 75
C6128	Three Little Pigs and Red Riding Hood Set, Salem	35 - 130
C6132	Mickey Plates, Salem	12 - 70
C6136	Divided Baby Dishes, Salem	15 - 75
C6140	Mickey and Friends Bowls, Salem	10 - 55
C6150	Welborn Pieces	5 - 25
C6155	Peter Pan Tea Set	75 - 250
C6158	Royal Orleans Mickey and Beanstalk Set	50 - 140

Also see A5000 AMERICAN POTTERY C0., A8050 ASH TRAYS & COASTERS, S3000 EVAN K. SHAW, and V3000 VERNON KILNS CERAMICS

C6300 CHRISTMAS LIGHTS AND SHIELDS

The NOMA Electric Corp. (NYC) made Mickey Mouse and Silly Symphony Christmas lights and bell shields from 1935-38. Paramount figural lights and replacement bulbs were made by Raylite Electric Corp. (Bronx, NY) 1958 and Sears sold a Winnie the Pooh set in the 60's.

Only the NOMA Mickey Mouse and Silly Symphony sets were sold in the U.S. However, a Snow White, a Pinocchio, and perhaps a Fantasia set were sold in Canada.

C6303	Mickey Mouse NOMA Light Set	35 - 135
C6304	Mickey Mouse NOMA Bell Set	20 - 80
C6305	Silly Symphony NOMA Light Set	25 - 120
C6306	Silly Symphony NOMA Bell Set	20 - 80
C6307	Snow White NOMA Light Set, Canadian	35 - 145
C6309	Pinocchio NOMA Light Set, Canadian	35 - 145
C6315	Paramount Figural Light Set	25 - 100

| C6316 | Paramount Replacement Light Set | 15 - 60 |
| C6320 | Winnie the Pooh Light Set | 4 - 18 |

C6600 CLOCKS

Mickey Mouse saved the Ingersoll-Waterbury Clock Company from bankruptcy in the 30's. The firm went on to be known as U.S. Time Corp. (1945) and, finally, Timex Corp. (1970). Bayard of France produced the animated clocks beginning in 1936 through 1969 without changing the design. Other companies produced clocks beginning in 1936 through 1969 on a limited basis.

C6601	Ingersoll Wind-up Mickey, square, 1933	200 - 850
C6602	Ingersoll Electric Mickey, square, 1933	200 - 850
C6603	Big Bad Wolf, wind-up, 1933	85 - 450
C6604	Ingersoll Wind-up Mickey, round, 1933	75 - 375
C6608	Ingersoll Desk Clock, 1934	125 - 600
C6615	Bayard Mickey	25 - 125
C6616	Bayard Snow White	45 - 145
C6617	Bayard Pinocchio	25 - 120
C6618	Bayard Donald	20 - 110
C6619	Bayard Pluto	20 - 110
C6635	Ingersoll Plastic Alarm, w/luminous hands, 1947	40 - 220
C6636	Ingersoll Plastic Alarm, 1947	40 - 200
C6637	Ingersoll Mickey Mouse, electric	40 - 200
C6638	Mickey Mouse, alarm	30 - 165
C6650	Allied Pluto, animated, plastic, 1953	45 - 225
C6652	Mickey or Lady Wall Clock, 1955	10 - 60
C6654	Sleeping Beauty	20 - 110
C6655	Clocks, 1960-1980	15 - 65
C6660	Mickey, Bradley	10 - 40
C6665	Bradley Mini Size Alarm, Mickey, Minnie, Donald, Cinderella, each	10 - 45

C7000 COMIC BOOKS AND DIGESTS -- NEWSSTAND

Four of the 1931-34 McKay books would qualify as comic books. The limited edition 1938 Whitman/K.K. black and white Donald Duck is often listed as the first comic, but "real" comic books weren't published until 1940 -- Dell Black and White Comic #16, Donald Duck and Donald Duck Dell Color Comics #4 (Feb). There are over 70 different comic book series and one shot titles catalogued by the Disney Archives. Walt Disney's Comics and Stories (Oct 1940) was undoubtedly the anchor of all titles. Over 500 issues were published before it was discontinued by Whitman. The Dell Four Color series produced the most collectible Disney comics. This series also spawned the regular Mickey Mouse, Donald Duck, and Uncle Scrooge series.

The artwork of Carl Barks weighs heavily in the value of many Disney "duck" comics. Barks wrote and drew the most desirable Four Color one shot Donald Duck stories. He created the character of Uncle Scrooge for Dell #178 -- "Christmas on Bear Mountain." Barks created other Disney ducks, too, Cousin Gladstone Gander, the Junior Woodchucks, and Gyro Gearloose among others. The first Barks comic was Four Color #9 -- "Donald Duck Finds Pirate Gold!"

Mickey Mouse's comic debut was Dell Color Comic #16 -- "Mickey Mouse vs. the Phantom Blot" drawn by longtime newspaper strip artist, Floyd Gottfredson. Uncle Scrooge became a quarterly series with the fourth issue in Dec 1953. Other series are based on Disney characters such as Pluto, Goofy, Scamp, The Beagle Boys and Zorro. Short special series based on Christmas, vacation time and Disneyland were also issued. One shots are usually based on animated features or TV shows. The Dell Color and Four Color series are the main focus of collector interest. The major ones are listed. A photo sample of other Disney comics is provided as an overview of available titles and how the books changed over the years. Dell distribution ended in July 1962 when Western Printing and Lithographing switched the series to the Gold Key banner and different distribution. Disney comics were never the same.

Disney comic books had been on sale for over 45 years when publication ceased in 1984. Many of the older stories had been republished in miniature form over the years in the 57 issues of Walt Disney Comics Digest (Jun 67 to Feb 76). In 1986, Gladstone Publishing div. of Another Rainbow, a company run by comic and art collectors, pumped new life into Disney titles. Gladstone is reprinting the best of older material done by U.S. and foreign publishers and developing some new stories. Gladstone also released a few Comics Digests.

Top investment grade comic books have largely been found. True mint copies are never really seen at antique or toy shows. What looks like new to most dealers or collectors would pale next to a mint copy. Prices in this guide ignore the investment grade books because preservation techniques would had to have been used since the day the issue was purchased new for it to survive in mint, investment condition. There is a chance you may find uncirculated comics Grandma hid in her cedar chest in Colorado or Arizona. Then you have something worthy of individual appraisal and the need for a dealer contact who knows top buyers. Otherwise, exposure to air, heat, and/or dampness have already accelerated the self-destructive acid in the paper.

C7000	Donald Duck, 1938, Whitman/K.K.Publications	150 - 400
C7001	Donald Duck, 1940, b & w, #16	40 - 180
C7002	Donald Duck, 1940, color, #4	200 - 600
C7003	Reluctant Dragon, 1941, color, #13	40 - 120
C7004	Mickey Mouse vs. the Phantom Blot, 1941, color, #16	150 - 600
C7005	Dumbo, the Flying Elephant, 1941, color, #17	30 - 95

Dell Four Color Comics

C7010	Donald Duck Finds Pirates Gold!, 1942, #9, first Barks	375 - 1,000
C7011	Bambi, 1942, #12	15 - 50
C7012	Thumper Meets the Seven Dwarfs, 1942, #19	15 - 60
C7013	Mickey Mouse and the 7 Colored Terror, 1943, #27	40 - 150
C7014	Donald Duck and the Mummy's Ring, 1943, #29	175 - 675
C7015	Bambi's Children, 1943, #30	15 - 50
C7016	Snow White and the Seven Dwarfs, 1944, #49	15 - 60
C7017	Donald Duck in Frozen Gold, 1945, #62	250 - 700
C7018	Three Caballeros, 1945, #71	50 - 150
C7019	Mickey Mouse in Riddle of the Red Hat, 1945, #79	50 - 160
C7020	The Wonderful Adventures of Pinocchio, 1945, #92	20 - 75
C7021	Donald Duck in the Terror of the River, 1946, #108	80 - 300
C7022	Mickey Mouse and the House of Many Mysteries, 1946, #116	15 - 60
C7023	Uncle Remus and His Tales of Brer Rabbit, 1946, #129	10 - 40
C7024	Mickey Mouse and the Submarine Pirates, 1947, #141	10 - 40
C7025	Donald Duck in Volcano Valley, 1947, #147	55 - 200
C7026	Mickey Mouse and the Beanstalk, 1947, #157	15 - 75
C7027	Donald Duck in the Ghost of the Grotto, 1947, #159	55 - 200
C7028	Mickey Mouse on Spook's Island, 1947, #170	12 - 40
C7029	Donald Duck Christmas on Bear Mountain, 1947, #178	60 - 200
C7030	Mickey Mouse in Jungle Magic, 1947, #181	12 - 30
C7031	Bambi, 1948, #186	12 - 30
C7032	Donald Duck in the Old Castle's Secret, 1948, #189	50 - 180
C7033	Mickey Mouse in the World Under the Sea, 1948, #194	12 - 30
C7034	Donald Duck in Sheriff of Bullet Valley, 1948, #199	50 - 180
C7035	Donald Duck in the Golden Christmas Tree, 1948, #203	12 - 120
C7036	Brer Rabbit Does It Again, 1949, #208	10 - 32
C7037	Mickey Mouse and His Sky Adventure, 1949, #214	20 - 80
C7038	Three Little Pigs and the Wonderful Magic Lamp, 1949, #218	10 - 30

C7039	Donald Duck Lost in the Andes, 1949, #223	50 - 180
C7040	Seven Dwarfs, 1949, #227	10 - 28
C7041	Mickey Mouse and the Rajah's Treasure, 1949, #231	10 - 28
C7042	Dumbo in Sky Voyage, 1949, #234	10 - 24
C7043	Donald Duck In Voodoo Hoodoo, 1949, #238	45 - 160
C7044	Thumper Follows His Nose, 1949, #243	10 - 25
C7045	Mickey Mouse and the Black Sorcerer, 1949, #248	10 - 28
C7046	Pinocchio, 1949, #252	8 - 22
C7047	Donald Duck in Luck of the North, 1949, #256	45 - 160
C7048	Mickey Mouse and the Missing Key, 1949, #261	10 - 30
C7049	Donald Duck in Land of the Totem Poles, 1950, #263	30 - 100
C7050	Mickey Mouse's Surprise Visitor, 1950, #268	10 - 30
C7051	Cinderella, 1950, #272	8 - 22
C7052	Donald Duck in Ancient Persia, 1950, #275	30 - 100
C7053	Mickey Mouse & Pluto Battle the Giant Ants, 1950, #279	10 - 30
C7054	Donald Duck and the Pixilated Parrot, 1950, #282	30 - 100
C7055	Mickey Mouse in the Uninvited Guest, 1950, #286	10 - 30
C7056	Donald Duck in the Magic Hourglass, 1950, #291	30 - 100
C7057	Mickey Mouse in Private Eye for Hire, 1950, #296	10 - 30
C7058	Donald Duck in Big Top Bedlam, 1950, #300	30 - 100
C7059	Mickey Mouse in Tom Tom Island, 1950, #304	10 - 30
C7060	Donald Duck in Dangerous Disguise, 1950, #308	25 - 90
C7061	Mickey Mouse in the Mystery of the Double Cross Ranch, 1951, #313	10 - 30
C7062	Donald Duck in No Such Varmint, 1951, #318	25 - 90
C7063	Mickey Mouse in the Haunted Castle, 1951, #325	10 - 30
C7064	Donald Duck in Old California, 1951, #328	25 - 85
C7065	Alice In Wonderland, 1951, #331	6 - 18
C7066	Mickey Mouse and Yukon Gold, 1951, #334	10 - 25
C7067	Donald Duck and the Magic Fountain, 1951, #339	10 - 25
C7068	Unbirthday Party with Alice In Wonderland, 1951, #341	10 - 25
C7069	Mickey Mouse in the Ruby Eye of Homar-Guy-Am, 1951,#343	10 - 25
C7070	Donald Duck The Crocodile Collector, 1951, #348	10 - 25

C7071	Mickey Mouse in the Mystery of Painted Valley, 1951, #352	10 - 25
C7072	Duck Album, 1951, #353	4 - 10
C7072	Donald Duck in Rags to Riches, 1951, #356	10 - 25
C7073	Mickey Mouse and the Smuggled Diamonds, 1951, #362	10 - 25
C7074	Donald Duck in a Christmas for Shacktown, 1951, #367	25 - 75
C7075	Mickey Mouse in the Inca Idol Case, 1952, #371	8 - 20
C7076	Donald Duck in Southern Hospitality, 1952, #379	8 - 20
C7077	Snow White and the Seven Dwarfs, 1952, #382	9 - 18
C7078	Uncle Scrooge in Only a Poor Old Man, 1952, #386	50 - 200
C7079	Mickey Mouse in High Tibet, 1952, #387	8 - 20
C7080	Donald Duck in Malayalaya, 1952, #394	8 - 20
C7081	Mickey Mouse and Goofy's Mechanical Wizard, 1952, #401	8 - 20
C7082	Li'l Bad Wolf, 1952, #403	4 - 10
C7083	Donald Duck and the Golden Helmet, 1952, #408	20 - 70
C7084	Mickey Mouse and the Old Sea Dog, 1952, #411	8 - 18
C7085	Robin Hood, 1952, #413	4 - 10
C7086	Donald Duck and the Gilded Man, 1952, #422	20 - 70
C7087	Mickey Mouse and the Wonderful Whizzix, 1952, #427	8 - 20
C7088	Pluto in Why Dogs Leave Home, 1952, #429	5 - 15
C7089	Little Hiawatha, 1952, #439	4 - 10
C7090	Peter Pan, 1952, #442	4 - 12
C7091	Captain Hook and Peter Pan, 1952, #446	5 - 15
C7092	Duck Album, 1953, #450	2 - 10
C7093	Uncle Scrooge in Back to the Klondike, 1953, #456	30 - 140
C7094	Goofy, 1953, #468	2 - 10
C7095	Li'l Bad Wolf, 1953, #473	2 - 8
C7096	Duck Album, 1953, #492	2 - 8
C7097	Uncle $crooge, 1953, #495	30 - 120

Donald Duck spun out of four color comic to become a series with #26, Mickey Mouse with #28, and Uncle $crooge with #4. Disney characters and movies were the subject of many more, but less collectible, issues. Carl Barks did all of the Donald Duck books from 1942 through 1950 and selective issues thereafter. Walt Disney Comics and Stories is the other major title of collecting interest. It replaced the Mickey Mouse Magazine with the Oct 1940 issue. The number one issue has reportedly sold for over $2,000 in mint condition. Nice fine copies were seen at the Big D Show in Dallas in 1988 and the Atlantic City show in 1989 for $1000. It still seems out of proportion to earlier Mickey Mouse magazines routinely selling for less than $100. Those interested in this run would do well to visit a number of comic dealers to check out condition and current selling prices as they vary widely.

The better short series titles and one-shot comics include:

C7501	Gyro Gearloose, 4-color by Barks, 4	5 - 20
C7510	Zorro, 4-color and Zorro series	4 - 12
C7550	Christmas Parade by Barks, 1949-50	45 - 160
C7565	Vacation Parade by Barks, 1950	45 - 160
C7575	Peter Pan Treasure Chest, 1952	20 - 55
C7576	Lady and the Tramp, Giant, 1955	5 - 15

Other Disney comics certainly have value. The definitive guide to this area is the *Comic Book Price Guide* by Robert M. Overstreet, mentioned under "Price Guides" in introductory material to this book.

C7600	Gladstone Disney Titles	2 - 4
C7800	Walt Disney Comics Digests	4 - 25
C7858	Gladstone Comics Disney Digest Titles	2 - 4

C7950 COMIC BOOK SUBSCRIPTION PREMIUMS, PROMOTIONS, AND ACKNOWLEDGEMENTS

Kay Kamen did the promotion for both *Mickey Mouse Magazine* and *Walt Disney's Comics and Stories* subscriptions. Four-page folders were mailed out to solicit subscriptions. Frequently a premium was offered. Acknowledgement or gift cards were sent to confirm the order was received. Premiums were slick prints of Disney characters or paperback versions of the Whitman Story Hour series starting at B5490.

C7951	Mickey Mouse Magazine Promotion Piece	18 - 50
C7952	Mickey Mouse Magazine Gift Card	15 - 40
C7955	Walt Disney Comics and Stories Mailers	15 - 45
C7956	Walt Disney Comics and Stories Gift Cards	20 - 50
C7957	Character Premium Prints 8 x 10's, each	5 - 25
C7965	Large Circus Premium Print	12 - 85

C8000 COMIC BOOKS -- PREMIUM AND GIVEAWAY

The color 10¢ comic book format began around 1938 and firmly took hold in 1940. Every kid was keen on comics, thus they made excellent premiums. *Travel Tykes Weekly* and *Dumbo Weekly* were among the first premium comic books. *Travel Tykes Weekly* was larger, like a newspaper, and had two cut-out stamps to paste on a map. It was dispensed in 4 page installments. The Dumbo D-X gasoline series was collected in an envelope or a binder. The Firestone comic giveaways, many by Barks, began in 1943. The miniature Cheerios and Wheaties comics ended the 40's on an upbeat note. The 3-D series that followed weren't as successful, the half size 50's premiums were too commercial. March of Comics were shoe and department store giveaways.

C8050	Travel Tykes Weekly, 1-20, Jan-Sept 1939, each	8 - 20
C8071	Dumbo Weekly, 1-16, 1941, each	6 - 18
C8087	Dumbo Binder	8 - 20
C8088	Dumbo Envelope	5 - 15
C8100	1943 Firestone Presents Comics by Walt Disney	55 - 175
C8101	1944 Donald and Mickey Firestone	6 - 70
C8102	1945 Donald and Mickey Firestone	50 - 150
C8103	1946 Donald and Mickey Firestone	50 - 150
C8104	1947 Donald and Mickey Firestone	50 - 150
C8105	1948 Donald and Mickey Firestone	50 - 150
C8106	1949 Donald and Mickey Firestone	15 - 50

The March of Comics Series included Disney titles from 1947 to 1951 plus two more half size books in 1963 and 1964. Differences in opinion on the value of these pulp comics is vast. Agreement on condition even tougher. Donald Duck was featured in numbers 4, 20, 41, 56, 69, and 263. Mickey Mouse was the subject of numbers 8, 27, 45, 60, and 74. The Sword in the Stone was #258.

Cheerios offered four sets of 4 miniature books in 1947 and three sets of 8 small 3-D comics in 1954. Wheaties issued four sets of 8 books in 1950-51. Sets B, C and D of the Wheaties books were found in great quantities in the mid-70's.

Cheerios (1947) Sets W, X, Y, and Z

C8200	Donald Duck and the Pirates, W-1	5 - 15
C8201	Bucky Bug and the Cannibal King, W-2	4 - 10
C8202	Pluto Joins the FBI, W-3	5 - 10
C8203	Mickey Mouse and the Haunted House, W-4	5 - 15
C8204	Donald Duck, Counter Spy, X-1	5 - 15
C8205	Goofy Lost in the Desert, X-2	5 - 15
C8206	Brer Rabbit Outwits Brer Fox, X-3	4 - 10
C8207	Mickey Mouse at the Rodeo, X-4	5 - 15
C8208	Donald Duck's Atomic Bomb, Y-1, Barks	25 - 75
C8209	Brer Rabbit's Secret, Y-2	4 - 10
C8210	Dumbo and the Circus Mystery, Y-3	4 - 10
C8211	Mickey Mouse Meets the Wizard, Y-4	5 - 15
C8212	Donald Duck Pilots a Jet Plane, Z-1	5 - 15
C8213	Pluto Turns Sleuth Hound, Z-2	4 - 10
C8213	The Seven Dwarfs and the Enchanted Mountain, Z-3	4 - 10
C8214	Mickey Mouse's Secret Room, Z-4	5 - 15
C8220	Donald Duck's Surprise Party, 1948, Icy Frost Twins	10 - 35

Wheaties Giveaways (1950-51) Sets A, B, C & D

C8230	Mickey Mouse and the Disappearing Island, A-1	4 - 12
C8231	Grandma Duck, Homespun Detective, A-2	4 - 12
C8232	Donald Duck and the Haunted Jewels, A-3	4 - 12

114

C8233	Donald Duck and the Giant Ape, A-4	4 - 12
C8234	Mickey Mouse Roving Reporter, A-5	4 - 12
C8235	Li'l Bad Wolf Forest Ranger, A-6	4 - 12
C8236	Goofy Tightrope Acrobat, A-7	4 - 12
C8237	Pluto and the Bogus Money, A-8	4 - 12
C8238	Mickey Mouse and the Pharaoh's Curse, B-1	3 - 8
C8239	Pluto Canine Cowpoke, B-2	3 - 8
C8240	Donald Duck and the Buccaneers, B-3	3 - 8
C8241	Mickey Mouse and the Mystery Sea Monster, B-4	3 - 8
C8242	Li'l Bad Wolf in the Hollow Tree Hideout, B-5	3 - 8
C8243	Donald Duck Trail Blazer, B-6	3 - 8
C8244	Goofy and the Gangsters, B-7	3 - 8
C8245	Donald Duck, Klondike Kid, B-8	3 - 8
C8246	Donald Duck and the Inca Idol, C-1	3 - 8
C8247	Mickey Mouse and the Magic Mountain, C-2	3 - 8
C8248	Li'l Bad Wolf Fire Fighter, C-3	3 - 8
C8249	Gus and Jaq Save the Ship, C-4	3 - 8
C8250	Donald Duck in the Lost Lakes, C-5	3 - 8
C8251	Mickey Mouse and the Stagecoach Bandits, C-6	3 - 8
C8252	Goofy Big Game Hunter, C-7	3 - 8
C8253	Donald Duck, Deep Sea Diver, C-8	3 - 8
C8254	Donald Duck in Indian Country, D-1	3 - 8
C8255	Mickey Mouse and the Abandoned Mine, D-2	3 - 8
C8256	Pluto and the Mysterious Package, D-3	3 - 8
C8257	Brer Rabbit's Sunken Treasure, D-4	3 - 8
C8258	Donald Duck, Mighty Mystic, D-5	3 - 8
C8259	Mickey Mouse and the Medicine Man, D-6	3 - 8
C8260	Li'l Bad Wolf and Secret of the Woods, D-7	3 - 8
C8261	Minnie Mouse, Girl Explorer, D-8	3 - 8
C8265	Ghosts of Waylea Castle -- Robin Hood Flour, 1952	3 - 15
C8266	The Miller's Ransom -- Robin Hood Flour, 1952	3 - 15
C8270	A New Adventure of Snow White and the Seven Dwarfs, 1952, Bendix	2 - 10
C8275	Cheerios 3-D Set 1, 1954	8 - 24
C8285	Cheerios 3-D Set 2, 1954	8 - 24
C8295	Cheerios 3-D Set 3, 1954	8 - 24

American Dairy Association (1955)

C8300	Brer Rabbit in Ice Cream for the Party	5 - 15
C8301	Cinderella in Fairest of the Fair	5 - 15
C8302	Lady and the Tramp in Butter Late Than Never	5 - 15
C8303	Snow White and the Seven Dwarfs in the Milky Way	5 - 15
C8308	New Adventures of Peter Pan presented by Admiral, 1953	10 - 30
C8325	Snow White and the Seven Dwarfs in Mystery of the Missing Magic	5 - 15

115

C9000 COOKIE JARS

Disney characters have been reproduced dramatically on cookie jars. Leeds China escalated interest with their famous Turnabout cookie jars. Unfortunately, Leeds painted on top of the ceramic glaze and paint is rarely, if ever, found in mint condition. Repainting often produces even worse results. A continuing flow of intriguing designs has followed. Also see other ceramic manufacturers such as Laguna, Evan K. Shaw and Vernon Kilns.

C9020	Mickey/Minnie, Turnabout	15 - 75
C9021	Donald/Joe Carioca, Turnabout	15 - 75
C9022	Dumbo, both sides, Turnabout	18 - 80
C9023	Pluto/Dumbo, Turnabout	18 - 80
C9024	Donald, figural, Leeds	8 - 28
C9028	Donald, figural no hat, American	15 - 50
C9035	Jar w/Mickey	10 - 55
C9036	Jar w/Donald	10 - 55
C9040	Donald, figural sitting	10 - 50
C9045	Thumper	8 - 35
C9088	Ludwig Lolly Pop Jar	8 - 35
C9100	Ludwig Von Drake, head	10 - 40
C9105	Musical Mickey Mouse, head	12 - 60
C9108	Donald Duck, head	10 - 45
C9110	Mickey, w/leatherette ears	10 - 55
C9115	Mickey Clock, Enesco	10 - 50
C9118	Donald, Pumpkin, figural	10 - 45
C9119	Winnie the Pooh, figural	10 - 45
C9120	Tigger, figural	10 - 50
C9126	Jar w/Mickey & nephews	5 - 15
C9128	Litho Can w/Mickey & Donald, Cheinco	4 - 12
C9130	Litho Can w/major characters, Cheinco	4 - 12
C9131	Chef Mickey	10 - 25

C9350 CRAFT SETS

Items in this class include paint-by-numbers, leathercraft, liquid embroidery, decoplaques, figure painting, mosaics, string and wire art, make 'n bake, glitter or sand decorating sets, copper tapping, wood burning, shrink art, jewelry making and other similar products.

C9360	Mickey Mouse Series -- Tinkersand	8 - 50
C9361	Snow White Series -- Tinkersand	8 - 45
C9365	Snow White Tap-A-Way Set	15 - 80
C9366	Snow White Wood Burning Set	15 - 85
C9375	Disneyland Medal Craft Tapping Set	12 - 75
C9377	Disneyland Woodburning Set	10 - 65
C9379	Leathercraft Kits	1 - 10

C9380	Jewelry Making Sets	4-25
C9381	Character String Art Kits	5-20
C9390	Paint-by-Numbers Sets	2-15
C9392	Spray and Play Airbrush, Ideal	3-20
C9393	Mickey Mouse Shrinky Dinks, set unused	2-10
C9394	Make 'n Bake sets	2-10

C9400 CRAYON AND COLORING SETS

Marks Brothers Company made crayon sets from 1933-39. Transogram made them from 1939-55. Hasbro started making various coloring activity sets in 1968 and have continued to 1984. Whitman issued Big Little Book coloring sets in the 30's and has included crayons with other products over the years.

C9401	Crayons, 1934, Marks Bros, set of 8	5-40
C9402	Mickey Mouse Crayon Set, Marks Brothers	60 - 250
C9403	Donald Duck Crayon and Paint Set, Marks Brothers	60 - 250
C9404	Mickey Mouse Big Little Set - Things To Do	20 - 150
C9405	Mickey Mouse Big Big Box	55 - 250
C9406	Donald Duck Paint and Color Box, #3061	55 - 250
C9407	Mickey Mouse Color Box	25 - 110
C9408	Snow White and the Seven Dwarfs Paint and Crayon Set	25 - 110
C9409	Snow White and the Seven Dwarfs Coloring Set	45 - 85
C9410	Mickey Mouse Crayon Set, Transogram	15 - 30
C9411	Donald/Mickey Giant Crayons, 12	15 - 28
C9412	Pinocchio Color Box	20 - 35
C9420	Magic Pictures, 40's, Jaymar	8-22
C9428	Mickey/Donald Giant Crayons, 10, 1949	10 - 25
C9430	Mickey Mouse and Donald Duck Crayons, 1950	8-20
C9432	Donald Duck Crayons	10 - 25
C9440	Peter Pan Crayons and Stencils	25 - 110
C9445	Magic Erasable Pictures	8-25
C9448	Mickey Mouse Club Magic Erasable Picture Book	5-22
C9449	Mickey Mouse Club - 12 coloring books & crayons, 1955, Whitman, boxed set	10 - 50
C9455	Annette Coloring Box, 1962, Whitman	10 - 55
C9482	Davy Crockett Pencil Craft Painting Box, Hasbro	8-50
C9485	Walt Disney Numbered Pencil Coloring Set, Hasbro	5-25

D3575 DISNEY DOLLARS

The Walt Disney Company decided to issue their own paper currency for use at Disneyland in 1987. Approximately $2 million worth of $1 bills featuring Mickey and $5 bills sporting Goofy were circulated. The company promises to redeem them in U.S. dollars upon demand. The issue was so successful the "funny money" was introduced to Walt Disney World the following November. Actually, this type of "script" money has been in existence since Disneyland opened in 1955. Ticket coupons and passports have always been good for admission or use anytime. When individual attraction tickets were eliminated, the company began redeeming them for the unused cash value.

The first Disney Dollars were the ones distributed at Mickey Mouse Club meetings held in theaters in the early 30's. Redemption, however, was limited to ice cream cones. There were Mickey play bucks printed on each Disney newspaper comic page and some interesting 30's play money you needed to keep about 45 years before any value was recognized.

The first theme park "Disney Dollar" was printed at Disneyland in 1964. Walt Disney World Recreation Coupons (1971) were designed to promote the expanded Disney concept of family entertainment and the vast sports facilities throughout the Walt Disney World complex. These are interesting because they are signed by Roy O. Disney who lived for only a brief period after Walt Disney World opened. There was a similar Disneyland "Discount Dollar" in 1980. These predecessors were amazingly similar to the "new" design for the Mickey buck. They were numbered and signed by Roy Disney, but were not redeemable in cash. Who wouldn't like to have a whole handful now?

D3577	Mickey Mouse Cone Dollars	6 - 20
D3578	Dollars cut from Sunday newspapers, each	1 - 2
D3580	Mickey Mouse Play Money, 30's, each	5 - 15
D3584	Disneyland 1964 Issue	?
D3585	Walt Disney World Recreation Coupons, each	8 - 20
D3586	San Diego Armed Forces Discount Dollar, 1980, each	2 - 10
D3587	Disney Dollar Announcement Flyer	.25 - .50
D3588	Disneyland $1 Bill, 1987	1 - 2
D3589	Disneyland $5 Bill, 1987	5 - 7
D3590	Disneyland or Walt Disney World $1 Bill, 1987	1 - 2
D3591	Disneyland or Walt Disney World $5 Bill, 1987	5 - 7

D4000 DISNEYKINS

Disneykins, miniature painted plastic figures (Hong Kong), were a product of Louis Marx & Company (NYC) from 1955 until 1980. The original 34 figures came in little individual boxes and several combinations of scene boxes and playsets. Larger sizes were sold as Disney kings and Disney Fun Pals. There were also special sets with accessories and premium sets for RCA and Jello Pudding. Rolykins were a variation. Regular Disneykins were used in at least one "Figure Picture Book" of *Snow White and the Seven Dwarfs*.

The first 34 figures were offered in various packages and playsets. They remained available for over 25 years. A few were even reproduced for the 1988 Sears Disneyland playset.

"New" Disneykins were introduced in 1961. The insert in each individual box depicted "36 Different Masterpieces", but playsets of New Disneykins included many not listed. The *Sleeping Beauty* and *Alice in Wonderland* playsets included "flat" hard plastic figures similar to the furniture, plants and other items included in previous playsets.

Packaging of Disneykin playsets was bizarre. The Three Pigs came with Brer Fox; Lady and Tramp with two clowns from *Dumbo*; two Lost Boys and Smee from *Peter Pan* came with Flower from *Bambi*; and Cinderella, Gus and Jaq with the owl from *Bambi*. A special *Lady and the Tramp* "kennel" package included 10 dogs and 2 cats -- Lady, Tramp, Bull, Pedro, Peg, Jock, Dachsie, Trusty, Toughy, Boris, Si and Am -- from the same film. Similar film sets were produced for *Pinocchio*, *101 Dalmatians* and *The Jungle Book*. Wild animals from non-Disney Marx playsets were included in some *The Jungle Book* playsets -- a rhinoceros, elephant, deer, giraffe and wolf were used for this purpose. The seven Disney designed *The Jungle Book* characters -- Col. Hathi, his son, Mowgli, Baloo, Bagheera, King Louie and Shere Khan -- were first offered as Jello Pudding premiums along with other Disneykins, then in with jungle animals in store sets. Prof. Ludwig Von Drake was an RCA premium -- boxed with four original Disneykins.

Morty and Ferdy are the same figure as are Dewey's brothers, Huey and Louie. Original paint distinctions have not been found by the author.

D4001	Castle Display of Original 34 Figures	200 - 450
D4002	Figures, original 34, boxed, each	3 - 10
D4003	Disneykin Scene Boxes, 10 different, each	5 - 20
D4014	Multi-Box of all 34 Figures, yellow	45 - 125
Disneykin Playsets, original figures only		
D4015	Mickey Mouse Scene	25 - 75
D4016	Donald Duck Scene	25 - 75
D4017	Panchito Western Scene	25 - 75
D4018	Dumbo Circus Scene	20 - 65
D4019	Pinocchio Scene	20 - 65
D4022	Babes In Toyland Display	125 - 250
D4023	Disneykings Display	150 - 350
D4024	New Disneykins Display	250 - 550
New Disneykins Playsets (D4025-D4030)		
D4025	Sleeping Beauty	55 - 300
D4026	Alice in Wonderland	75 - 400
D4027	Cinderella Mice, plus Wendy and Owl	25 - 125
D4028	Peter Pan Lost Boys, Smee plus Flower	25 - 125
D4029	Standing Lady & Tramp plus Clowns	25 - 125
D4030	Three Pigs plus Brer Fox	25 - 125

Larger and Special Packaging

D4050	Lady and Tramp Kennel Box, 10 figures	100 - 400
D4065	RCA Premium Boxed Set	20 - 85
D4066	Ludwig Von Drake Playsets, 4 different, each	15 - 55
D4067	101 Dalmatians, boxed sets of 8, each	45 - 195
D4068	The Jungle Book Sets, 3 different, each	40 - 175
D4069	Snow White and the Seven Dwarfs Figurine Picture Book, 1968	75 - 150
D4070	Blister Packs of 8 figures, w/new Disneykins (6), each	20 - 100

Triple Playsets (D4071-D4073)

D4071	Pinocchio	75 - 175
D4072	Snow White	80 - 175
D4073	Combination of Pinocchio, Snow White and Dumbo sets	80 - 175
D4075	Rolykins, wheels, boxed, each	3 - 9
D4085	Rolykins, ball bearings, boxed, each	3 - 9
D4086	Rolykins, ball bearings, blister pack	10 - 35
D4095	Disney on Parade Playset, J.C. Penney	50 - 125
D4100	101 Dalmatians, boxed sets of 8, each	75 - 300
D4110	Disney Fun Pals, blister packs, each	15 - 50
D4115	Disneykings, boxed, each	4 - 12
D4130	The Jungle Book Sets, 3 different, each	40 - 175

INDIVIDUAL FIGURES, NOT IN BOXES, SCENES, OR PLAYSETS

Original 34 Characters

D4201	Snow White	2 - 5
D4202	Grumpy	1 - 4
D4203	Sneezy	1 - 4
D4204	Sleepy	1 - 4
D4205	Dopey	1 - 4
D4206	Bashful	1 - 4
D4207	Doc	1 - 4
D4208	Happy	1 - 4
D4209	Donald	2 - 5
D4210	Dewey	1 - 4
D4211	Daisy	1 - 4
D4212	Morty	1 - 4
D4213	Mickey	2 - 5
D4214	Minnie	2 - 5
D4215	Pluto	2 - 5
D4216	Goofy	2 - 5
D4217	Geppetto	2 - 5
D4218	Pinocchio	1 - 5
D4219	Jiminy Cricket	1 - 4
D4220	Figaro	1 - 4
D4221	Alice	1 - 4

D4222	Tinker Bell	1 - 5
D4223	Blue Fairy	1 - 4
D4224	Peter Pan	2 - 5
D4225	Captain Hook	2 - 5
D4226	Pecos Bill	1 - 4
D4227	Bambi	1 - 4
D4228	Panchito	1 - 4
D4229	Timothy	1 - 4
D4230	Dumbo	2 - 5
D4231	Ring Master	1 - 4
D4232	Brer Rabbit	1 - 4
D4233	Thumper	1 - 4
D4234	Joe Caricoa	1 - 4

Bambi additional figures

D4235	Flower	15 - 30
D4236	Owl	15 - 30

Babes in Toyland soldiers (approx. 1")

D4237	In Boat w/cannon	5 - 15
D4238	In Gray PT Type Boat	5 - 15
D4239	Rifle on Shoulder	5 - 15
D4240	Rifle at the Ready	5 - 15
D4241	w/Drum	5 - 15
D4242	w/Trumpet	4 - 12

The Three Little Pigs characters

D4244	Practical Pig	15 - 30
D4245	Fiddler Pig	15 - 30
D4246	Piper Pig	15 - 30

Alice in Wonderland characters

D4247	White Rabbit	15 - 30
D4248	Mad Hatter	20 - 38
D4249	March Hare	20 - 38
D4250	Queen of Hearts	15 - 30

Cartoon Short and TV characters

D4259	Prof. Ludwig Von Drake	15 - 35
D4260	Uncle Scrooge	20 - 45
D4261	Chip	18 - 40
D4262	Dale	18 - 40

Cinderella characters

D4264	Jaq	15 - 30
D4265	Gus	15 - 30

Pinocchio additional characters

D4266	Stromboli	15 - 30
D4267	Foulfellow	15 - 30
D4268	Lampwick	15 - 30
D4269	Cleo	18 - 35

Peter Pan additional characters

D4270	Lost Boy No. 1	15 - 30

D4271	Wendy	15 - 30
D4272	Lost Boy No. 2	15 - 30
D4273	Smee	15 - 30

Sleeping Beauty characters

D4274	Maleficent	25 - 65
D4275	Fauna	18 - 35
D4276	Flora	18 - 35
D4277	Merryweather	18 - 35
D4278	Sleeping Beauty	20 - 50
D4279	Prince Charming	20 - 50

Miscellaneous characters

D4280	Willie the Whale	25 - 75
D4281	Bongo	25 - 75
D4282	Brer Fox	15 - 30
D4283	Toby Tortoise	25 - 75

Dumbo additional characters

D4284	Regular Clown	15 - 30
D4285	Fireman Clown	15 - 30

Lady and the Tramp characters

D4286	Lady, standing	15 - 30
D4287	Lady, sitting	20 - 40
D4288	Tramp, standing	15 - 30
D4289	Tramp, sitting	20 - 40
D4290	Bull	18 - 35
D4291	Pedro	18 - 35
D4292	Peg	20 - 40
D4293	Jock	18 - 35
D4294	Dachsie	18 - 35
D4295	Trusty	18 - 35
D4296	Toughy	18 - 35
D4297	Boris	18 - 35
D4298	Si	18 - 35
D4299	Am	18 - 35

The Jungle Book characters

D4300	Col. Hathi	10 - 25
D4301	Sonny (his son)	5 - 15
D4302	Mowgli	5 - 15
D4303	Baloo	5 - 15
D4304	Bagherra	5 - 15
D4305	King Louie	10 - 25
D4306	Shere Khan	5 - 15

101 Dalmatians characters

D4310	Pongo	25 - 75
D4311	Perdita	25 - 70
D4312	Cruella De Vil	35 - 100
D4313	Jasper	25 - 75
D4314	Horace	25 - 75

D4315	The Colonel (sheepdog)	20 - 60
D4316	Sergeant Tibs	20 - 60
D4317	Nanny	25 - 75
D4320	Puppies, 35 different, each	10 - 25

Flat, hard plastic characters

D4370	Sampson	20 - 40
D4371	Goon	10 - 25
D4372	Cheshire Cat	20 - 45
D4373	Caterpillar	20 - 45
D4374	Ace of Spades	15 - 35

D5000 DISNEYLAND

This section includes publications and materials unique to Disneyland theme park operations and guest relations. Most souvenirs, toys, and items such as pennants, postcards, games, etc., are found at other classifications. Disneyland revolutionized the amusement park concept with fresh new ideas worthy of study by sociologists and businessmen alike. Operation excellence was the result of planning, training, strict policies, and creative entertainment. Job applicants, for example, aren't hired, they are cast in a part. Supervisors have the "lead" roles.

There are always new things happening to encourage repeat visits. The development of the concept is reflected in park publications, in promotions, and the attention given to the smallest details. The main items are maps, pictorial guide books, tickets, event booklets, history books, employee materials, and promotion pieces. Various park licensees have also issued material found at this class. The promotional material listed is but a small representation of the thousands of items generated annually as part of the "show". The author is grateful to Bruce and Linda Cervon, noted Disneyland collectors, for the information they provided. Disneyland memorabilia commands the highest prices in California. East coast collectors tend to associate with Walt Disney World attractions.

D5001	The Story of Disneyland Guide Book, 1955	75 - 200
D5002	Disneyland in Natural Color, 1955	90 - 250
D5003	At Disneyland the Story of Aluminum, 1955	18 - 55
D5004	Monsanto Hall of Chemistry, fold out booklet, 1956	20 - 65
D5005	Disneyland -- A Complete Guide Book to ... , 1956	15 - 55
D5006	Clyde Beatty's "African Jungle Book", 1956, Richfield	10 - 20
D5006	Give-away Map/Guide Folders	
	-- 1955 or 56	10 - 45
	-- 1957, 58 or 59	8 - 30
	-- 1960 - 65	6 - 20
	-- 1966 - 75	5 - 10
	-- 1976 - 87	2 - 5

D5007	Autopia Driver's License	3-10
D5008	Same as D5003, but with 1957 in upper right corner	12 - 35
D5009	Walt Disney's Sleeping Beauty Castle, 1959	10 - 30
D5012	Walt Disney's Guide to Disneyland, 1958	10 - 30
D5014	Gate Flyers	
	-- promoting newest attractions -- The Columbia, Alice in Wonderland and the Grand Canyon, 1958	5-15
	-- Enchanted Tiki Room and Below Decks, 1964	5-15
D5016	Disneyland Summer, 1959, 4 pages	5-15
D5017	Same as D5012, but w/1959 copyright & minor changes	10 - 30
D5020	Walt Disney's Guide to Disneyland, 1960	8-25
D5021	Plastic Home of the Future, 1960, 2-color	10 - 30
D5022	Walt Disney's Guide to Disneyland, 1961, red	12 - 35
D5024	Walt Disney's Guide to Disneyland, 1962, yellow	12 - 35
D5025	Monsanto Home of the Future, 1963, 4-color	10 - 28
D5026	Walt Disney's Guide to Disneyland, 1963, orange	12 - 35
D5027	Walt Disney's Guide to Disneyland, 1964	10 - 30
D5028	Walt Disney's Disneyland, 1964, Whitman	8-20
D5029	Walt Disney's It's A Small World, 1964	15 - 40
D5030	The Moving Magic of Global, 1964	5-20
D5031	Walt Disney's Disneyland, 1964, hard cover	10 - 25
D5032	Walt Disney's Pictorial Souvenir Book of Disneyland, 1965	10 - 30
D5033	Disneyland World of Flowers, 1965, hard cover	10 - 30
D5034	Walt Disney's Disneyland, 1965, hard cover	10 - 25
D5035	Disneyland USA Summer '67	20 - 45
D5036	Club 33, Royal Street, New Orleans Square, 1967	20 - 45
D5037	Schwinn Take A Trip to Disneyland, 1966	5-25
D5038	Grad Nite Albums, each	4-20
D5040	Walt Disney's Disneyland, A Pictorial Souvenir Book, 1968	12 - 28
D5041	Walt Disney's Pirates of the Caribbean, 1968	15 - 45
D5043	Adventure Thru Inner Space, postcard cover booklet	8-30
D5044	Walt Disney's It's A Small World, 1969	8-25
D5050	Walt Disney's Disneyland, A Pictorial Souvenir and Guide, 1971	5-20
D5054	Same as D5050, but w/1972 copyright (& Guide removed)	5-20
D5056	Same as D5054 w/1973 copyright & interior changes	5-20
D5058	Same as D5054 w/1974 copyright & changes	5-20
D5060	Walt Disney's Pirates of the Caribbean, 1974	5-20
D5061	Walt Disney's It's A Small World, 1974	5-20

D5064	Same as D5054 w/1975 copyright & changes	5-20
D5066	Same as D5054 w/1976 copyright & changes	5-20
D5067	Walt Disney's Disneyland, new cover, 1976	5-18
D5070	Same as D5067 w/1977 copyright & changes	5-18
D5072	Same as D5067 w/1978 copyright	5-18
D5073	It's A Small World, souvenir booklet, 1978	5-15
D5075	Disneyland -- The First Quarter Century, 1979, blue hard cover	5-15
D5078	Same as D5067 w/1980 copyright & changes	5-15
D5080	Same as D5067 w/1981 copyright & changes, maroon cover	4-10
D5086	Same as D5067 w/1983 copyright & changes	3-8
D5090	Silver cover and castle photo, no date	1-2
D5120	The Disneyland News - Monthly tabloid newspaper sold on Main Street. Vol 1 No 1, July 1955 to Vol 2 No 9, Mar 1957, each	5-35

Disneyland maps have been available since 1958. They didn't change each year, however. Modifications were usually made every few years when major additions required new map art to be created. Apparently The Art Corner shop sold them framed for a time. Maps from 1958 to 1964 show Edison Square and Liberty Street which were never built.

D5140	Your Trip to Disneyland, records and map, 1955, Mattel	5-50
D5142	Map of Tom Sawyer Island, 1957, original version lists "Tom and Huck's Tree House" as the "highest point in Disneyland." Later version (but also copyrighted 1957) deletes such mention, and uses dark green shading to make trails stand out, each	5-15
D5143	Map of Disneyland USA, 1958	25-85
D5149	Map of Disneyland USA, 1964	23-75
D5153	Walt Disney's Guide to Disneyland, 1968	20-60
D5157	Same as D5153, adds Bear Country, 1972	15-55
D5160	Dial Guide to Disneyland, 1976	5-20
D5161	Disneyland Map, 1979, Big Thunder	8-25
D5162	Dial Guide to Disneyland, 1979	5-20
D5164	Disneyland Map, 1983, New Fantasyland	3-10
D5200	New Employee Package	15-50
D5210	The Disneyland Story 20th Year Employee Book	15-50
D5215	The Disneyland Story 25th Year Employee Book	8-35
D5216	Family Open House Book	5-20
D5350	Main Street Light Post Signs, various promotions	65-350
D5400	Employee Policy and Job Related Books	8-25
D5500	Opening Day Press Ticket	100-300
D5510	Press Tickets	
	-- Captain EO	5-15
	-- Star Tours	5-15

D5515	Cast Tickets -- Star Tours	2-10
D5525	Walt Disney Story, press giveaway	75 - 200
D5530	America Sings, Sam the Eagle, press giveaway, 1974	90 - 250
D5532	Space Mountain, press giveaway, 1977	50 - 125
D5538	Key to New Fantasyland and Booklet	20 - 45
D5620	Declaration of Independence and Quill Pen, INA	45 - 100
D5640	Art Corner Magic Mirror Movies	15 - 35
D5650	30th Year Hats, 5 different - one for each land, each	2-10
D5700	Souvenir Tickets	3-15
D5700	1986 Gift Giver Ticket	1 - 2
D5701	Old Coupon Ticket Books, complete w/admission ticket	25 - 100
D5702	Old Coupon Ticket Books, part used	2 - 8
D5703	Designated Attraction Tickets, each	2 - 10
D5800	Giveaway Guide Books, 60's, 70's, 80's, each	1 - 5

D6100 DOLLS

Charlotte Clark, an enterprising Los Angeles housewife, got the idea of making a Mickey Mouse doll upon seeing her first Mickey cartoon. When she learned a license was needed to reproduce the copyrighted character, she obtained one and hired several seamstresses to make dolls for the Studio and small retail accounts. The Studio had licensed the rights to produce dolls to George Borgfeldt and Sons of New York. Borgfeldt had presented the Dean Rag Book Co. design produced in London (1930), but the Disneys preferred the design of Mrs. Clark. Roy Disney tried for over a year to get Borgfeldt to adapt to a quality doll similar to the Clark design without success. In frustration, Disney permitted the McCall Company to print a 35¢ pattern (No. 91) for the Charlotte Clark doll. It could be used to make Mickey or Minnie dolls in three sizes (8", 13" and 18"). Borgfeldt turned to Margarete Steiff & Co. of Germany to finally improve quality. Kay Kamen solved the doll problem by licensing the Knickerbocker Toy Company of New York. Mrs. Clark served as a consultant to Knickerbocker and other doll licensees for many years. Madame Alexander was also licensed in 1933 for higher priced dolls. Richard G. Krueger produced the Three Little Pigs, Big Bad Wolf, and Red Riding Hood dolls in 1934. Ideal became a licensee around the time of Snow White until war shortages ended mass production. The Gund Manufacturing Company produced the majority of post war collectible dolls.

A doll vs. a figure or plush stuffed toy is generally a stuffed or other figure dressed with separate clothing and/or accessories. Borgfeldt dressed wood Minnie figures appear at F7200.

D6101	Charlotte Clark, signed, 1930 - 1934	
	-- Mickey or Minnie 8-1/2"	50 - 200
	-- Mickey or Minnie 12-1/2"	50 - 200
	-- Mickey or Minnie 18"	600 - 1,800
	-- Larger promotional sizes	2,500 - up
D6109	Charlotte Clark Donald, signed	200 - 700
D6110	Charlotte Clark, made from McCall pattern	
	1931-39 -- these are still being made	35 - 100
D6200	Dean Rag Book Co. Mickey, 1930-31	
	Mickey or Minnie 5" to 9"	140 - 400
	Mickey or Minnie 12", 14" or 16"	250 - 700
	Mickey or Minnie 18" or 21"	750 - 1,500
D6220	Dean Safety-First Mickey	1,000 - 3,000
D6221	Dean Jazzer Mickey	1,000 - 3,000
D6222	Dean Triketoy, Mickey on tricycle	2,000 - 4,500
D6225	Dean Mickey Mouse Dancers	3,000 - 7,000
D6226	Dean Mickey Mouse Skater	750 - 1,500
D6227	Dean Li-Vo Mickey	1,000 - 3,000

Steiff w/ear button and paper neck tag (The Steiff US license was for 1931, but Bambis in three sizes (1942) were somehow imported.

D6251	Mickey or Minnie 5"	250 - 700
D6253	Mickey or Minnie 7"	450 - 1,500
D6255	Mickey or Minnie 9"	1,000 - 2,500
D6257	Mickey or Minnie, 10" or taller	2,500 - 5,000
D6260	Donald 5"	250 - 750

1934

D6275	Ross Mickey	375 - 600
D6280	Krueger Three Little Pigs, each	50 - 150
D6281	Krueger Big Bad Wolf or Riding Hood, each	30 - 100

Knickerbocker Toy Co., 1934-1941 Designs were modified over the years. The years of the different designs are best guesstimates.

D6301	Mickey, 3 sizes, w/cloth shoes	350 - 700
D6302	Minnie, 3 sizes, w/cloth shoes	450 - 800
D6305	Big Bad Wolf	75 - 280
D6306	Red Riding Hood	60 - 190
D6307	Three Little Pigs, each	40 - 75
D6310	Krueger Wolf	30 - 180
D6311	Red Riding Hood	20 - 130
D6312	Three Little Pigs, each	15 - 30
D6315	Borgfeldt Red Riding Hood	60 - 190

1935 Knickerbocker

D6325	Mickey w/composition shoes	35 - 250
D6326	Minnie w/composition shoes	35 - 250
D6327	Clown Mickey	750 - 1,200
D6328	Six-Gun Mickey, suede chaps	850 - 2,000

1936 Knickerbocker

D6335	Donald, composition	500 - 1,100

Knickerbocker Toy Co. produced some of the earliest and most collectible Disney dolls.

128

D6336	Two-Gun Mickey, tufted chaps	475 - 1,100
D6337	Western Minnie	350 - 800
D6340	Donald, stuffed, 2 sizes	350 - 950
D6341	Drum Major Donald	500 - 1,000

1936 Krueger

D6350	Big Bad Wolf	45 - 125
D6351	Robber Kitten	35 - 85
D6352	Toby Tortoise	30 - 75
D6353	Elmer Elephant	30 - 75
D6354	3 Orphan Kittens, each	15 - 45
D6355	Donald Duck, w/sailor hat	65 - 195
D6356	Pluto the Pup	35 - 175

1938 Snow White and the Seven Dwarfs

D6368	Alexander Snow White	250 - 450
D6369	Alexander Dwarfs, each	45 - 150
D6370	Ideal Snow White, 3 sizes	150 - 500
D6371	Ideal Dwarfs, each	30 - 90
D6374	Knickerbocker Snow White, 3 sizes	135 - 280
D6375	Knickerbocker Wicked Queen	180 - 450
D6376	Knickerbocker Dwarfs, 2 sizes	60 - 175
D6377	Knickerbocker Forest Animals, each	20 - 60
D6380	Krueger Snow White, velvet or organdy	60 - 175
D6381	Krueger Dwarfs, sharkskin or velvet	20 - 60
D6382	Krueger Fawn, birds, chipmunk or bunny, each	15 - 40

1938-1941 Knickerbocker (D6390-D6420)

D6390	Western Donald	450 - 900
D6391	Mexican Mickey or Donald	475 - 950
D6393	Russian Donald	475 - 950
D6394	Major Mickey	550 - 1,100
D6395	Ferdinand the Bull, composition or stuffed	20 - 65
D6397	Donald's Nephews, stuffed, 2 sizes, each	15 - 45
D6400	Dwarfs, stuffed	20 - 55
D6410	Pinocchio, jointed composition or stuffed	125 - 325
D6411	Jiminy Cricket, jointed composition or stuffed	125 - 325
D6413	Figaro, jointed composition or mohair	75 - 185
D6415	Cleo the Goldfish	25 - 60
D6417	Donkey, 2 sizes	20 - 60
D6420	Dumbo	50 - 200
D6440	Crown Pinocchio, 3 composition versions	80 - 350
D6445	Ideal Pinocchio, wood jointed or "Flexy"	120 - 250
D6447	Krueger Pinocchio, wood jointed or cloth	100 - 220
D6450	Krueger Ferdinand the Bull	30 - 75
D6451	Krueger Donald, w/band leader's hat	100 - 250
D6460	Steiff Bambi, 3 sizes, each	35 - 200
D6480	Panchito, Joe Carioca or Donald, Character Novelty, each	50 - 150
D6500	Bongo or Lulubelle, 1947, Gund	35 - 100

Walt Disney's PINOCCHIO is a perfect inspiration for articles of this sort. 12" doll, fully clothed, has movable arms, legs and head. Banks have lock and key. All of durable wood pulp composition. Brilliantly colored. They look like much more than their low retail prices and will sell on sight.

To Retail at 25c to $1.00

DOLLS · BANKS · STATUETTES

CROWN TOY MFG. CO., INC.

200 Fifth Avenue, New York, N. Y.

Factory: 494 Dumont Avenue, Brooklyn. N. Y.

Crown Toy Manufacturing Company was a Disney licensee from 1937 through 1941 and produced an interesting variety of composition dolls, figures and banks.

D6501	Mickey or Donald, 1947, Gund	55 - 135
D6503	Pluto, 1947, Gund	50 - 125
D6504	Mother Pluto and 3 Pups, 1948, Gund	70 - 150
D6505	Pluto, 1949, Gund	50 - 110
D6510	Mickey or Minnie, 1949, Gund, each	60 - 150
D6512	Dumbo, 1949, Gund	40 - 90
D6513	Danny the Black Lamb, w/fair ribbon	50 - 110
D6514	Three Little Pigs, 1949, Gund, each	15 - 50
D6517	Donald's Nephews, 1949, Gund, each	20 - 50
D6525	Gus or Jaq, 1950, Gund, each	20 - 60
D6526	Cinderella, 1950	65 - 175
D6529	Cinderella, 1950, story book	30 - 65
D6530	Cinderella, 2-headed topsy-turvy, 18"	40 - 100
D6540	Pinocchio and the Blue Fairy, 1951, Duchess	30 - 95
D6541	Snow White, 1951, Duchess	25 - 60
D6542	Cinderella, 1951, Duchess	25 - 60
D6543	Alice In Wonderland, 1951, Duchess	30 - 75
D6550	Alice in Wonderland, 1951, movie doll	40 - 100
D6551	Alice in Wonderland, 1951, story book	30 - 65
D6570	Peter Pan, 1952, Ideal	35 - 110
D6576	Tinker Bell, 1952-59, various sizes	15 - 65
D6590	Mickey or Minnie, 1952, Sun Rubber w/clothes, each	15 - 40
D6620	Baby Princess Sleeping Beauty, 1959	25 - 65
D6625	Talking Ludwig Von Drake, w/tape & controls	80 - 250
D6650	Cinderella, removable heads, set, 1964, Horsman	40 - 120
D6651	Cinderella in ball gown, 1964, Horsman	30 - 70
D6775	Small World Dolls, 12" female characters from Japan, Africa, Mexico, France & others, 1963, each	15 - 45
D6800	Mary Poppins, 1964, 36" walking doll	40 - 120
D6801	Mary Poppins, 1964, Horsman, 3 sets, each	25 - 90
D6835	White Rabbit, promotional	50 - 110
D6850	Miniature Disney Favorites, Gund, each	12 - 35
D6862	Mickey or Minnie Rag Doll, each	5 - 20
D6863-6868	Mickey Costume series (c.1975) Durham, Super Mickey, Chef, Drum Major, Ring Master, Sailor and Cowboy, movable arms and legs, heads turn, each	10 - 25
D6875	Dolls by Jerri	55 - 300
D6880	Mickey & Minnie, w/stands, 1985, Applause, each	15 - 50
D6881	Mickey/Minnie, wedding or Mouseketeers, 1986, Applause, each	8 - 20

D7800 DOLLS -- PAPER

Paper dolls were usually published in book form. However, boxed sets appeared as early as 1959. Saalfeld produced a Mickey and Minnie book in 1933. Whitman has been the dominant publisher ever since.

D7801	Mickey/Minnie Cut-Out Doll Book, 1933	75 - 400
D7805	Snow White Cut-Out Doll & Dresses, vertical, 1938	60 - 175
D7806	Snow White Cut-Out Doll & Dresses, 1938,	60 - 150
D7807	Snow White and the Seven Dwarfs, 10¢ paper dolls,1938	60 - 150
D7808	Snow White and the Seven Dwarfs Paper Dolls, 1938	60 - 150
D7810	Pinocchio Doll Cut Outs, 1939	60 - 150
D7830	Annette Mouseketeer Cut-Out Dolls, 1958	10 - 25
D7832	Linda Mouseketeer Cut-Out Dolls, 1958	8 - 20
D7834	Sleeping Beauty Dolls w/Magic Stay-On Dresses, 1959	15 - 45
D7835	Sleeping Beauty, 6 Cut-Out Dolls, 1959	8 - 25
D7838	Pollyanna, 1960	8 - 20
D7842	Annette in Hawaii, 1961, Whitman #1969	8 - 20
D7848	Annette Movie & TV Doll, boxed, 1962, Whitman	15 - 45
D7850	Hayley Mills in Summer Magic, 1963, Whitman #1966	8 - 25
D7852	Paper Doll Activity Book featuring Mary Poppins, 1964	5 - 20
D7853	Annette Cut Out Doll, 1964, Whitman #1953	6 - 20
D7855	Mary Poppins 4 Paper Dolls, 1964, Whitman #1982	5 - 18
D7856	Jane and Michael, Mary Poppins, 1964	5 - 18
D7857	Hayley Mills in That Darn Cat, 1965, Whitman #1955	6 - 20
D7859	Cinderella, 1965	5 - 18
D7860	Mary Poppins Paper Dolls, 1966	5 - 18
D7861	It's a Small World, 1966	5 - 18
D7875	Other Paper Dolls, 1967-1984, each	4 - 12

D8000 DONALD DUCK PRODUCTS

The Florida Citrus Canners Cooperative (later Citrus World) found a unifying symbol with Donald Duck in 1941. National Oats Co. used Donald on oatmeal in 1943, followed by Nash-Underwood mustard & peanut butter in 1944. By 1948 Donald Duck was endorsing over two dozen product categories. Mickey and the other Disney characters were used to endorse food and drink products throughout the 30's, but food licensing became more important in the 40's. War material shortages curtailed the production of many toy items right at the time character merchandise income from animated features was becoming significant. Donald was the most popular cartoon character of the time and was featured on most products. Kay Kamen eventually formed a special division for licensing Donald Duck products. Food product merchandising was discouraged when Disney entered TV programing to avoid sponsor conflicts.

D8001	Orange Juice cans, 40's	10 - 30
D8030	Other citrus drink and fruit cans, 40's	10 - 30
D8050	Citrus products cans, 50's and later	1 - 15
D8150	Oatmeal, 1943-45, 2 sizes	40 - 135
D8155	Peanut Butter, 1944, Nash-Underwood	15 - 45
D8157	Mustard, figural jar, bank lid	20 - 75
D8160	Orange Juice container, 1946, Foremost Dairies	35 - 125
D8165	Peanut Butter, 1947, Cinderella Foods	15 - 45
D8166	Salad Dressing	25 - 65
D8167	Mayonnaise	25 - 65
D8168	Sandwich Spread	25 - 65
D8170	Rice, packaged	20 - 55
D8190	Macaroni or Spaghetti	30 - 85
D8192	Apple Juice, Apple Butter, or Applesauce	20 - 65
D8195	Coffee	30 - 85
D8196	Peas or canned field peas	20 - 65
D8198	Chowder	20 - 50
D8199	Pimentos	20 - 50
D8200	Catsup, Cocktail Sauce or Chili Sauce	20 - 65
D8204	Tomato Juice, various sizes	15 - 45
D8208	Whole Tomatoes, canned	15 - 45
D8209	Tomato Puree	15 - 45
D8210	Corn, canned	20 - 50
D8211	Pumpkin, canned	20 - 50
D8214	Corn Syrup, Atlantic	20 - 50
D8215	Chocolate Flavor Syrup, Atlantic	15 - 35
D8220	Corn syrup products, American	20 - 50
D8225	Bread, various bakeries	5 - 25
D8260	Popcorn	10 - 30
D8265	Cola or other soft drink bottles	4 - 16
D8266	Soft drink six bottle carton	40 - 80
D8267	Bottle caps, each	1 - 2
D8268	Promotional glass, each	8 - 25
D8275	Frozen confection bags, each	1 - 10
D8290	Donald Duck products, labels only, each	1 - 15

D8500 DRAWING SETS & MATERIALS

A drawing set differs from a crayon, coloring, or paint set. Drawing sets, by various means, facilitate the actual drawing or creating of the

Disney character. The set usually contains pictures to be reproduced in some manner along with a "desk", light table, or a drawing device.

D8501	Marks Brothers Pantograph #954	150 - 600
D8503	Mickey and Minnie's Merry Moments Stencil Outfit, c.1931, Spear's/Borgfeldt	135 - 325
D8504	Mickey Mouse Art Set, Dixon #2670	35 - 140
D8505	Dixon Mystery Art Set #2900	40 - 150
D8600	Mousekartooner, Mattel	10 - 25
D8610	Toon-A-Vision Designer, 1968	10 - 25
D8625	Light Up Drawing Desk, Lakeside	8 - 20

F1000 FAN CARDS

A fan card is a free promotional illustration or photo that is sent to fans who send fan letters or otherwise request a photo. It was a popular pastime to do so in the 30's and continues to date. In recent years the size has been reduced. Cards were produced for all animated features and most live action films. The animated character cards are the most prized and collected.

F1001	Mickey and Butch, newspaper offer	40 - 150
F1005	Mickey-Sincerely Yours	40 - 140
F1008	Mickey and Minnie	30 - 80
F1010	Mickey and Pluto	25 - 80
F1020	Mickey, Pluto & Three Little Pigs	25 - 80
F1030	Donald	25 - 70
F1040	Snow White and the Seven Dwarfs	20 - 65
F1041	Dopey	15 - 55
F1048	Snow White and the Seven Dwarfs, premium	4 - 15
F1050	Pinocchio and Jiminy Cricket	15 - 50
F1051	Pinocchio and Geppetto	15 - 50
F1055	Pinocchio, premium	4 - 15
F1070	Bambi	10 - 35
F1085	Song of the South	15 - 50
F1087	Fun and Fancy Free, Mickey and Donald	20 - 60
F1088	Fun and Fancy Free, Bongo	15 - 50
F1089	Melody Time	15 - 50
F1090	So Dear to My Heart	10 - 40
F1092	The Adventures of Ichabod and Mr. Toad	15 - 50
F1095	Cinderella	15 - 50
F1097	Alice In Wonderland	15 - 50
F1098	Peter Pan	10 - 40
F1099	Walt Disney	10 - 40
F1100	Mickey's 25th Birthday	2 - 5
F1105	Lady and the Tramp	10 - 40
F1106	Lady and the Tramp, reissue	2 - 6

F1115	Sleeping Beauty	3-10
F1118	Shaggy Dog	3-10
F1125	101 Dalmatians	3-10
F1136	The Sword in the Stone	3-10
F1138	Donald, engineer	1-4
F1139	Mickey and Pluto, at the fireplace	3-10
F1148	Mary Poppins	3-10
F1155	The Jungle Book	3-10
F1160	The Love Bug	3-8
F1162	Walt Disney and main characters	3-8
F1165	Winnie the Pooh	2-5
F1170	The Aristocats	2-5
F1173	Mickey (costumed) at Walt Disney World	2-5
F1175	Bedknobs and Broomsticks	2-5
F1178	Robin Hood	3-10
F1180	50 Happy Years	5-15
F1185	New Mickey Mouse Club	2-5
F1188	The Rescuers	2-5
F1190	Pete's Dragon	2-5
F1192	Mousekedays at Disneyland	2-5
F1200	Mickey's 50th Portrait, EPCOT Center	2-5
F1201	Mickey's 50	3-10
F1203	Snow White, reissue	2-5
F1205	The Fox and the Hound	2-5
F1208	TRON	2-5
F1210	Mickey's Christmas Carol	2-5
F1215	Splash	2-5

F2500 FIGURES -- CARDBOARD

F2510	Movie Studio, Standard Toykraft	50-135
F2520	Hingees, King, Larson & McMahon, came in individual envelope or in set w/other comic characters	
	-- Individual	5-25
	-- Set	25-75
F2530	Slotties, CCA, set of 6	20-50
F2540	Joinies, CCA, Kellogg Raisin Bran premiums Original set of 8, plus vocational set of ?, each	4-8
F2555	Alice in Wonderland, stand-up figures, Whitman, set of 15, #5613	15-35
F2556	Peter Pan, playtime statuettes, Whitman, set of 11, #5616	15-40
F2600	Mickey Mouse Peg Pals, Colorforms, 1978	2-8

Also see B3100 BOOKS -- CUT OR PUNCH OUT and D7800 DOLLS -- PAPER

F3000 FIGURES -- CELLULOID

Celluloid was an early plastic-like substance. Two types of figures are produced from this material -- miniature solid pieces and the more recognized thin, hollow figures. They were produced from the early 30's to the early 50's -- mainly in Japan. The major importer was Borgfeldt. Celluloid wind-up toys were perhaps more common than static figures and celluloid figures were used on some tin wind-up and mechanical toys of the 40's and 50's. The market has been one of the strongest Disneyana performers.

F3011	Mickey 5", movable arms	250 - 650
F3012	Minnie 5", movable arms	250 - 650
F3015	Donald and Mickey in boat	1,200 - 3,000
F3025	Donald 3", long bill, movable arms & legs	60 - 120
F3026	Donald 5", long bill, movable arms & legs	150 - 300
F3027	Donald 7", long bill, moveable arms & legs	450 - 900
F3030	Mickey, on celluloid bridge, wood base	200 - 400
F3031	Mickey, pie-cut eyes, no moving parts, various sizes	220 - 450
F3032	Two walking Mickeys on celluloid base, large one hollow	120 - 300
F3034	Donald, long bill, no moving parts, various sizes	120 - 250
F3048	Cleo the Goldfish	30 - 60
F3050	Mickey, regular eyes	50 - 100
F3060	Donald, regular eyes, short bill	40 - 90

Also see N6500 NODDERS and W7000 WIND-UP TOYS

F3300 FIGURES -- CERAMIC

Major ceramic makers such as American Pottery, Brayton's Laguna Pottery, Leeds China Company, Evan K Shaw, National Porcelain Company, Hagen-Renaker and Vernon Kilns are listed in their own classifications. Bisque figures are also listed separately. What remains is largely an unidentified group of foreign manufacturers and importers. Some from the early 30's and others who have supplied ceramic figures to the Disney theme parks since 1955. The 30's pieces were made mainly in Japan and Germany and imported by Borgfeldt. A Tinker Bell piece from the 50's has a foil sticker that reads "Ucago Ceramics -- Japan." Another Mickey piece has the letters "UCGC -- Japan." United China and Glass of New Orleans was the supplier of both. Pieces available in the parks in the 70's are simply marked with a copyright notice and the word "Japan." Some pieces from the 60's and 70's are credited to Enesco Imports, Inc. An Enesco *Baloo* figurine is copyright 1965. During the 70's ceramic figure designs for popular characters changed every 2 or 3 years. Catalog stock numbers are shown for 70's and 80's figures, when available. The 0553 item code prefix has been deleted. These numbers appeared in catalogs and on the original price

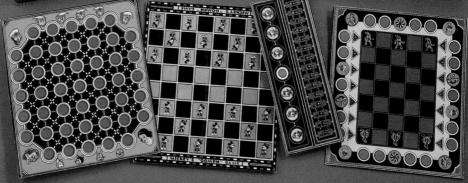

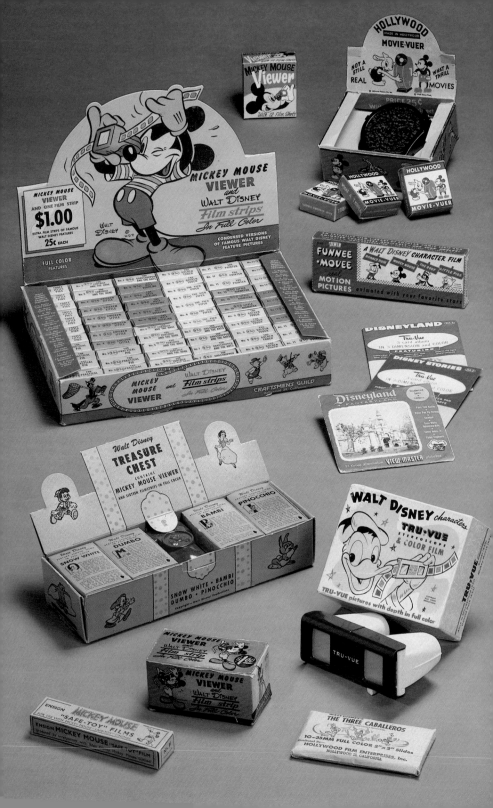

MICKEY MOUSE

CUT OUT DOLL BOOK

No. 980

The Saalfield Publishing Co., Akron, Ohio
Made in U. S. A.

Roger Rabbit

- Limited Edition of 3,000.
- Full one-sheet size (27x41")
- Printed on 100 lb. coated paper.

"P-p-p-p-please take me home and frame me!" **Roger Rabbit**

It's the story of a man, a woman, and a rabbit in a triangle of trouble.

Time to Toon in again!

Jessica Rabbit #2

- Limited Edition of 500.
- Full one-sheet size (27x41")
- Printed on Gold mylar paper.

"I'm good, and I'm finally drawn that way!" **Jessica Rabbit**

Please fill in the information on this form (facsimiles are acceptable) and include it with your order. Include payment in the form of check or money order, please, US funds only.

Send orders to:
Kilian Enterprises
1643 Burns
Wichita, KS 67203

tag only. Sizes and numbers for identical looking pieces did change.

F3305	Mickey, w/teeth, various sizes	75 - 800
F3310	Mickey's Band, gold or colored instruments, 1-1/4", each	25 - 100
F3320	Mickey figures, Germany, 30's	250 - 1,000
F3330	Mickey figures, Japan, up to 7", 30's	150 - 750
F3340	Ucago figures, each	10 - 40
F3400	Enesco figures, each	10 - 25
F3500	Mickey (9017), Minnie (9018), or Pluto (0333), each	5 - 15
F3503	Mickey (0327) or Minnie (0328), pie-cut eyes, each	5 - 15
F3506	Donald (0329), Daisy (9050), or Nephews (9051), each	5 - 15
F3511	Uncle Scrooge (9049)	5 - 15
F3515	Alice (9016), White Rabbit (9001) or Cheshire Cat (9023), each	15 - 40
F3518	Mad Hatter (9000) or March Hare (9003), each	20 - 50
F3525	Snow White, lifting dress (0332)	15 - 35
F3526	Seven Dwarfs, standing (9008-9014), each	6 - 12
F3540	Lady (9019) or Tramp (9020), each	25 - 50
F3542	Trusty (9021) or Jock (9022), each	12 - 25
F3545	Pongo (9034) or Perdita (9035), 7", each	75 - 150
F3547	Dalmatian Pups, six different (9036), 4" to 5", each	25 - 50
F3555	Mary Poppins (0017)	6 - 12
F3556	Tinker Bell (0331), Bambi (0018) or Dumbo (9002), each	5 - 15
F3560	Pinocchio (9015) or Jiminy Cricket (9007), each	5 - 15
F3562	Jaq (9004) or Gus (9006), each	5 - 20
F3564	Brer Fox, Brer Rabbit or Brer Bear, set	10 - 40
F3570	Cinderella (9467) or Prince, kneeling (9468), each	5 - 15
F3572	Gus (9469) or Jaq (9470), each	4 - 12
F3575	Snow White, standing (9459), 5-1/2"	5 - 15
F3576	Seven Dwarfs, standing, sitting & reclining (9460-9466), each	4 - 10

2" Earthenware figurines

F3580	Mickey, standing (9490), resting (9491) or sitting (9492), each	4 - 8
F3583	Minnie, standing (9493), sitting (9494) or bowing (9495), each	4 - 8
F3586	Pluto, sitting (9496) or laying down (9497), each	4 - 8
F3588	Donald, standing w/left arm raised (9498)	4 - 8

3" Earthenware figurines, Mickey's band (12)

F3590	Mickey, band leader (9550), w/tuba (9551) or w/trumpet (9552), each	4 - 8

145

F3593	Minnie, w/drums (9553), cymbals (9554) or sax (9555), each	4 - 8
F3596	Goofy, w/bass (9556) or bass drum (9557), each	4 - 8
F3598	Donald, w/trumpet (9558) or guitar (9559), each	4 - 8
F3600	Daisy, w/sax (9560) or flute (9561), each	4 - 8

4" Earthenware figurines

F3610	Mickey, pie-cut eyes, standing (9434), legs crossed (9438) sitting down, dangling legs (9439) or on stomach (9436), each	4 - 10
F3614	Minnie, pie-cut eyes, standing (9441), sitting, legs to one side (9445), legs crossed (9446) or on stomach (9443)	4 - 8
F3619	Pluto, sitting (?), walking (9125) or laying down (?), each	4 - 8
F3622	Donald, standing (9452), sitting (9453) or on stomach (9454), each	4 - 8
F3625	Daisy, standing (9456)	4 - 8
F3626	Nephews, standing, sitting or on stomach, set	6 - 18

F4700 FIGURES -- COMPOSITION

Some of the very first Mickey Mouse figures were made of wood composition -- basically a material of sawdust mixed with paste -- similar to papier-mache. Composition figures were molded, dried and painted. If the paint was damaged, moisture could get to the composition material and cause the figure to decompose. Therefore, surviving specimens are usually in fairly good condition. Composition was widely used for doll heads, torsos, and complete figures.

F4705	Barefoot Mickey, 2-1/2"	75 - 150
F4710	Mickey, w/lollypop hands	450 - 1,400
F4715	Dixon Pencil Holder	95 - 195
F4716	Dixon Pencil and Eraser Holder	95 - 195
F4720	Mickey, from Lionel Circus Train set	85 - 150
F4724	Knickerbocker Mickey w/o a costume	500 - 1,100
F4725	Knickerbocker Donald w/o a costume	500 - 1,100
F4735	Seven Dwarfs, each	20 - 50

Knickerbocker Ferdinand, Pinocchio, Jiminy Cricket, Figaro, plus costumed versions of Donald and Mickey see D6335 thru D6420.

Crown and Ideal Pinocchios see D6440 and D6445.

Also see W7000 WIND-UP TOYS

F5500 FIGURES -- PLASTIC

Plastic figures date from the 40's. Louis Marx & Co. started producing a line of plastic figures in 1953. Many varieties were produced over the next 25 years -- painted and unpainted. Original unpainted Marx figures reappeared in the 60's as Disney Fun Pals. Smaller versions of the same designs were sold as Disneykins (see D4000). New figures were created for Marx Playsets (see P3810). The last series (1971-72) consisted of 10 unpainted 5"-6" figures. Durham, Multiple Products, Sutton and other toy makers have produced a wide variety of plastic figures for individual sale and as part of other toy products.

In addition, there were three large horse and rider sets -- Zorro (also came in three smaller sizes), Johnny Tremain, and Sleeping Beauty and the Prince. There was a Peter Pan boxed set of 5 figures and other sets packaged in plastic bags. Linemar did a 12" Babes in Toyland soldier set and Auburn did some special sets for Disneyland. Vanity Fair Electronics Corp. produced StoryKins sets of plastic figures accompanied by thin red plastic records. Snow White has combable hair and the figures of the Seven Dwarfs had bristle-like beards. Mattel produced 12 clear crystal-like hard plastic figures under the name of Little Treasures in 1975.

Plastic figures are another hot area of Disneyana.

F5550	Hard plastic, 2-3/4", each	5-15
F5570	Hard plastic on wheels, each	5-15
F5600	Marx unpainted, 1-1/4" to 2-3/4", include Mickey, Minnie, Morty, Ferdie, Donald, Daisy, Huey, Louie, Dewey, Pluto, Snow White, Seven Dwarfs, Pinocchio, Jiminy Cricket, Geppetto, Figaro, Blue Fairy, Dumbo, Timothy, Ringmaster, Fireman Clown, Clown, Alice, Queen of Hearts, White Rabbit, Mad Hatter, March Hare, Peter Pan, Captain Hook, Smee & Tinker Bell, each	5-10
F5635	Peter Pan, boxed set	35 - 85
F5638	Lady and Tramp	20 - 55
F5649	Auburn Disneyland sets, each	65 - 135
	Zorro on horse w/all accessories (see Z5034)	
F5650	Disney Fun Pals, same as F6100, painted, each	3 - 8
F5660	Additional Fun Pals -- Goofy, Pecos Bill, Panchito & others, each	3 - 8
F5670	Big Bad Wolf and Three Little Pigs, painted, each	10 - 20
F5675	Robin Hood, Marx figures, each	5-15
F5685	Davy Crockett, Marx figures, each	5-15
F5690	Marx Snap-eeze moveable figures of Mickey, Donald, Pluto, Dalmatian, Mad Hatter, March Hare, Babes in Toyland Soldier, Captain Hook, Panchito, Practical Pig, Figaro, Brer Bear, Brer Fox, Dopey and Ludwig Von Drake, each	5-10
F5721	Johnny Tremain & Horse, w/all accessories	25 - 65
F5722	Sleeping Beauty and Prince, horse w/all accessories	50 - 100
F5724	Babes in Toyland Flexible Soldiers, Linemar	20 - 50
F5725	Zorro & Horse, 5" or 7", in package	15 - 45

F5730	Donald Duck's Express & Figures, 1968	25 - 55
F5731	Mowgli's Hut-Mobile & Figures, 1968	35 - 75
F5732	Mickey Mouse's Tin Lizzie & Figures, 1968	25 - 50
F5733	Donald Duck's Whirlybird & Figures, 1968	25 - 50
F5734	Mickey Mouse's Hot Rod & Figures, 1968	30 - 60
F5737	StoryKins Snow White and Doc	20 - 50
F5738	StoryKins remaining 6 Dwarfs	20 - 50
F5770	Marx 5" - 7" figures, Mickey, Minnie, Donald, Goofy, Pluto, Snow White, Dopey, Pinocchio, Jiminy Cricket, Bambi, Peter Pan & Tinker Bell, 1971-72, each	3 - 6
F5783	Same as F6500, but painted eyes only	3 - 7
F5800	Little Treasures clear hard plastic figures of Mickey, Donald, Tinker Bell, Bambi, Thumper, Flower, Snow White, Dopey, Doc, Pinocchio, Jiminy Cricket & Figaro, each	2 - 5
F5812	Little Treasures, packaged sets (4), each	15 - 30

F6000 FIGURES -- PORCELAIN BISQUE

Porcelain bisque figures are made of a special clay. The "green ware" from the mold is generally fired in a kiln just once before painting. If a glaze was applied after painting and the piece fired again, it would be porcelain ceramic. The paint on early bisque figures had no protection and often chipped or wore off easily. Truly mint specimens are rare. Miniature bisque figure and candy stocking stuffers once sold for a penny. A pair of 6" Mickey and Minnie bisques with movable arms wholesaled for 80¢ per dozen pairs or 3¢ each. The retail was probably 5¢ to 10¢ for the pair. A mint pair today would sell for close to $2,500. New Grolier Enterprises limited edition (15,000) bisque figures sold for over $50. Capodimonte of Italy produced individual figures and limited edition scenes from animated features that sold for over $1,500. There have been hundreds of bisque figures in between. These have been made in two periods: 1931-41 and 1971-present. George Borgfeldt imported figures from Mickey cartoons, Silly Symphonies, Snow White and the Seven Dwarfs (in five sizes), Ferdinand the Bull and Pinocchio. Walt Disney Distributing Co. commissioned bisque figures starting in 1971. Most were sold at theme parks, but for a couple of years some special figures were marketed through gift ware dealers. These are marked "Disney Gift-Ware" with an image of Mickey with a paint brush. A foil seal identifying "UCGC-Taiwan" (United China and Glass) as the maker also appeared on the bottom of some pieces. Original art for this series has been sold at collector shows. Few of the early Borgfeldt bisque figures were advertised. The list below would not be as complete if it weren't for a couple special people the author wishes to acknowledge. This section has been compiled in cooperation with Bernie Shine and *Collectors' Showcase* magazine. A substantial number of the descriptions accompanying this classification originally appeared in *Collectors' Showcase* articles titled "Early Disney Bisque Figures Part I" (Nov/Dec '84) and "Part II" (Mar/Apr '85) by Bernie Shine. Use of this copyrighted material has been granted by both the author Bernie Shine and co-publisher Keith Kaonis. The first number is the height of the figure in inches; the second, if any, the incised number found on the bisque near the copyright notice. SFTBH is an abbreviation for Single Figure Toothbrush Holder. Other manufacturers listed if not Borgfeldt or 70's Walt Disney Distributing Co.

The Market for bisque figures is brisk. The Capodimonte series continues to be expanded. Individual figures of Donald Duck, Snow White and each Dwarf, Pinocchio, Mickey as the Sorcerer's Apprentice, and Peter Pan have been added. The 50th anniversary of Snow White scene was sold for $3200.

Christmas bisques from Grolier continue and the theme parks began issuing a new series in 1985 based on the studio Christmas card 50 years previous. The first two were one year off, but the series got in sync with the 1987 Snow White issue.

F6000	Mickey, 1, smallest Mickey bisque	35 - 100
F6001	Bulbous head, 4-3/4, 2 moveable arms, believed first	500 - 1,100
F6002	Mickey, 1-1/4, waving right hand	35 - 100
F6003	Mickey, 1-1/2, waving right hand	35 - 85
F6004	Mickey, 1-3/4, right hand at hip, left at side	35 - 100
F6005	Mickey, 1-7/8 x 3-1/4, riding in canoe	600 - 1,200
F6006	Mickey, 2-3/4, two moveable arms	300 - 600
F6007	Mickey, 2-3/4, S504, hands on hip	15 - 45
F6008	Mickey, 2-3/4, S442, sitting position (also see F6009)	40 - 110
F6009	Complete Mickey/Minnie tea set (includes F6009 & F6086 plus table, 2 chairs & miniature china set)	200 - 650
F6010	Mickey, 3-3/4, S15, holding flag in right hand, sword on left	55 - 125
F6011	Mickey, 3-1/4, S16, holding sword in right hand	35 - 85
F6012	Mickey, 3-1/4, S17, holding rifle, wearing ammo packs, head slightly to right	35 - 85
F6013	Mickey, 3-1/4, S429, holding rifle	35 - 85
F6020	Mickey, 2-3/8, S26?, baseball glove on left hand	25 - 65
F6021	Mickey, 2-3/8, baseball glove on left hand, ball in right	35 - 85
F6022	Mickey, 2-3/8, holding baseball bat	45 - 95
F6023	Mickey, 2-3/8, w/catcher's gear & mitt	45 - 95
F6024	Mickey, 3-1/4, S64, baseball glove on left hand	35 - 85
F6025	Mickey, 3-1/4, S65, baseball glove on left hand, ball n right	35 - 85
F6026	Mickey, 3-1/4, S66, holding baseball bat	35 - 85

Millions of cheap bisque figures were produced in Japan and
imported by George Borgfeldt for sale principally in 5¢ & 10¢ stores.
Large quantities were purchased by florists for use in arrangements
for sick children. Old flower stores have been the source of several
large bisque figure fines over the years.

F6027	Mickey, 3-1/4, S67, w/catcher's gear & mitt	35 - 85
F6030	Mickey, 3-1/4, bulbous figure w/conductor's baton, 2 moveable arms, white feet	125 - 250
F6031	Mickey, 3-1/4, bulbous figure w/song book, white feet	125 - 250
F6032	Mickey, 3-1/4, bulbous figure playing accordion, white feet	125 - 250
F6033	Mickey, 3-1/4, bulbous figure playing banjo, white feet	125 - 250
F6034	Mickey, 3-1/4, bulbous figure playing French horn, white feet	125 - 250
F6035	Mickey, 3-1/4, bulbous figure playing drum, white feet	125 - 250
F6040	Mickey, 3-3/4, C72, playing snare drum	20 - 60
F6041	Mickey, 3-3/4, C73, playing French horn	20 - 60
F6045	Mickey, 3-3/4, S1390, nodding head attached to body w/cord	600 - 1,200
F6047	Mickey, 3-3/4, S177, wearing hat, holding cane	25 - 70
F6048	Mickey, 4, S33, wearing hat, holding cane	25 - 60
F6049	Mickey, 4, in tuxedo, holding top hat and cane	400 - 850
F6050	Mickey, 4, S1277, wearing nightgown	35 - 70
F6052	Mickey, 4-1/2, A567, bank, standing next to garbage can or light	750 - 1,500
F6053	Mickey, 5-1/4, standing on green platform, hands on hip	600 - 1,200
F6054	Mickey, 5-1/4, A116, hands on hips	175 - 350
F6060	Mickey, 5, SFTBH, bulbous head, moveable right arm, straight	115 - 225
F6061	Mickey, 5, SFTBH, head to left, moveable right arm, straight	115 - 225
F6062	Mickey, 5, C103, SFTBH, head to left, moveable right arm, slightly curved	115 - 225
F6063	Mickey, 5, two moveable arms	300 - 750
F6064	Mickey, 5-3/4, C106, two moveable arms	450 - 900
F6068	Mickey, 5-1/4, playing accordion	325 - 650
F6069	Mickey, 5-1/4, playing French horn	325 - 650
F6070	Mickey, 5-1/4, playing banjo	325 - 750
F6071	Mickey, 5-1/4, playing drum	325 - 750
F6072	Mickey, 5-3/4, S36, playing French horn	600 - 1,200
F6079	Mickey, 7-1/2, S509, standing on green base, two moveable arms	1,000 - 2,000
F6080	Mickey, 8-3/4, standing on green base, two moveable arms, largest Mickey bisque	1,500 - 3,700
F6085	Minnie, 2-3/4, S505, hands on hip	15 - 45
F6086	Minnie, 2-3/4, S443, sitting position (also see F6009)	40 - 110

F6087	Minnie, 3-1/4, S18, holding nurse's kit in right hand next to right leg, left hand on chest	35 - 85
F6088	Minnie, 3-1/4, S493, holding nurse's kit under right arm, left hand on hip	35 - 85
F6090	Minnie, 3-1/2, C69, playing mandolin	20 - 40
F6091	Minnie, 3-1/2, C71, playing accordion	20 - 40
F6092	Minnie, 3-1/2, S424, pushing wheelbarrow, used as pincushion	700 - 1,400
F6094	Minnie, 3-1/4, S178, wearing hat, holding umbrella & purse	25 - 70
F6095	Minnie, 4, S34, wearing hat, holding umbrella & purse	25 - 60
F6096	Minnie, 4, S1276, wearing nightgown	35 - 70
F6097	Minnie, 5, bank, standing next to garbage can	750 - 1,500
F6100	Minnie, 5, standing on green platform, hands on hips	600 - 1,200
F6101	Minnie, 5-1/4, A117, hands on hips	175 - 350
F6102	Minnie, 5, SFTBH, bulbous head, moveable right arm, straight	120 - 235
F6104	Minnie, 5, SFTBH, head turned right, left arm moveable, straight	120 - 235
F6105	Minnie, 5-1/4, C104, SFTBH, head turned right, left arm moveable, slightly curved	120 - 235
F6106	Minnie, 5-3/4, S3?, playing violin	750 - 1,500
F6109	Minnie, 5, two moveable arms	300 - 750
F6110	Minnie, 6, C105, two moveable arms	450 - 900
F6120	Pluto, 3-1/4, S433, seated next to guard house	50 - 125
F6121	Pluto, 2-1/4, sitting position	25 - 50
F6122	Pluto, 2-3/4, S35, sitting position	25 - 50
F6130	Donald, 1-3/4, M-1, head turned to right, hands on hip	55 - 125
F6131	Donald, 3, 3, bill open, hands at sides	35 - 85
F6135	Donald, 3-1/4, S1333, holding flag	55 - 125
F6136	Donald, 3, S1334, holding bugle	45 - 85
F6137	Donald, 3, S1335, holding rifle	45 - 85
F6138	Donald, 3, S1336, holding sword	45 - 85
F6140	Donald, 3-1/4, walking, bill in air	30 - 75
F6143	Donald, 3-1/4, 1, sitting on rocking horse	100 - 200
F6144	Donald, 3-1/4, 2, sitting on scooter	100 - 200
F6145	Donald, 3-1/4, 3, standing on scooter	100 - 200
F6147	Donald, 3, in admiral's hat & coat	40 - 95
F6150	Donald, 4, ??9, two moveable arms, medium bill	500 - 1,000
F6152	Donald, 4-1/2, S1278 hands on hips	125 - 250
F6153	Donald, 4, holding paintbrush & can of paint	500 - 1,000
F6155	Donald, 4, S1158, playing mandolin	100 - 200
F6156	Donald, 4, S1130, playing violin	100 - 200

Walt Disney's PINOCCHIO dolls and figurines look like much
more than their low retail prices. The 10½" mechanical doll winds
with a key. The little puppet is of wood and the one large figure
and set of six characters are of Bisque. An unusually attractive line.

Retail Prices — 5c, 10c, 25c and $1.00

MECHANICAL DOLLS • FIGURINES

The Borgfeldt Company produced bisque, composition, wind-up
and wood figures for Pinocchio in 1940. They cost 5¢, 10¢, 25¢ and
$1.00 . . . back then.

F6157	Donald, 4, S1131, playing accordion	100 - 200
F6158	Donald, 4-1/2, S1130, playing violin	175 - 350
F6159	Donald, 4-1/2, S1131, playing accordion	175 - 350
F6160	Donald, 4-3/4, toothbrush holder, standing next to a pillar (see T6414)	
F6162	Donald, 5-1/4, toothbrush holder, profile of Donald looking right	
F6165	Donald, 5-3/4, S1128, two moveable arms	900 - 1,800
F6175	The Goof, 1-3/4, right hand in back, left hand to side	50 - 100
F6176	The Goof, 3-1/2, right hand in back, left hand to side	30 - 60
F6177	Horace, 1-7/8, hands to side	50 - 100
F6178	Horace, 3-3/4, hands to side	40 - 80
F6179	Horace, 5, arms folded across chest	250 - 500
F6183	Clarabelle, 5, hands on dress	250 - 500
F6185	Mickey & Pluto, 2-1/4, Mickey riding Pluto	15 - 45
F6186	Mickey & Donald, 1-7/8 x 3-1/4, in canoe	600 - 1,200
F6190	Mickey & Pluto, 5-1/2, S178, Mickey & Pluto side by side, Mickey's right arm moveable	500 - 1,000
F6192	Three Little Pigs, 3-1/2, dancing, thimble base, each	20 - 40
F6193	Three Little Pigs, 3-1/2, S162, S165 and S?, standing w/instruments, each	15 - 35
F6194	Big Bad Wolf, 1-3/4	50 - 100
F6195	Big Bad Wolf, 3-3/4	40 - 80
F6200	Elmer Elephant, 4-1/2, S1407, two moveable arms	75 - 150
F6201	Elmer Elephant, 1-1/2	40 - 80
F6202	Elmer Elephant, 4-1/2	50 - 100
F6210	Snow White, 4 sizes, 2-1/4 to 6-1/2, standing	40 - 140
F6215	Dwarfs, 4 sizes, 3 to 5, standing, each	10 - 20
F6257	Dwarfs, 2-1/2, w/musical instruments, each	10 - 25
F6260	Ferdinand the Bull, 1-3/4	20 - 45
F6261	Ferdinand the Bull, 3	18 - 35
F6270	Pinocchio, 6	35 - 75
F6271	Pinocchio, 3 or Figaro, 2-1/2	30 - 60
F6273	Honest John, Giddy, Geppetto or Jiminy Cricket, 3	20 - 45

Walt Disney Distributing Co. began in 1971 and ceased operations in 1977. Many of the bisque units designed and marketed by them were continued at theme parks. Items marked Disney Gift-Ware were discontinued. Only three figures from the Robin Hood set were sold (Robin Hood, Prince John and Sir Hiss). The Spirit of '76 was sold mainly at Disneyland. Bea Jones, cast lead for the Disneyana Shop at the time, told the author only 429 of these pieces were sold. The popularity of bisque figures has prompted Grolier Enterprises to produce three different series based on 18 animated films -- Magic Memories (limited to 15,000 @ $52.50 each), Musical Memories (limited to 19,950 @ $57.50 each) and Heroes and Villains (limited to 24,750 @ $57.50 each). The Heroes and Villians set was discontinued before it was completed. Royal Orleans (United China & Glass Co.) has produced traditional and Christmas character bisques. Capodimonte of Italy has produced scenes depicting Snow White, Donald Duck and his nephews, Cinderella, Pinocchio and Sleeping Beauty originally selling for 1000 - 3200 each. Individual pieces were made available for Snow White and the Seven Dwarfs and other scenes. A total of ten features were slated to be the subjects of Capodimonte bisques. Most of the theme park bisque designs as well as the Big Bad Wolf and individual music boxes featuring the Three Little Pigs, Mickey as conductor and Minnie playing the harp are kept in regular supply. Theme park bisques were originally made in Japan, but have since been produced in Taiwan and Korea. Designs have been resculpted each time and differences occur according to country of origin. New designs are being issued as well. Original art used to guide the manufacturer's sculptors has been selling for 30 - 100. This art normally consists of several views and one color overlay.

F6300	Disney Gift Ware Figures, each	10 - 35
F6340	Theme Park, 6 figures, each	12 - 40
F6350	Theme Park, 4 figures, each	5 - 10
F6450	Theme Park, 2 - 3 figures, each	4 - 8
F6475	Theme Park Multi Figures	18 - 55
F6485	Royal Orleans, Show White, Pinocchio or Cinderella, each	20 - 60
Grolier Christmas bisques		
F6500	Mickey, Minnie and Pluto at Lamppost, 1979	25 - 60
F6501	Lady and Tramp, 1980	15 - 30
F6502	Santa and Mickey, (short run), 1981	35 - 100
F6503	Dumbo pulling sleigh, 1982	15 - 35
F6504	Scrooge Christmas Surprise, 1983	15 - 30
F6505	Happy Birthday Donald, 1984	15 - 30
F6506	Mickey and Donald as Santa's Helpers, 1985	15 - 30
F6507	Musical We Wish You A Merry Christmas, 1986	20 - 35
Disneyland/Walt Disney World Christmas bisques		
F6550	1985, based on 1934 Studio Christmas card	25 - 85
F6551	Individual Mickey and Minnie from F6550, each	10 - 18
F6552	1986, based on 1935 Studio Christmas card	25 - 40
F6553	1987, based on Snow White card, one of 2 for 1937	New 75
F6554	Individual figures from 6553, each	2 - 4

F7000 FIGURES -- RUBBER

Seiberling Latex Products Co. (Akron) manufactured a line of solid

Seiberling Latex Products Company of Akron, Ohio produced squeeze type and solid rubber figures from 1934 to 1942. Hollow figures of the Three Little Pigs, Big Bad Wolf and Snow White are very rare due to the relatively rapid decay of rubber. Solid figures of Mickey, Donald and the Seven Dwarfs were very popular and are still seen at most toy shows.

)hard) and hollow rubber toys from 1934-42. The solid variety have survived well. Hollow rubber figures have mostly rotted. Sun Rubber Company (Barberton, OH) produced post-war rubber figures as did their Canadian counterpart, Viceroy Manufacturing Company, Ltd. Bayshore Industries, Inc. (Elkton, MD) produced foam rubber and "bend-me" figures from 1952 to 1962. Diener Industries, Inc. (Van Nuys, CA) made rubber "jigglers" and other figures 1968-72.

The 1934 Kay Kamen merchandise catalog shows the Seiberling Three Little Pigs and Big Bad Wolf came in two versions -- with only minor paint and fully decorated. Later editions show only the full paint version. There was also a set of flat, 4-color Snow White and the Seven Dwarfs from Seiberling.

F7010	Big Bad Wolf, 2 versions	200 - 450
F7011	Three Little Pigs, 2 versions, each	40 - 125
F7020	Mickey, 6", full paint	125 - 350
F7021	Mickey, 6", black w/highlight paint	100 - 225
F7022	Mickey, 3-1/2", black w/highlight paint	35 - 125
F7025	Donald, 6", moveable head	125 - 350
F7026	Donald, 5", moveable head	100 - 275
F7027	Donald, 6", squeeze toy	80 - 200
F7030	Pluto, 7" wide, red or yellow	15 - 60
F7032	Pluto, 3-3/8" wide, red or yellow	10 - 45
F7034	Elmer Elephant, hollow	25 - 75
F7040	Snow White, hollow	100 - 450
F7041	Seven Dwarfs, each	20 - 45
F7048	Seiberling Snow White and the Seven Dwarfs, flat w/4-color transfers, set in box	275 - 450
F7048A	Individual figures from F7048, each	10 - 30
F7049	Ferdinand the Bull	10 - 35
F7050	Pinocchio	20 - 75
F7051	Jiminy Cricket	20 - 75
F7052	Figaro or Cleo, each	15 - 55
F7054	Donkey	5 - 55
F7065	Mickey, 1949, Sun Rubber	10 - 50
F7066	Donald, 1949, Sun Rubber	8 - 35
F7067	Pluto, 1949, Sun Rubber	8 - 35
F7068	Thumper, 1949, Sun Rubber	8 - 35
F7080	Bayshore foam rubber figures, each	5 - 50
F7090	Diener "jigging dolls", each	2 - 10

F7200 FIGURES -- WOOD

George Borgfeldt & Company (NYC) sold wood Mickey and Minnie figures in 1931. Pluto figures followed in 1934, Donald in 1935 or 36 and Pinocchio in 1940. Bert B. Barry (Chicago) made non-Disney looking Pinocchio figures in 1940-41.

F7205	Mickey, w/lollypop hands	500 - 1,300
F7207	Mickey, w/disc hands, w/decal	600 - 1,100
F7210	Mickey or Minnie, knob hands, 4", each	55 - 125
F7212	Mickey or Minnie, 4 finger hands, 5", each	125 - 250
F7214	Mickey or Minnie, 4 finger hands, 8", each	350 - 650
F7220	Pluto, 3+" long, w/dog house	125 - 250
F7220	Pluto, 3+" long, only	35 - 75
F7221	Pluto, 5-1/2+" long	125 - 250
F7225	Donald, 3"	25 - 125
F7227	Donald, 5"	375 - 750
F7235	Pinocchio	25 - 85
F7250	Line-Mar Mickey, Donald or Pluto, each	20 - 75

Also see D6100 DOLLS, F7600 FISHER-PRICE

F7500 FILMS, SLIDES AND VIEWERS

Recreating the Disney film magic in the home has been the inspiration of a wide variety of home movies, film strips, slides and accompanying viewers. Hollywood Film Enterprises (Hollywood) distributed 16mm films (some sound) 1932-43, 8mm films 1944-50 and slides (1947). Tru-Vue and View-Master are noted for 3-D images. The Craftsmen's Guild made the most popular film strip viewer, besting many that preceded it. Hollywood Film Ent. product came in 25', 50', 100', 200' and 400' black and white abridged versions of popular cartoons. Titles were usually different than theatrical versions. 16mm sound films are still collected, but boxes for the silent versions maintain the most interest. The cartoons are mostly available on video tape or disc, and the majority of old film is brittle or otherwise unshowable. Regular 8 and Super 8 (many sound) were very popular for over 30 years.

Hollywood Films and Boxes 1932-1950 (F7510-F7520)

F7510	Safety Film, Mickey w/projector, boxed	5 - 20
F7515	Mickey Mouse Films, 16mm or 8mm	4 - 20
F7518	Walt Disney Character Films, 16mm or 8mm	4 - 15
F7520	Walt Disney Cartoons, 16mm or 8mm	3 - 15
F7521	Pepsodent's Snow White Moving Picture Machine (cardboard viewer) 1938 premium	60 - 160
F7522	Mickey Mouse "Safe Toy" Films, each	2 - 10
F7525	Hollywood Movie Viewer & Film Loops	25 - 75
F7526	Extra Character Film Loops, 8 for F7525, each	2 - 5
F7528	Funnee Movee Viewer & Films, Irwin	5 - 35
F7529	Extra Character Films for F7528, each	2 - 5
F7530	Craftsmen's Guild Viewer & Film	10 - 50
F7531	Extra Character Films, 13 different for F7530, each	2 - 5
F7531A	Display Box of Extra Films, complete	80 - 150

F7532	35mm Color Slide Sets, 6, Hollywood, 1947, each	5 - 20
F7534	Walt Disney Characters Tru-Vue Viewer & Filmstrip	4 - 24
F7535	Extra Character Filmstrips for F7534	2 - 5
F7536	Mickey Mouse Viewer & 12 Films	2 - 12
F7540	View-Master Sets, depending on age & subject	5 - 30
F7541	View-Master Reels, in illustrated envelope	5 - 20
F7542	Tru-Vue 3-D Card Viewer & 1 Card Set	3 - 20
F7543	Extra Character View Card Sets for F7542, each	4 - 10
F7544	Magic Eyes Story Sets for F7542, each	5 - 15
F7550	GE Show 'n Tell Filmstrips & Records, each	2 - 10
F7555	Super 8 and Super 8 Sound Home Movies	5 - 25

F7600 FISHER-PRICE TOYS

Fisher-Price (East Aurora, NY) manufactured wooden pull toys with printed paper laminated sides from 1935-1958. During this time they also made Donald Duck and Pluto paddle puppets. Many products during the 30's thru the 60's were produced for use as Easter candy and egg containers. The company was also licensed for the years 1963-64 and produced 8mm cartridge movie viewers from 1975 - 84. In addition, talking books were introduced during this time.

Publication of a Fisher-Price collectors guide has influenced this area of Disneyana.

F7610	Mickey/Pluto drum & cymbal (Mickey Mouse Band)	225 - 450
F7612	Donald/Pluto cart	250 - 650
F7613	Walking Donald carting Mickey's nephews	250 - 650
F7614	Long bill Donald flapping wings	50 - 200
F7618	Carnival w/Donald, Pluto, Elmer & Mickey, in box	125 - 250
F7620	Easter Parade w/Donald, Clara Cluck & 3 Bunnies, in box	125 - 250
F7630	Pluto paddle puppet	15 - 40
F7631	Donald paddle puppet, rubber wings	75 - 150
F7635	Base drum & cymbal Mickey	125 - 350
F7636	Mickey Choo Choo	30 - 75
F7637	Short bill Donald w/flapping arms	40 - 125
F7638	Donald (profile) xylophone	50 - 155
F7640	Doc & Dopey hammering drum	65 - 185
F7644	Struttin' Donald Duck	75 - 225
F7645	Mickey xylophone, solid black oval eyes	70 - 195
F7647	Plucky Pinocchio, on donkey	50 - 160
F7648	Pinocchio express, cart	65 - 185
F7649	Donald Duck drum major	35 - 115

Fisher-Price was an early producer of wooden Disney pull toys. Many of their products had carts which doubled as Easter baskets when the Bunny delivered candy. Donald Duck was more Easter-oriented and hence is the predominate Disney character used on Fisher-Price toys.

F7650	Same as F7649 w/cart	40 - 125
F7655	Dumbo circus car	75 - 225
F7670	Donald Duck Choo Choo	20 - 65
F7671	Donald Duck cart, pupil eyes	20 - 85
F7672	Mickey Mouse or Donald Duck drummer	25 - 65
F7673	Donald xylophone, pupil eyes, 3/4 head view	40 - 125
F7678	Donald w/plastic feet & paper on all surfaces	15 - 55
F7679	Mickey Policeman on Motorcycle	20 - 75
F7682	Mickey Mouse puddle jumper	10 - 35
F7700	Cartridge film viewer	3 - 15
F7701	Extra film cartridges for F7700, each	2 - 10

G1000 GAMES

Disney games have been broken down into seven classifications. Most manufacturers produced games in more than one classification, so check the chronological order in each classification to find the game of interest. Some game boxes were revised as animated features were re-released.

G1001 GAMES -- BOARD

Most board games came boxed. The high range values given are for the boxed game complete with all playing pieces and instructions. Missing game parts detract from the value of a game and sometimes it is difficult to determine if any parts are missing. The instructions for many games list the playing pieces. If instructions are missing it's usually a good indication playing parts are also absent.

G1010	Mickey Mouse Coming Home Game, 2 sizes, Marks	50 - 150
G1011	Mickey Mouse Scatter Ball, Marks	75 - 250
G1012	The Game of Who's Afraid of the Big Bad Wolf?, Marks	25 - 75
G1015	Walt Disney's Own Who's Afraid of the Big Bad Wolf?, Parker	25 - 75
G1016	Walt Disney's Own Game -- The Pied Piper of Hamelin, Parker	25 - 75
G1017	Walt Disney's Own Red Riding Hood, Parker	25 - 75
G1020	Mickey/Minnie Ball Game, Marks #267	125 - 375
G1021	Mickey Mouse Circus Game, also Marks #267	125 - 375
G1029	Snow White Game, Tek toothbrush premium	25 - 60
G1030	The Game of Snow White and the Seven Dwarfs, MB	25 - 75
G1031	Walt Disney's Own Game Snow White and the Seven Dwarfs, Parker	25 - 75
G1032	Walt Disney's Game Parade, American Toy	45 - 150

G1035	Walt Disney's Own Game Ferdinand the Bull, Parker	20 - 55
G1036	The Game of Ferdinand the Bull in the Arena, Whitman	25 - 75
G1038	Walt Disney's Own Game Donald Duck Party Game, Parker	20 - 75
G1040	Pinocchio the Merry Puppet Game, MB	20 - 75
G1041	Walt Disney's Pinocchio Game, Parker	20 - 75
G1042	Pitfalls -- a Pinocchio Marble Game, Whitman	25 - 65
G1100	Walt Disney's Big Track Meet, ONTEX	10 - 35
G1150	Walt Disney's Uncle Remus Game ZIP, Parker	15 - 45
G1175	Donald Duck's Party Game for Young Folks, Parker	10 - 40
G1180	Walt Disney's Cinderella Game, Parker	10 - 35
G1184	Peter Pan -- A Game of Adventure	8 - 30
G1185	Peter Pan -- A Game of Adventure, Transogram	8 - 30
G1190	Walt Disney's Official Frontierland Game, Parker	8 - 25
G1191	Walt Disney's Adventureland Game, Parker	8 - 25
G1192	Walt Disney's Fantasyland Game, Parker	8 - 25
G1193	Walt Disney's Tomorrowland Rocket to the Moon Game, Parker	10 - 30
G1195	Walt Disney's Disneyland Game, Transogram	10 - 35
G1196	Hardy Boys Treasure Game	10 - 30
G1198	Walt Disney's Davy Crockett Adventure, Gardner	10 - 40
G1200	Mickey Mouse Club Game in Disneyland, Whitman	10 - 35
G1225	Walt Disney's Sleeping Beauty Game, Whitman	10 - 30
G1226	Sleeping Beauty Castle, litho tin	10 - 30
G1227	Mickey Mouse Tic-Tac-Toe, litho tin	10 - 30
G1235	One Hundred and One Dalmatians	8 - 25
G1240	Mary Poppins Game, w/magic wheel	10 - 30
G1241	Mary Poppins Carousel Game, Parker	8 - 25
G1245	Disneyland (10 Anniversary), w/magic wheel	15 - 45
G1260	Robin Hood	5 - 15

G2000 GAMES -- CARDS

Mickey Mouse ice cream cones probably beat Whitman with the first card game. Whitman did adult bridge tally sets and regular playing card decks, as well as children's Old Maid and other card games. Russell Manufacturing Co. had been a major card game producer until the company ceased being a Disney licensee in 1986, ending a 41 year relationship. Whitman took over as the major supplier in this classification.

Playing card collecting became a fad in the early 50's and a number of collector's trading cards were issued. Theme parks have been the source of an ever changing array of regular playing card decks.

| G2005 | Mickey Mouse Cones -- imprinted w/the names of dairies -- an early Kay Kamen promotion | 10 - 60 |
| G2008 | Card game from Post Toasties box | 4 - 15 |

Whitman (G2010 thru G2035)

G2010	Mickey Mouse Old Maid Cards, 3 designs, in box	15 - 50
G2011	Mickey Mouse Playing Cards, in box	10 - 45
G2012	Mickey/Minnie Bridge Cards & Tally Set, in box	20 - 95
G2013	Three Little Pigs Playing Cards	10 - 35
G2014	Three Little Pigs Bridge Tally Set	20 - 85
G2015	Miniature Mickey Mouse Playing Cards	10 - 35
G2016	Clarabelle & Horace Playing Cards, 2 deck set	30 - 120
G2020	Dopey Playing Cards, 2 deck set	20 - 65
G2021	Miniature Snow White Playing Cards	20 - 45
G2025	Pinocchio Playing Card Game	20 - 50
G2026	Pinocchio & Jiminy Cricket Playing Cards, set	25 - 65
G2035	Donald Duck Playing Card Game	10 - 40
G2050	War Insignia Trading Cards, each	2 - 6
G2060	Mickey Mouse Library of Games, Russell	15 - 65
G2067	Donald Duck Card Game, 1st design	10 - 35
G2068	Donald Duck Card Game, 3 box designs, Whitman	10 - 25
G2073	Mickey Mouse Canasta Junior, Russell	8 - 25
G2080	Alice in Wonderland/White Rabbit Bridge Decks, set	12 - 30
G2090	Mickey Mouse Club Card Games, Russell, each	3 - 8
G2100	Disneyland Collector's Cards, 12, Whitman, set	12 - 48
G2119	Disneyland Card Game, Whitman	5 - 20
G2120	Disneyland Playing Card Decks, each	3 - 15
G2150	Mickey Mouse Funny Rummy	3 - 10
G2160	Mary Poppins Card Game, Whitman	2 - 8
G2164	Library of Games -- 60's version, in train or monorail box	8 - 25
G2170	Ed-U-Cards, Mickey Mouse, Pinocchio, The Jungle Book & others, each	2 - 8
G2190	Walt Disney World Playing Cards, castle or miniatures	2 - 8
G2195	Mickey Mouse Round Playing Cards	5 - 20
G2196	Mickey Mouse Jumbo Playing Cards	2 - 8
G2197	Mickey Playing Cards, traditional or jester, each	2 - 5
G2199	Old Witch Card Game, 2 versions, each	1 - 2
G2200	Goofy Card Tricks, Whitman	1 - 4

G2500 GAMES -- EDUCATIONAL

There have been many educational materials with Disney characters, including puzzle and teaching machine type games found at other classifications. A series of first learning games dealing with letters, numbers, colors, animals and friends were issued by Western Publishing

Co. (Racine, WI) in the 60's. Value 2 - 10 each.
Also see G2900 GAMES -- ELECTRIC AND ELECTRONIC and G3000 GAMES -- PUZZLE.

G2900 GAMES -- ELECTRIC AND ELECTRONIC
These games are AC or battery operated. Atari also developed a game for home computers in 1983.

G2905	Mickey Mouse Funny Facts Game, Einson-Freeman	300 - 600
G2930	Disneyland Electric Quiz, Jacmar	10 - 25
G2931	20,000 Leagues Under the Sea Electric Quiz, Jacmar	5 - 15
G2933	Disneyland Electric Tours w/Davy Crockett -- 4 Games In One, Jacmar	15 - 50
G2934	Sleeping Beauty -- An Electric Game, Jacmar	10 - 30
G2938	Mickey Mouse Electric Treasure Hunt, Tudor	15 - 55
G2939	Atari Game Cartridge	5 - 20
G2950	TRON Hand Held Electronic Game, Tomy	10 - 35

G3000 GAMES -- PUZZLE
A number of Disney games mixed play action with puzzles. The popular Lotto games provided a race for young children to see who could get all the Disney character shapes into the correct openings first.

G3005	Walt Disney Jigsaw Lotto, 3 sizes, Jaymar	15 - 65
G3007	Jig Saw Lotto, small size, Jaymar	10 - 40
G3008	Character SCRAMBLE, Plane Facts	15 - 60
G3019	Mickey Mouse Comic Picture Puzzle, Parker	10 - 28
G3020	Donald Comic Picture Puzzle, Parker	10 - 28
G3030	Mickey Mouse Mix-Up-Game, Parker	5 - 20
G3040	Mickey Mouse Pop 'N Play, Gabriel	5 - 15

G3200 GAMES -- SKILL
Skill games are ones where motor practice can improve physical performance. Target, toss, pinball, table top sports and hand held games are included in this section. Higher values are for games in original boxes.

G3210	On the Warpath Shooting Game, 1932, Borgfeldt	150 - 500
Marks Brothers Co. (G3225-G3244)		
G3225	Bean Bag Game	75 - 300
G3226	Target, 2 sizes	100 - 350

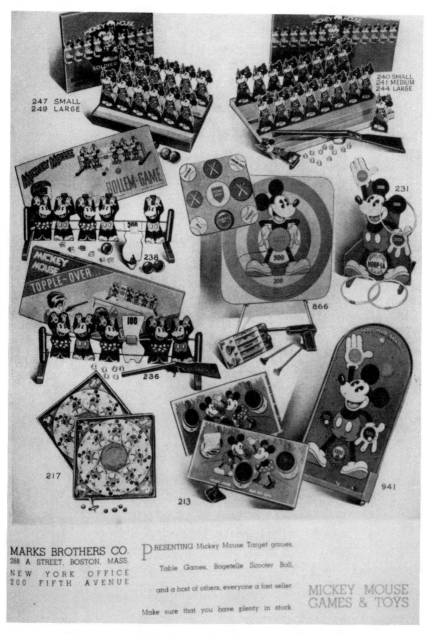

The Marks Brothers Company of Boston was one of the earliest manufacturers of Mickey Mouse games. Some were board games, but most were target, toss or other type of skill games. Marks Brothers also produced early Mickey puzzles, a toy piano, kites, and party favors. Their colorful products are all highly collectible.

165

G3228	Bagatelle, 2 types	200 - 500
G3229	Hoop-La Game, 2 types	115 - 375
G3230	Mickey Soldier, set, 18	75 - 450
G3231	Pop Game	150 - 575
G3232	Hand Held Ball Puzzle Games, 3, each	20 - 95
G3235	Topple-Over Shooting Game	175 - 575
G3236	Mickey Rollem Game	150 - 425
G3237	Mickey/Minnie Rollem Game	150 - 425
G3240	Snow White Moving Target	250 - 600
G3244	Mickey/Donald Soldier Set, 8	55 - 250
G3248	Jacks Set, U. S. Lock and Hardware	20 - 60
G3249	Bow & Arrow Set, Wilson	25 - 85
G3252	Dopey Bean Bag Game, Parker	95 - 225
G3253	Donald Duck Bean Bag Game, Parker	95 - 225
G3256	Mickey Ski Jump Target Game, American	110 - 300
G3257	Snow White and the Seven Dwarfs Target Game, American	110 - 300
G3260	Pinocchio Ring Toss, De-Ward	15 - 45
G3280	Donald Duck Tiddley Winx, Jaymar	10 - 35
G3281	Donald Duck Tiddley Winx, Jaymar	10 - 35
G3290	Target Set, Lido	10 - 40
G3291	Shooting Gallery, Lido	12 - 45
G3293	Donald Duck Pins, Pressman	10 - 35
G3295	Mouskatennis, Pressman	8 - 20
G3298	Mickey Mouse Basketball, Gardner	10 - 35
G3299	Donald Duck Bean Bag Game, Gardner	10 - 35
G3300	Casey Jr. Game, Gardner	10 - 35
G3314	Mickey Mouse or Davy Crockett Target Sets, Daisy	20 - 50
G3315	Davy Crockett Bow & Arrow Set, Withington	20 - 50
G3316	Davy Crockett Bow Gun, Withington	25 - 65
G3320	Disneyland Dipsy Doodles, 3 designs, each	2 - 10
G3330	Tiddly Winks, Whitman	5 - 15
G3331	Ludwig Von Drake Tiddly Winks, Whitman	5 - 15
G3334	Ludwig Von Drake Score-A-Matic Ball Toss Game, Transogram	15 - 45
G3345	Donald Duck Fun Ball, Gardner	4 - 18
G3358	Pinocchio Pic Ups	1 - 8

G3500 GAMES -- OTHER

This miscellaneous group includes traditional games like dominoes, bingo and pin the tail on Mickey to Whizzer wheel and magic printing machine games.

G3520	Mickey Mouse Dominoes, Halsam	30 - 95
G3525	Mickey Mouse Party Game (Pin the Tail)	15 - 45

G3526	Same as G3525, but in box, Marks Bros.	20 - 65
G3530	Pin the Nose on Pinocchio, Parker	15 - 45
G3535	Picture Dominoes, Transogram	10 - 30
G3540	Double Dominoes	15 - 35
G3545	Bingo, Lido	15 - 40
G3550	Magic Printing Machine Game, Norstar	5 - 20
G3570	Pin the Tail on Mickey Mouse, Hallmark	2 - 6

G4000 GLASSES -- DRINKING

Disney character premium tumblers were used to promote the sale of cottage cheese from 1933 to 1941 and 1947-48. There were main character, Snow White, Pinocchio and Disney All Star sets. Many of the one-color glasses came in a variety of different colors and sizes. Bosco drink mix offered a special small size. Libbey Glass division of Owens-Illinois Glass Co. was the major producer. There was a multi-colored Snow White set also. Character glasses have been popular theme park souvenirs since Disneyland opened. The 70's gave rise to collector's sets of 3 to 8 glass tumblers issued by soft drink and fast food companies.

The promotional character collector's sets are often issued regionally. There are also variations from one fast food chain to another.

G4003	Mickey, milk glass tumbler, 2 designs	25 - 75
G4005	Three Little Pigs, glass breakfast set, Krueger, 1934	45 - 150
G4010	Main character cottage cheese premiums, Mickey, Minnie, Donald, Pluto, Clarabelle, Horace, Three Little Pigs, Big Bad Wolf, Elmer Elephant & Funny Bunny, each	5 - 15
G4025	Snow White & Seven Dwarfs, dairy premiums, each	5 - 12
G4033	Snow White & Seven Dwarfs, Bosco, each	5 - 20
G4034	Snow White & Seven Dwarfs, full color, set	45 - 125
G4048	Kraft Snow White premium set	35 - 70
G4055	Disney All Star Parade series, 10, 1939, each	8 - 25
G4070	Pinocchio premiums, 12, each	5 - 15
G4083	Pinocchio, glass promotion folder	5 - 35
G4099	Calox Pinocchio safedge glass, McKesson & Robbins, each	5 - 15
G4100	Character pair glasses, 40's -- Mickey/Minnie, Donald/Daisy, Pluto/Goofy, Pinocchio/Jiminy Cricket, 2 sizes, each	5 - 15
G4110	Cinderella set, 8, each	5 - 12
G4120	Alice in Wonderland set, 8, each	5 - 15
G4128	Peter Pan, 4, each	5 - 15
G4135	Lady and the Tramp, each	5 - 15
G4150	Character glasses, Disneyland souvenir	5 - 12
G4180	Procter & Gamble Sleeping Beauty set, each	5 - 15

G4190	The Jungle Book, each	7 - 20
G4220	Theme park character glasses	1 - 5
G4250	Coca-Cola character set, 6, each	5 - 12
G4257	Mickey's Christmas Carol, 3, each	4 - 12

G4980 GLOBE OF THE WORLD

Rand McNally & Co. (Skokie, IL) made character world globes and a world globe game with magnetic characters in 1955. Globes alone are valued at 15 - 50, the games at 20 - 300. A theme park globe for Walt Disney World was done in 1971. Value 35 - 75.

G5500 GOEBEL

Goebel, the German company famous for Hummel overglaze figurines, produced a continuous series of Disney figures from 1950-67. The Goebel 50th Anniversary book lists them as being sold in the U.S. from 1952-54; however, Ebeling & Reuss Co. (Philadelphia, PA; now Devon, PA) was licensed to import "Disney Hummel figures" as of Feb 24, 1955 for an undetermined period. The vast majority of the 220 pieces in the first series were based on the film *Bambi*. Many merely used the same figures on different bases, bookends, ashtrays, or as salt and pepper shakers. The Goebel Disney figures sold in America had a "full bee" mark (a bee in the letter V) on the underside of each piece, along with the word "Germany." Two figures, Bambi and Mickey as the Sorcerer's Apprentice, were made for sale at theme park Disneyana shops in the late 70's. These and a new series of 10 figures are marked "Goebel." The "full bee" figures were painted in earthier tones and shading very close to Hummel figures. More modern figures are brighter with less shading. Values of "full bee" figures range from under $50 for a small Bambi to several hundred for larger multi-figure scenes. The full bee set of Snow White and the Seven Dwarfs did not include the Prince. This piece was added in a later remake of the set. A third and smaller Snow White set was issued in 1984, also without a prince. In the early 80's only one of Goebel's three U.S. distributors was responsible for importing the Disney line -- Goebel United States (formerly Hummelwerk), a wholly-owned subsidiary of Goebel Art GmbH, West Germany, based in Pennington, NJ. Schmid took over the sole distributorship in the late 80's.

The sculptors who modeled the original series included Arthur Moeller, Reinhold Unger, Karl Wagner with additional pieces being done by artists Aschermann, Wolf and Wehlte. Following is a complete list of Disney Goebel figures as recorded by the company. The specific character is not always listed nor the description too accurate from the German translations. Read rocking figures as nodders, and the term "lips" refers to the indentation for a cigarette on an ashtray. Figures found most often in the U.S. include Snow White and the Seven Dwarfs,

168

Bambi characters, Dumbo on the edge of the cliff, Elmer Elephant and Tillie the Tiger, Pinocchio, Honest John, Giddy and Figaro. These are all in the list, but positive identification still needs to be made on many pieces. It is fairly clear only selected pieces were sold in the U.S. The literature distributed by Ebeling & Reuss depicted only 35 pieces ... the ones usually found in this country. A complete list of values is not possible at this time, but trading experience is noted where possible. The list is presented as it was received from Goebel for collector interest. The Goebel number is the last digit(s) of the Tomart number. Disney figures were numbered and each number was preceded by the letters DIS. The incised number is legible on some pieces. To determine exact Goebel identification, read G5001 as DIS 1; G5014A as DIS 14A.

A quantity of Tinker Bells (DIS 188) incised dated 1959 were imported in what remained of a 2,000 numbered edition firing. The source was Germany. The Disney theme parks are also selling new editions of many original mold Bambis and other figures. Some of the reissue Bambis have flies rather than the original butterflies on their tails.

Values listed are for "full Bee" marked figures.

G5001	Dwarf "Bashful", 1950	25 - 75
G5002	Dwarf "Sleepy"	25 - 75
G5003	Dwarf "Happy"	25 - 75
G5004	Dwarf "Grumpy"	25 - 75
G5005	Dwarf "Sneezy"	25 - 75
G5006	Dwarf "Dopey"	25 - 75
G5007	Dwarf "Doc"	25 - 75
G5008	Thumper, ashtray w/lip on tail	80 - 185
G5009	Bambi, ashtray	70 - 160
G5010	Standing Deer & Jumping Rabbit, on base	--
G5011	Standing Bambi, w/o base	--
G5012	Snow White	50 - 100
G5013A	Larger Bambi, w/its head turned backwards, a butterfly is sitting on its tail	--
G5013B	Small Bambi, w/its head turned backwards, a butterfly sitting on its tail	--
G5014A	Small Flower, sitting on its hind legs	25 - 65
G5014B	Small Flower, standing	--
G5015	Ashtray w/two lips & a dressed duck in the ash-bowl	--
G5016	Pig, w/hat, "Seier Pig"	--
G5017	Little Indian "Hiawatha"	--
G5018	Sitting Up Rabbit, beside a vessel	--
G5019	Standing Rabbit, beside a vessel	--
G5020	Standing Duck, beside a vessel	--
G5021	Lying Bambi, w/o base	20 - 55
G5022	Standing Deer, on base w/stem	--
G5023	Sitting Rabbit, the ears are on the back	--

169

G5025	Sitting Skunk, w/a flower in both its paws	--
G5026	Sitting Laughing Rabbit, spreading out its paw	--
G5027	Owl, sitting on a branch, w/stem as vase	--
G5028	Owl, spreading out its wings on tray w/two lips	90 - 200
G5029	Flying Owl, w/book as wall ornament	--
G5030	Owl of G5029, beside a vessel as wall-vase	--
G5031	Cigarette box, on its cover the deer of G5021	--
G5032	Rabbit of G5023, as salt shaker	--
G5033	Skunk of G5025, as salt or pepper shaker, set	45 - 95
G5034	Rabbit of G5026, as salt shaker	--
G5035	Bird, sitting on a branch w/its tail raised	--
G5036	Sitting Rabbit, w/its forelegs hanging down	--
G5037A	Owl, sitting on stem, bookend	--
G5037B	Rabbit, sitting beside stem, bookend	--
G5038	Rabbit, lying flat on face, hind legs spread out	--
G5039	Sitting Rabbit, vessel on back	--
G5040	Rabbit of G5036, as salt shaker	--
G5041	Rabbit of G5039, as salt shaker	--
G5042A	Stem & Bambi, looking right, vase	80 - 175
G5042B	Stem & Bambi, looking left, vase	80 - 175
G5043	Sitting Rabbit, hind legs stretched, foreleg raised	--
G5044	Bird, sitting on branch, looking downward	--
G5045	Pig of G5016, as ashtray	--
G5046	Duck of G5020, as ashtray	--
G5047	Rabbit of G5019, beside round vessel, toothpick holder	--
G5048	Indian of G5017, beside round vessel, toothpick holder	--
G5049	Indian of G5017, as ashtray	--
G5050	Rabbit of G5024, as salt shaker	--
G5051	Dwarf of G5001, as vase	--
G5052	Dwarf of G5002, as vase	--
G5053	Dwarf of G5003, as vase	--
G5054	Dwarf of G5004, as vase	--
G5055	Dwarf of G5005, as vase	--
G5056	Dwarf of G5006, as vase	--
G5057	Dwarf of G5007, as vase	--
G5058	Standing Man, w/top hat, "Mad Hatter", 1951	--
G5059	Standing Figurine, w/crown, "King"	--
G5060	Female Figurine, w/animal under her arm, "Queen	--
G5061	Standing Rabbit, w/spectacles, heart on its chest	--
G5062	Standing Girl, w/hands at her skirt, "Alice"	--
G5063	Standing Man, w/top hat and cigar, "Walrus"	--
G5064	Standing Man, w/paving stone on head, "Carpenter"	--
G5065	Two Men, w/caps standing side by side, "Dee and Dum"	--

G5066	Standing Bird, w/pipe, "Dodo"	--
G5067	Standing Man, playing card as body, "Gardener Cards"	--
G5068	Wall-vase w/deer Bambi & rabbit	--
G5069	"Queen", as rocking figurine	--
G5070	"King", as rocking figurine	--
G5071	Dressed Bird,w/pipe as ashtray, 1952	--
G5072	Sitting Elephant, stretching up its trunk as ashtray	--.
G5073	Standing Duck, as ice-hockey player on a round bowl	--
G5074	Small Duck, as ice-hockey player on a round bowl	
G5075	"Mickey Mouse", as hunter, beside stem, as vase	175 - 325
G5076	Running Dog, w/artificial ears & tail	--
G5077	Kneeling Mickey Mouse, going hunting	140 - 300
G5078	Mickey Mouse, w/book sitting on a stem	90 - 200
G5079	Sitting Dog, "instructions for hunting"	--
G5080	Round bowl w/lips at rim, as ashtray	--
G5080A	Not on list, but apparently a Dumbo ashtray	--
G5081	Standing Mouse, w/left hand raised	--
G5082	Standing Mouse, w/hands on belly "Father"	--
G5083	Standing Mouse, w/left hand at ear "Mother"	--
G5084	Sitting Cat, w/flower on its head	--
G5085	Laughing Cat, lying on its back w/its forelegs crossed on its chest	--
G5086	Sitting Elephant, w/large ears & vessel on back	--
G5087	Dressed Rabbit, lying flat on face w/forelegs propped up	--
G5088	Standing Man, w/top hat, hands on hips	--
G5089	Standing Man, w/coffee pot in his hand	--
G5090	Standing Man, w/cigar in right hand	--
G5091	Running Rabbit, w/watch in hand	--
G5092	Sitting Elephant, w/trunk raised as ashtray	--
G5093	Standing Thick Man, as rocking figurine	--
G5094	Cinderella & Prince, on round base	--
G5095	Cinderella, on staircase w/lost shoe	--
G5096	Cinderella, w/groom	--
G5097	Standing Thick Man, w/stick & cigar as rocking figurine	--
G5098A	Sitting Cat, w/head raised	25 - 60
G5098B	Sitting Cat, w/head turned to left	25 - 60
G5099	Sitting Pinocchio	50 - 175
G5100	Running Pinocchio, w/plumed hat & apple in hand	85 - 250
G5101	Elmer Elephant & Tillie	85 - 250
G5102	Dressed Fox, w/top hat & walking stick	100 - 350
G5103	Dressed Cat, w/top hat & walking stick	90 - 275

G5104	Round weaved small basket w/a cat on its cover	60 - 195
G5105	Cat,standing on bowl w/wavy rim	--
G5106	Figurine of G5068, as ashtray w/two lips	--
G5107	Figurine of G5065, as ashtray w/two lips	--
G5108	Figurine of G5066, as ashtray w/two lips	--
G5109	Rabbit of G5039, w/o vase	--
G5110	Standing Thick Man, w/cigar as liquor bottle	--
G5111	Large Bambi & Frog, on an oval base	300 - 500
G5112	Bambi of G5111, w/o base	--
G5113	Standing Bambi & Sitting Thumper	100 - 250
G5114	Standing Bambi & Sitting Skunk	--
G5115	Bambi of G5114, w/o base	--
G5116	Bambi of G5022, w/o base	--
G5117	Standing Bambi, w/butterfly on tail	--
G5118	Sitting Duck, opening bill	--
G5119	Two Kissing Skunks	100 - 350
G5120	Two Sitting Rabbits, on oval base	100 - 350
G5121	Standing Owl, spreading wings	--
G5122	Dumbo of G5080A, as single figurine	100 - 225
G5123	Duc of G5073, as single figurine	--
G5124	Duck of G5074, as single figurine	--
G5125	Cat w/large ball	60 - 195
G5126	Duck of G5015, as single figurine	--
G5127	Duck of G5046, as single figurine	--
G5128	Large Playful Rabbits, w/o base	200 - 400
G5129	Frog of G5111, as single figurine	--
G5130	Skunk of G5114, as single figurine	--
G5131	Rabbit of G5113, as single figurine	--
G5132	Open book w/standing figurine as display plaque	--
G5133	Open book w/standing boy as display plaque	--
G5134	Standing Bearded Man, w/apron as liquor bottle	--
G5135	Cat, w/upright tail "Lucifer"	--
G5136	Rabbit of G5050, w/o holes	--
G5137	Rabbit of G5034, w/o holes	--
G5138	Cat Box of G5104, w/holes	75 - 225
G5139	Bambi of G5117, w/artificial butterfly	--
G5140	Lying Deer & Bambi	--
G5141	Sitting Dog, "Bruno"	--
G5142	Standing Duck, w/a hole in its bill for an artificial fly	--
G5143A	Dressed Pig, w/violin	--
G5143B	Dressed Pig, w/flute	--
G5143C	Dressed Pig, w/mouth organ	--
G5144	Standing Bird, w/scarf	--
G5145A	Rabbit of G5120, as single figurine	--
G5145B	Rabbit of G5120, as single figurine	--

G5146	Bambi of G5021, as ashtray w/lip	--
G5147	Bambi of G5012, as ashtray w/lip	--
G5148	Dwarf of G5005, as ashtray w/lip	--
G5149	Sitting Dog, "Pluto", as perfume spender, has light inside	185 - 300
G5150	Standing Bambi, as perfume spender, w/light, 1953	185 - 300
G5151	Rabbit standing on its hind legs as perfume spender	--
G5152	Open book, w/Mickey Mouse as display plaque	--
G5153	Standing Boy, hands on hips "Peter Pan"	--
G5154	Standing Boy ,w/teddy, "Peter Pan" & Michael	--
G5155	Kneeling Water Sprite, on a round base, "Mermaid"	--
G5156	Standing Girl, w/wings "Tinker Bell"	--
G5157	Sitting Boy, "Peter Pan"	--
G5158	Standing figurine w/a club in his left hand, "Cubby"	--
G5159	Standing figurine made up as a fox, "Foxy"	--
G5160	Cat of G5105, as ashtray w/lip	--
G5161	Dog of G5149, as lamp stand, 1954	--
G5162	Ashtray G5148, w/o lip	--
G5163	Bambi of G5022, beside oval bowl	--
G5164	Boy of G5100, beside and oval bowl	--
G5165A	Standing Duck, w/butterfly on its tail as music box	--
G5165B	Standing Duck, w/butterfly on its bill as single figurine	--
G5166	Pig of G5143, beside a round bowl	--
G5167	Sitting Dog, "Susi", 1955, Lady	--
G5168	Sitting Dog, w/its foreleg raised, "Strolch", Tramp	--
G5169	Sitting Bloodhound, Trusty	--
G5170	Sitting Terrier, "York", Jock	--
G5171	Sitting Dachshund, "Dachsie"	--
G5172	"Bulldogge"	--
G5173	Pekinese, "Peg"	--
G5174	Sitting Cat, "Si"	--
G5175	Sitting Greyhound, "Boris"	--
G5176	Sitting Dog, "Toughy"	--
G5177A	Boy, w/rifle, bookend	--
G5177B	Bear, standing on hind legs, bookend	--
G5178	Drinking cup w/handle & a kneeling boy in relief	--
G5179	Bowl w/two jumping bears in relief	--
G5180A	Standing Boy, w/rifle, salt shaker	--
G5180B	Standing Bear, pepper shaker	--
G5181	Standing Bambi ,as perfume spender, 1956	--
G5182	"Susi", Lady, w/two brown dogs at one chain	--
G5183	"Strolch", Tramp, w/two dogs at one chain	--

173

G5184   "Susi", Lady and "Strolch", Tramp, as group
        of dogs   --

Prices listed are for Stylized Bee

G5186   Bambi of G5112, beside stump as lamp
        stand, 1957   --
G5187   Bambi of B5139, beside stem as lamp stand   --
G5188   Standing figurine w/wings, "Tinker Bell", 1959   50 - 90
G5189   Kneeling figurine w/wings, "Tinker Bell"   --
G5190   Group of Dogs, w/chain   --
G5191   Group of Dogs, w/chain   --
G5192B Standing Dog   --
G5193   Two Bambis of G5111, as a group w/o base,
        1960   --
G5194   Bambis of G5116 & G5021, as a group w/o base   --
G5195   Bambis of G5111 & G5116, on base   --
G5197   Sitting Dalmatian, 1961   --
G5198   Lying Dalmatian   --
G5199   Sitting Dalmatian, holding a heart in its muzzle   --
G5200   Barking Small Dalmatian   --
G5201   Sitting Small Dalmatian, w/a bone in its muzzle   --
G5202   Wall lamp "Donald Duck", in the vessel, 1962   --
G5203   Wall lamp "Donald Duck", w/a ball in his hands   --
G5204   Basket Amendment Set, rabbit of G5040 as
        salt & pepper shaker in a basket   --
G5205   Group of Dogs, w/chain, 1962   --

Prices listed after 1964 have name "Goebel" in mark

G5206   Sitting Bear, w/a little boy on its belly, 1965   --
G5300   Snow White, plate (see P3690)
G5301   Mickey or Bambi, theme park designs   25 - 75
G5310   Reissue of G5001-7, plus G5012 & new Prince
        figure, set   100 - 200
G5330   New design approach, 10 figures, Mickey or
        Minnie jogging; Mickey Tennis, stamp collecting
        or in garden; Donald fishing, playing video game
        or boating; or Minnie embroidering or working
        out, each   10 - 55
G5240   Snow White (5-3/4") and Dwarfs (2-3/4"), set   50 - 125

H1000 HAGEN-RENAKER CERAMICS

Hagen-Renaker (Monrovia, CA) famous for miniature ceramic Disney figures, was licensed through a sales representative firm, George Good Co. (LA) from 1955-61. *Lady and the Tramp* figures were sold exclusively at Disneyland the first year. In 1956 the company added figures from *Alice in Wonderland, Bambi, Cinderella, Dumbo* and *The Mickey Mouse Club*. Larger figures were distributed nationally under the Designer's Workshop name: Snow White, the Seven Dwarfs,

Jiminy Cricket and other characters. Banks and cookie jars were 1956 DW products. More miniatures were soon included. The *Peter Pan* and *Fantasia* figures were added in 1957; *Snow White and the Seven Dwarfs* miniatures in 1958; and *Sleeping Beauty* characters in 1959. Banks and cookie jars were made for Hagen-Renaker by other potteries. A larger set of Hagen-Renaker *Fantasia* figures were produced for sale at theme park Disneyana shops in the mid-80's. Additional figures for this series and a Country Bear Jamboree set were planned, but not produced. The detail on Hagen-Renaker ceramics captures the interest of most collectors fortunate enough to find one. They are truly masterworks in miniature.

H1001	Lady (sold later as "non-Disney"), orig.	20 - 65
H1002	Tramp	125 - 250
H1003	Scamp, Ruffles or Fluffy, each	25 - 65
H1006	Scooter, Jock or Trusty, (sold later as "non-Disney"), each	45 - 95
H1009	Si or Am, each	50 - 100
H1011	Pedro or Dachsie, each	50 - 110
H1013	Peg or Bull, each	70 - 145
H1015	Alice	175 - 375
H1016	Mad Hatter, March Hare or Caterpillar, each	160 - 350
H1019	Cinderella	175 - 375
H1020	Gus or Jaq, each	90 - 200
H1022	Bambi or Faline, each	70 - 150
H1024	Flower or Thumper, each	35 - 95
H1026	Dumbo or Timothy Mouse, each	70 - 145
H1030	Mickey, as band leader	85 - 195
H1031	Pluto or Goofy	70 - 160
H1033	Donald Duck	85 - 195
H1034	Scrooge McDuck, w/dollar	80 - 175
H1035	Huey, Louie or Dewey, playing baseball, each	50 - 110
H1038	Chip or Dale, each	65 - 135
H1040	Peter Pan	85 - 195
H1041	Wendy or Michael, each	80 - 175
H1043	John	125 - 275
H1044	Michael's Teddy Bear (sold later as "non-Disney") or Nana	80 - 175
H1046	Tinker Bell , flying	250 - 500
H1047	Tinker Bell , kneeling	125 - 275
H1048	Tinker Bell, shelf sitter	200 - 500
H1049	Reclining Mermaid, blonde or redhead, each	90 - 185
H1051	Kneeling Mermaid, blonde or redhead, each	100 - 200
H1055	Bacchus	75 - 165
H1056	Faun #1, #2 or #3, each	65 - 145
H1059	Unicorn	100 - 200
H1060	Baby Unicorn or Baby Pegasus, each	85 - 180

H1063	Greek Column	5 - 25
H1065	Snow White	65 - 135
H1066	Seven Dwarfs, set	140 - 280
H1075	Sleeping Beauty	120 - 250
H1076	Prince Phillip	60 - 150
H1077	Maleficent & Raven	300 - 650
H1078	Flora, Fauna, or Merryweather, each	40 - 135
H1081	King Stefan or King Hubert, each	115 - 250
H1083	The Queen	90 - 195
H1084	Samson	250 - 650
H1085	Rabbit, Squirrel, Owl, Cardinal or Bluebird, each	50 - 110

Larger (about 3" to 4 1/2") Designer's Workshop Figures

H1090	Bambi or Flower, each	60 - 175
H1091	Jiminy Cricket or Figaro, each	115 - 350
H1092	Snow White	200 - 600
H1093	Seven Dwarfs, each	70 - 200
H1094	Dumbo	80 - 200
H1100	Practical Pig, Thumper, Dumbo or Figaro cookie jar, each	200 - 400
H1103	Practical Pig, Thumper, Dumbo, Figaro or Lady bank, each	150 - 350

3" Figures Circa 1985

H1120	Mickey, as the Sorcerer's Apprentice	35 - 100
H1121	Broom, w/water bucket	25 - 55
H1122	Bacchus	20 - 45
H1123	Baby Pegasus, pink, blue or black, each	20 - 45
H1126	Ostrich	40 - 100
H1127	Mushroom, 3/4"	5 - 10

J2000 JEWELRY (EXCEPT RINGS)

Character jewelry has been produced in materials ranging from plastic to platinum set with diamonds. Cohn & Rosenberger produced some of the most collectible jewelry (1931-36). Brier Manufacturing runs a close second with collectors. Cartier was a jewelry licensee for early animated features and again since 1981. Others are listed below.

Cohn & Rosenberger, Inc. (J2020-J2058)

J2020	Mickey Lapel Button or Brooch, 1931-32, each	40 - 115
J2022	Mickey Necklace, 1931-36	50 - 125
J2023	Mickey Bracelet, solid or chain, 1931-36, each	25 - 100
J2025	Mickey Silver Belt Buckle, 1931-32	15 - 75
J2026	Mickey Bib Holder, 1931-32	20 - 75
J2030	Three Little Pigs Necklace, 2 designs, 1933, each	18 - 70
J2032	Three Little Pigs Enameled Bracelet, 3 designs, each	20 - 80
J2035	Three Little Pigs Wide Band Enameled Bracelet	45 - 125

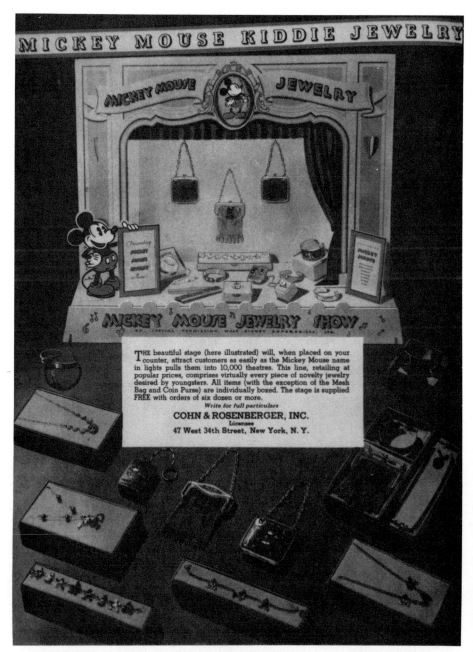

Cohn & Rosenberger, Inc. was licensed to produce Mickey Mouse and other character jewelry from 1931-36 and 1941-42. They made enameled rings, necklaces, bracelets, pins and mesh bags featuring Mickey, Minnie and the Three Little Pigs.

J2036	Three Little Pigs Sweater Enameled Pin	25 - 90
J2037	Three Little Pigs Pendant, 2 designs, each	25 - 90
J2040	Mickey Enameled Bracelet, 2 designs, 1934, each	25 - 90
J2042	Mickey "Jeweled" Pendant	35 - 150
J2044	Minnie "Jeweled" Bracelet	35 - 150
J2045	Mickey or Minnie Illustrated Mesh Purse, each	75 - 250
J2047	Mickey Disc Pendant	27 - 80
J2050	Three Little Pigs Mesh Coin Purse	40 - 175
J2051	Mickey/Minnie Mesh Coin Purse	50 - 250
J2052	Mickey Mesh Coin Purse	55 - 250
J2053	Three Little Pigs Enameled Purse	30 - 185
J2054	Mickey/Minnie World's Fair Enameled Purse	60 - 300
J2055	Mickey/Minnie/Pluto Enameled Purse	50 - 250
J2056	Mickey/Minnie Enameled Purse	50 - 250
J2058	Three Little Pigs Match Safe, green or orange, each	25 - 65
J2060	Mickey Glass Bubble Tie Bar	15 - 55

Brier Manufacturing Company (J2074-J2140)

J2074	Box for Brier Mfg. Company Jewelry	10 - 25
J2075	Mickey or Minnie Cloisonne Pin, each	25 - 85
J2077	Donald or Pluto Cloisonne Pin, each	25 - 85
J2079	Mickey/Minnie, Mickey/Pluto or Mickey/Donald Sweater Clasp, each	40 - 100
J2082	Pendant Necklace - Mickey, Minnie, Donald or Pluto, each	20 - 60
J2086	Bracelet -- same character choice as J2082, each	20 - 60
J2100	Snow White or Dwarf Enameled Pin, each	14 - 38
J2108	Snow White or Dwarf Painted Wood Composition Pin, each	12 - 45
J2116	Mickey Wood Composition Pin, playing violin, trumpet or drum, each	15 - 60
J2119	Donald Wood Composition Pin, playing piccolo	15 - 55
J2120	Ferdinand the Bull Wood Composition Pin	10 - 35
J2122	Mickey, Donald or Pluto, giant wood composition pins, each	10 - 45
J2130	Pinocchio, Jiminy Cricket or Cleo, plastic character pins, each	10 - 30
J2135	Same characters as J2130 as pendants, each	15 - 35
J2140	Pinocchio/Jiminy Cricket Sweater Clasp or Bar Pin, each	15 - 35
J2150	Cartier Gold Enameled Character Pins -- Snow White, Dwarfs, Ferdinand, Pinocchio & others, each	100 - 400
J2165	Cartier Character Money Clip	75 - 300
J2170	Ferdinand, rear view, against rhinestone fence	8 - 35

Brier Manufacturing Company was the major producer of Snow White and the Seven Dwarfs jewelry when the film was first released in 1938. Metal and a wood-like substance was used in their creations.

J2173	Authentics Wood Carved Pieces, each	25 - 100
J2175	Speidel Character Disc Bracelets, Necklaces, Bar Pins -- Pinocchio & probably Snow White, each	15 - 65
J2180	Hop Low, China Relief	10 - 50
J2200	Alpha-Craft Pins, each	6 - 32
J2220	Charmore Gold Plated Character Pins -- Mickey, Minnie, Donald, Pluto, Thumper, Practical Pig & others, each	10 - 32
J2240	Eastern Jewelry Character Pins, plastic or metal. Heads moved on metal pins. Metal	10 - 40
	Plastic	5 - 20
J2260	Dexter Character Pins; Cuff Links; Tie Tack & Bars; & Necklaces -- Mickey, Lady and the Tramp, Davy Crockett & Sword in the Stone, plus Snow White re-release, heavy non-precious metal. Arden Range	3 - 15
J2290	Sword in the Stone Pins, Bracelets, Key Ring & Pendants, 1963, Arden Range	4 - 12
J2400	Theme park souvenir jewelry, 50's and 60's	7 - 35
J2470	Theme park souvenir jewelry, post 70's	3 - 15

SPECIAL NOTICE- There are many jewelry pieces sold at Disney theme parks and elsewhere which look old, but are not. There are metal bracelets that resemble early Cohn & Rosenberger designs. An "antique jewelry" line depicting Steamboat Willie and pie-cut eyes Mickey and Minnie is particularly deceptive. None of these sold new for over 15. Most sell in the 3 - 15 price range.

K5000 KNIVES, POCKET

Imperial Knife made Mickey Mouse knives in the 30's and Davy Crockett styles in the 50's. An early enameled penknife looks to have been made by Cohn & Rosenberger. A 1933 Chicago World's Fair knife is an infringement, made in the 70's.

K5010	Knife, enameled	40 - 200
K5020	Mickey Penknife, 2 styles, Imperial	25 - 90
K5022	Mickey 2-Blade Knife, Imperial	40 - 120
K2023	Mickey 4-Blade Knife, Imperial	65 - 150
K5040	Davy Crockett Frontier Knife	10 - 25
K5041	Davy Tomahawk Knife, w/cap lifter	15 - 35
K5042	Davy 3-Blade Frontier Knife	10 - 28
K5060	Jackknives (Richards of Sheffield), 5 designs, Mickey, Goofy, Donald, Baloo, Little John, each	5 - 15

Also see S3500 SILVER CUPS, PLATES, BOWLS, SILVERWARE AND FLATWARE

The Soreng-Manegold Company produced popular Mickey Mouse
lamps from 1934 to 1938. Green and tan bases are the most often
seen. Illustrated shades are difficult to find. The company also
produced yarn and thread holders from the same tooling. Lamp
bases, however, cannot be used for these purposes.

181

L1000 LAMPS, LAMPSHADES AND NIGHTLIGHTS

There are many classic Disney lamps. Finding one with its original shade is rare. The extra wide price spreads in this section take this factor into consideration. The top price is for a mint lamp with a fine to mint grade original shade, except for night lights which had no shade.

L1010	Krueger Musical Three Little Pigs Lamp, 1933	250 - 650

Soreng-Manegold Company (L1020-L1028)

L1020	Mickey Lamps, green or tan, 3 shade styles, 1935 each	35 - 100
L1023	Same as L1020, but new shade, 1936	35 - 100
L1025	Mickey or Donald Wall Lamp, each	250 - 900
LI027	Mickey, in chair	450 - 1,200
L1028	Donald, standing at post	500 - 1,300
L1030	Mickey, Donald or Dopey, battery operated "Kiddy-Lites", Micro-Lite, each	60 - 185
L1034	Dopey, at kettle, LaMode	125 - 350
L1035	Snow White, at wishing well, LaMode	125 - 350
L1036	Snow White, Dopey, Grumpy, Doc, Mickey or Donald, plaster lamp & shade, LaMode, each	65 - 275
L1042	Bookend Lamps or Night Lights, LaMode, same characters as L1036, each	75 - 300
L1048	Same characters as bookends only, set of 2, each	45 - 150
L1050	Multi-Products Pinocchio, Jiminy Cricket, Geppetto,Lampwick figures, Flexo table lamp, each	70 - 250
L1054	Multi-Products Wall Plaques, 3, Flexo Wall Lamps, each	70 - 250
L1063	Mickey, Minnie, Donald, Joe Carioca, Panchito (Evan K. Shaw design) or Dopey Table Lamps, each	85 - 275
L1069	Snow White's Bluebirds, Donald or Pluto Wall Lamps, Railley, each	60 - 225
L1073	Ceiling Globe	25 - 65
L1074	Donald, Dopey and others, Leeds China designs, each	40 - 125
L1200	Snow White Nite-Lite, Hankscraft	25 - 75

L2500 LEEDS CHINA COMPANY

Leeds China Company (Chicago) was a licensee from 1944-1954. Flower shops were major customers. Planters and pitchers with flower arrangements were basic products. The product line was diverse. (see B1350 BANKS, C9000 COOKIE JARS and S1000 SALT AND PEPPER SHAKERS) Earlier pieces were painted overglaze and the paint

UTILITY CERAMICS

Ceramics with a purpose—Walt Disney Character planters, cookie jars, banks, and others. Customers readily buy these appealing Disney items, each beautifully decorated with fired-on colors. Priced right for substantial volume sales.

Donald Duck, Mickey Mouse and Dopey Planters, each to retail at	$1.25
Thumper Cotton Picker to retail at	$1.00
Dumbo Water Pitcher to retail at	$1.50
Mickey Mouse, Donald Duck and Joe Carioca Cookie Jars, each	$1.75
Dumbo, Donald Duck, and Mickey Mouse Banks, each to retail at	89c
Mickey and Minnie Mouse, Donald Duck, Dumbo and Pluto Table Shakers, each pair to retail at	59c
Dumbo Range Shakers, each pair to retail at	79c
Donald Duck Baby Plate (regular style) to retail at	$1.50
Donald Duck Baby Plate (face-type) to retail at	$1.50

LEEDS CHINA COMPANY
2715 ARCHER AVE., CHICAGO, 8, ILL.

The Leeds China Company of Chicago was one of the most prolific manufacturers of Disney ceramic pieces from 1944 to 1954. Chinaware, cream and sugar sets, salt and pepper shakers, banks, cookie jars, pitchers and planters were some of the company's leading products.

flaked off. Later pieces were airbrushed with lighter pastel colors under glaze. These remain in excellent condition, but are seen less often. Lamp bases were perhaps made for a different manufacturer. The designs seem endless. Paint variations add to the variety. Some are even edged in gold. Assortments for 1947 and 1949 are pictured along with some individual pieces. Prices are listed by category.

L2501	Figurines, overglaze, each	10 - 55
L2530	Figurines, underglaze, each	10 - 60
L2560	Planters, overglaze, each	6 - 25
L2600	Planters, underglaze, each	8 - 35
L2670	Child's Feeding Dishes	15 - 60

L5000 LOBBY CARDS

A set of lobby cards, usually 8, was issued with each release of a Disney film. The design of the title card in each set changes when a film was re-released. Other cards changed or ones from a previous release were re-used. They were printed and in color vs. still photos which were usually black and white. The standard size was 11" x 14". Older animation sets sell well at film collector conventions. Sets from animation films since *Lady and the Tramp* go for 20 - 60 in their illustrated envelopes. Individual animated feature lobby cards can be found for .50 - 4 each.

Selected lobby card sets have been sold at theme park Disneyana shops (as available) starting at $10 for complete 8 card sets in the envelope. The use of lobby cards has been abandoned with the advent of multi-screen theaters.

L9000 LUNCH BOXES AND KITS

Four licensees have provided an almost continuous supply of lunch boxes in non-war years. Each one since the 50's came with a thermos bottle. Prices are for complete units. Scratches and rust rapidly deplete value.

L9005	Mickey Mouse Lunch Kit, 1935-37	150 - 550
L9008	Snow White Lunch Box, Libbey	15 - 65
L9010	Pinocchio Lunch Box, Libbey	10 - 45
L9011	Pinocchio Lunch Pail, Libbey	10 - 55
L9025	Mickey/Donald, Liberty	8 - 35
L9026	Davy Crockett, Liberty	8 - 35
L9030	Disney School Bus	5 - 20
L9031	Disney Fire Engine	5 - 25

Aladdin Industries has participated in virtually every major Disney promotional event since 1956 with a metal or plastic lunch kit.

L9035	Aladdin Lunch Kits, 50's	8 - 50

L9100	Aladdin Lunch Kits, 60's	5 - 30
L9150	Aladdin Lunch Kits, 70's	3 - 15
L9200	Aladdin Lunch Kits, 80's	2 - 10

M3200 MATCHES AND MATCH SAFES

There were two enameled match safe designs in the early 30's. Matchbooks from the studio commissary, the China Relief, and the Pepsi-Cola WWII insignia series offer examples from the late 30's and 40's. The vast majority of matchbooks have been generated by theme park events, shops, restaurants, and hotels. It is an area of Disneyana that offers a wide variety of graphics for little or no cost to theme park visitors.

M3203	Three Little Pigs Match Safe, orange or green enamel	25 - 65
M3204	Mickey/Minnie Match Safe	30 - 85
M3206	Studio Commissary, each	5 - 15
M3210	China Relief	5 - 15
M3220	Disneyland 50's or 60's	2 - 6
M3240	Disneyland 70's or 80's	1 - 2
M3250	Walt Disney World or EPCOT	.10 - 1
M3260	Tokyo Disneyland	1 - 2

M3900 MERCHANDISE CATALOGS

Kay Kamen initially went to work as Roy and Walt Disney's special representative for character merchandising. Building on the United Artists exhibitors campaign book of 1932 Kamen did a series of special Christmas promotion books. When sub-licensing contracts with Borgfeldt and Levy ran out (see The Disney Time Line) Kamen became sole character licensing agent and issued the first full merchandise catalog in 1934. The other issues were 1935, 1936-37, 1938-39, 1940-41, 1947-48 and 1949-50. Following Kamen's death, the company reclaimed all merchandising rights and issued catalogs on a different basis.

In 1950-51 a pocket folder with insert pages was used. A newspaper format was adopted in 1952 and two thin books were done in 1953. Promotion was done on a film-by-film basis until 1970. Walt Disney Distributing Co. was formed in 1971 and operated until 1977. They issued one catalog, portfolios of catalog pages and then loose-leaf catalogs. Magic Kingdom Club and theme park mail order catalogs are condensed, but provide some reference.

Catalogs from Kay Kamen and the Disney Merchandise Licensing Division provided a great deal of the reference for Tomart's Disneyana series. Several other types of merchandise catalogs and listings have been published by Disney. These include licensee lists, the Disney Family Gift Catalogs being issued by the Mail Order Division and Merchandise

185

Catalogs being prepared by the theme parks.

M3901	United Artists Campaign Book	300 - 600
M3902	Christmas Promotion Books	100 - 350
M3909	Envelopes for Kay Kamen Catalogs	20 - 50
M3910	Merchandise Catalogs, Kamen	175 - 600
M3919	Reproduction of 1935 & 1938 Catalogs	10 - 20
M3920	Merchandise Division Catalogs	45 - 125
M3955	Licensee Lists, each	2 - 15
M3970	Walt Disney Distributing Co. Catalogs	20 - 50
M3980	Family Gift Catalogs or Theme Park Merchandise Catalogs	1 - 5
M3990	Theme Park Mail Order Catalogs, each	1 - 5

M4500 MICKEY MOUSE CLUBS

The first Mickey Mouse Club was created in Sept 1929 by Harry W. Woodin, manager of the Fox Dome Theater in Ocean Park, CA. He later joined the Disney organization to create clubs in theaters across the nation. A typical club meeting was held at noon on Saturday before the matinee. There was a club meeting with merchant tie-ins, contests, prizes, and giveaways. Officers received special badges and conducted meetings. They changed every 8 weeks. Theaters paid Disney only $25 plus supplies. They received a General Campaign book, Club song sheets, officer badges, etc. The club drummed home good behavior, got kids involved with theaters and merchants, didn't cost much and was a huge success. At its peak in 1932 the national Mickey Mouse Club had over a million members from over 800 theaters, each with memberships in the 1,000 to 5,000 range. The idea grew so fast the club operations became difficult to handle and it was decided to let the clubs die a natural death. It took till the 1950's in one Florida theater. The second Mickey Mouse Club was the ABC television version. It first aired Oct 3, 1955 and became a national phenomenon. It was syndicated in the early 60's. SFM Entertainment acquired the rights to re-syndicate the black and white TV episodes in the mid-70's. The success they enjoyed led to the creation of the New Mickey Mouse Club in Jan 1977 after a "nation-wide" talent search. The show didn't click and was cancelled in its second season. The logos of the second and third clubs are similar. In some cases the 50's logo was used on 70's merchandise. The earliest design has a large "M" around Mickey's head and the word "Mouseketeers." The 3rd club had open face, bold letters spelling out the words "Mickey Mouse Club." Listed at this classification are club promotion items, membership cards and a few items that fit in. Toys, magazines, pinback buttons, etc. are found at other classifications. The 4th Club was introduced in 1989. This time the shows were produced at the company's new Florida studios for The Disney Channel.

First Mickey Mouse Club -- Movie Theaters 1929-35

M4501	General Campaign Manual	100 - 250
M4502	Membership Application	2 - 8
M4503	Membership Card	10 - 30
M4504	Birthday Card Postcard, sent by theaters	10 - 35
M4505	Promotional Banners or Supplies	95 - 500
M4506	Reproductions of M4505 Signs	2 - 10
M4515	Newsletters, each	40 - 80

ABC Television Mickey Mouse Club 1955-59 and reruns

M4600	Membership Application or Card	2 - 10
M4601	Membership Card/Certificate Mailer	5 - 25
M4625	Mouseketeer Cast Photo Album	8 - 20

Regular licensees such as Whitman, Aladdin (lunch boxes) and a few others supported the 3rd Club, but the program didn't attract viewer interest and failed to provide the impact needed for more extensive merchandising. Items produced aren't very collectible as they were sold by the pound at deep discount prices when the show was cancelled.

M4900 MICKEY MOUSE CLUB MAGAZINES AND ANNUALS

The official Mickey Mouse Club magazine was issued quarterly before it became a bi-monthly publication in Dec 1956. Seven issues were titled *Walt Disney's Mickey Mouse Club Magazine* before the name was shortened to *Walt Disney's Magazine*. The last six issues were smaller. Ads show many Mickey Mouse Club toys and premiums. Annuals reprint selected features from earlier magazines.

M4901	Volume 1 -- Number 1, Winter 1956	15 - 50
M4902	Volume 1 -- Number 2, Spring 1956	15 - 45
M4903	Volume 1 -- Number 3, Summer 1956	12 - 40
M4904	Volume 1 -- Number 4, Fall 1956	12 - 40
M4905	Volume 2 -- Number 1, December 1956	8 - 30
M4906	Volume 2 -- Number 2 through Volume 2 -- Number 6, each	5 - 20
M4913	Volume 3 -- Number 1 through Volume 3 -- Number 6, each	5 - 10
M4919	Volume 4 -- Number 1 through Volume 4 -- Number 6, Oct 1959, each	5 - 10
M4926	Annual #1	15 - 30
M4927	Annual #2	10 - 20

M5400 MICKEY MOUSE MAGAZINES

The first published *Mickey Mouse Magazine* (9 issues) -- Vol 1, No 1 (Jan 33) thru Vol 1, No 9 (Sept 33) -- was distributed through theaters

and department stores. A new series beginning Nov 33 was part of Kay Kamen's dairy campaign. There were 24 giveaway issues -- two volumes of 12 each
-- ending with the Oct 35 publication. The second style *Mickey Mouse Magazine* was published by Hal Horne, Inc. (NYC). They sold on newsstands for 10¢ each (except #1 and Dec 36 Christmas issues which sold for 25¢ each). The initial Summer issue (released May 1935) and the eight following were produced by Hal Horne (monthly except Jan 36 -- no issue). Kay Kamen took over after the June 36 number and managed the magazine through its conversion to *Walt Disney's Comics and Stories* in Oct 1940. The magazine changed sizes three times -- after the 1st, 2nd and Aug 1939 issue. The newsstand version had great art and many ads for early Disneyana.

M5401	First Series, Jan-Sept 1933, each	35 - 125
M5410	Dairy Series # 1, Nov 1933	40 - 100
M5411	Dairy # 2, Dec 1933	35 - 85
M5412	Dairy #'s 3 - 12, Jan 34 - Oct 34, each	15 - 50
M5422	Dairy #'s 13 - 24, Nov 34 - Oct 35, each	10 - 40
M5435	Newsstand #1, Summer (May) 1935	130 - 375
M5436	Newsstand #2, Oct 1935	100 - 275
M5437	Newsstand #3, Nov 35 - #9, June 36, each	75 - 175
M5444	Newsstand #10, July 36 - #61, Sept 40, each	25 - 100

M6200 MILK BOTTLES AND COLLARS

Owens-Illinois Pacific Coast Co. (San Francisco) was licensed to produce "glass containers" for 1936-37. The Owens-Illinois Can Company (Toledo, OH) took over for the years 1938-41. Pint, half-pint, and quart bottles were produced featuring the main cartoon characters and those from Snow White, Ferdinand the Bull, and Pinocchio. Nearly 40 different regular and creamer designs are known. Images on the bottles can be silk screened or a colored glass transfer.

The Wolf Envelope Co. (Cleveland, OH) and Neber-Whitehead & Co (St. Louis) were the major producers of paper advertising collars. These slipped over the neck of the bottle most often to advertise character glass tumblers packed with cottage cheese or sour cream.

M6300 MIRRORS

Theodore Diamond introduced a classic series of Mickey Mouse mirrors in 1936. Galax Minor Company was licensed for 1938-39 and there have been many producers of theme park merchandise.

M6310	Theodore Diamond, 3 designs, each	200 - 500
M6315	Galax Mirrors, each	25 - 100
M6335	Mirrors, 50's and later, each	25 - 85

M6500 MODEL KITS

Revell, a leading name in model airplane and car kits, and other manufacturers have produced some unusual Disney model kits over the years. These are all figural when constructed, but the most collectible are unassembled kits in the original boxes.

M6525	Perri the Squirrel	25 - 65
M6527	Tomorrowland Rocket	75 - 150
M6528	Peter Pan's Pirate Ship, from Disneyland,	
	3 versions	18 - 75
M6550	The Robin Hood Characters, 5	10 - 25
M6551	The Royal Coach, Elephant & Prince John	10 - 25

Pirates of the Caribbean "Zap-action" models (MPC)

M6555	Ghosts of the Treasure Guard	10 - 20
M6556	Dead Men Tell No Tales	10 - 20
M6557	Dead Man's Raft	10 - 20
M6558	Hoist High the Jolly Roger	10 - 20
M6559	Condemned to Chains Forever	12 - 25
M6560	Fate of the Mutineers	10 - 20
M6561	Freed in the Nick of Time	12 - 25

M7000 MOVIE STILLS

Movie stills are created for publicity purposes. Older ones were displayed in theaters as well. The size is normally 8" x 10". Older stills that came from studio still books had cloth backs and a binding tab. Stills are abundant for features and newer shorts. Most are black and white, but there were some early tinted stills and colored ones are routine for post-50's films. Value 2 - 5 each. Older cartoon stills are rarer, but are easily reproduced. Repros are usually seen in the 1 - 2 range. This has tended to keep values down. The value of tinted and rarer cartoon stills must be judged on an individual basis.

Also see L5000 LOBBY CARDS

N2500 NATIONAL PORCELAIN COMPANY

The National Porcelain Company, Inc. (Trenton, NJ) was a licensee from 1939-42. The 2-1/2" and 3-1/4" figures were produced in white, pastel green or tan. Only the Pinocchio figures are known to the author. They are Pinocchio, Jiminy Cricket, Geppetto, Figaro, Cleo, Honest John, Gideon and a donkey. Value 15 - 50 each.

N6500 NODDERS

A nodder is a figure with its head balanced on a wire axis, hinge or spring. Tilting the head in one direction, then releasing, triggers a nodding or bouncing head action.

N6505	Mickey, celluloid	800 - 1,800
N6510	Donald, celluloid	500 - 1,400
N6530	Mickey, plastic, Irwin	25 - 60
N6531	Donald, plastic, Irwin	25 - 60
	Alice in Wonderland figures, Tweedledee, Tweedledum, or the Queen of Hearts, each	See Goebel
N6575	Mickey, Donald or Pluto, papier mache, Brechner, each	10 - 30
N6580	Mickey or Goofy Walt Disney World Souvenir	2 - 12

O5000 ORIGINAL COMIC ART

Black and white art for comic books, newspaper daily and Sunday strips, plus art done for non-film promotional or licensee purposes has been sold over the years. A run of the mill daily strip may bring as little as 25 - 100 whereas a Sunday or comic book page by a collected artist may command several hundred. Comic art, in general, has never reached the level of animation drawings and cels. Original work of Carl Barks and Floyd Gottfredson are the lone exceptions. Here again is an area where each individual piece must be judged on its own merit. Signed Barks and Gottfredson art can command several hundred to several thousand dollars depending on the subject matter.

O8000 OSWALD THE LUCKY RABBIT

Oswald the Lucky Rabbit was a character developed by the Disney Studio in 1927. His first film released was *Trolley Troubles*. In all, 26 titles were done by Disney before the copyright owner "hired" most of Walt's animators and went into production for himself. As a result of this crisis Mickey Mouse was created.

Oswald the Lucky Rabbit was the first Disney character merchandised on consumer products and thus played a historic role in Disneyana. There is, however, a complicating factor. Oswald merchandise was sold for many years after he ceased to be a Disney character. An Oswald comic was published until 1962. To further complicate matters, both the Disney and non-Disney films were distributed by Universal, the name in which all early Oswald character merchandise was copyrighted.

The Disney Oswald had longer, floppier ears than his successor, who was more generally known as Oswald the Rabbit. The positively identified Disney Oswald merchandise includes a pinback button, candy wrapper and display sign, celluloid figure and a stencil set. Merchandise known to exist, but uncertain to be Disney connected, includes a Fisher-Price pop-up puppet, stuffed Oswald, and mechanical Oswald walking doll.

O8001	Stencil Set, Universal Toy & Novelty Co.	100 - 250
O8002	Pinback Button, Philadelphia Badge Co.	85 - 275

O8005	Candy Wrapper, Vogan Candy Corp.	?
O8006	Candy Display Sign, Vogan Candy Corp.	?
O8010	Crib Toy Celluloid Figure	145 - 400

P0400 PAINT BOXES AND SETS

There is overlap between paint, crayon and drawing sets. Products listed here are ones where paints of some type were the dominant factor -- metal box of water colors, water color paint sets, paint by numbers, magic water paints, etc. Marks Brothers first produced such sets in 1934. Transogram has probably been the largest producer over the years. Page of London water color sets are widely distributed in the U.S.; imported by F. J. Stanton Co., Inc. (NYC).

P0415	Mickey Mouse Paint Set, Marks Brothers #204	145 - 350
P0416	Mickey Mouse Paint Set, Marks Bros. #206	95 - 200
P0417	Mickey Mouse Easel Paint Set, Marks Bros. # 254	125 - 250
P0420	Donald Duck Paint Set, 1936, Whitman	75 - 150
P0425	Walt Disney Character Paint Set, Standard Toykraft	50 - 100
P0430	Pinocchio Color Box, 1940, Transogram	15 - 40
P0435	Mickey Mouse Paint Box, Transogram	10 - 30
P0436	Donald Duck Paint Box, Transogram, 8 colors	10 - 30
P0437	Donald Duck Paint Box, Transogram, 21 colors	15 - 45
P0440	Donald Duck Paint Sets, Transogram, in paperboard boxes, 3 sizes	15 - 60
P0450	Mickey Mouse Paint Box, space suits, Transogram	5 - 20
P0460	MagicPaint Pictures, paint with water, Artcraft, each	5 - 15
P0468	Disneyland Color by Number Oil Set	15 - 40
P0490	Spray & Play Air Brush Set, Ideal	4 - 15
P0500	The Jungle Book Paint & Crayon Set, Hasbro	4 - 15
P0505	Mickey Mouse Club Oil Painting by Numbers	10 - 28

Page sets vary dramatically from 8 color to 48 color and perhaps larger. There are no U.S. records to show the years of license, but paint boxes found indicate a period of at least 20 years.

| P0540 | Larger and older Page sets w/40's style drawings | 2 - 25 |
| P0542 | Smaller Page sets (listing Strauss as the distributor) | 3 - 9 |

Marks Brothers Company of Boston was also one of the earliest manufacturers of Mickey Mouse paint, drawing and craft sets.

P1000 PENCIL SHARPENERS

There were early Mickey and long billed Donald celluloid figural pencil sharpeners. The most common early Disney pencil sharpeners are products of Plastic Novelties (1935-55). They were produced in several different series sold over the years. See descriptions below. Condition of decal is the principal factor in determining value of Plastic Novelties sharpeners. There have been wall or desk mount units and many other "pencil box" sharpeners as well.

P1005	Mickey, figural celluloid	120 - 350
P1008	Donald, figural celluloid	120 - 350
P1020	Plastic Novelties, figural sharpeners, Mickey, Donald, Snow White, Dopey, Pinocchio, Lampwick, Jiminy Cricket, Figaro, Ferdinand or Dumbo, each	15 - 35
P1030	Plastic Novelties, rectangular sharpeners, same characters as P1020, each	8 - 24
P1040	Plastic Novelties, circular sharpeners, same characters as P1020, each	8 - 24
P1050	Same as 1040, but w/brass frame, each	8 - 28
P1060	Plastic Novelties, circular w/convoluted edge, Mickey, Pluto, Goofy, Donald, Joe Carioca, Panchito, Brer Rabbit, Brer Fox, Brer Bear, Casey, Peter (& the Wolf), Hep Cats and Baby Hep, each	5 - 20

P1300 PENS, PENCILS AND PENCIL BOXES

The Inkograph Company made pens and mechanical pencils starting in 1935 after the Joseph Dixon Crucible Co. set the pace with a broad line of pencil boxes beginning in 1931. Dixon also made wooden and color pencils for "sketching, drawing, and map coloring." Ingersoll sold ballpoint pens with watches and rings in the late 40's. Hasbro was the major maker in the late 40's and 50's and from 1968-84.

P1305	Mickey Ink-D-Cator Fountain Pen, Inkograph	35 - 95
P1306	Mickey Fountain Pen, Inkograph, not made w/Mickey's head like others	90 - 185
P1307	Inkograph Mechanical Pencil	35 - 95
P1308	Inkograph Pen Holder & Point, fountain feed pen	50 - 100
P1310	Dixon Wooden Lead Pencil	25 - 65
P1311	Dixon Colored Pencil Set, 2 versions, each	25 - 75
P1325	Ingersoll Mickey or Donald Ballpoint Pen	15 - 50
P1400	Dixon Pencil Box, no drawer	15 - 35
P1401	Dixon Pencil Box, one drawer	15 - 50
P1402	Dixon Pencil Box, two drawers	20 - 85

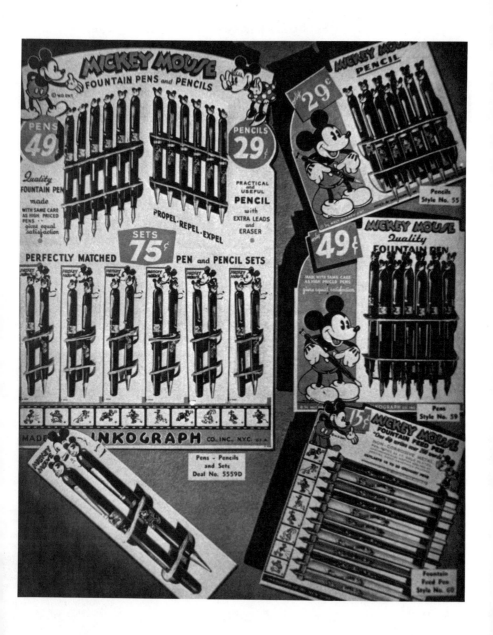

The Mickey Mouse Inkograph fountain pen and pencil set originally cost 49¢ for the pen, 29¢ for the pencil or 75¢ for the set. Today the pair could cost $150 easily. The pen used with a desk inkwell is even rarer.

P1405	Dixon Figural Pencil Box, Mickey (2 versions), Minnie or Red Riding Hood, each	70 - 200
P1410	Dixon Military Insignia Pencil Box	15 - 55
P1411	Mickey Ballpoint Pin, Charmore	35 - 100
P1420	Hasbro Pencil Boxes, each	8 - 25
P1421	Hasbro Pencils, each	3 - 10
P1445	Empire Pencil Boxes or Cases	5 - 20
P1449	Hasbro Pencil Boxes since 1968	3 - 10

P1850 PIE BIRD

There was one Donald Duck ceramic pie bird known to the author. It doesn't appear in any merchandise catalogs. The piece has been seen nationwide and has been traced to a variety of estates. There are no marks to indicate the manufacturer, only the incised words "Donald Duck" on one side and "© Walt Disney" on the other. There have been many pie birds made for use in venting steam from the bottom of the pie during baking. Have seen this item priced from 50 - 200.

P1900 PINBACK BUTTONS, PINS AND BADGES

In 1927 Oswald the Lucky Rabbit was the first Disney character to appear on a pinback button. The first Mickey Mouse Club got off the ground in 1929 and was the subject of pinback buttons for several years. Newspaper comic strips, advertising sponsor buttons and Kay Kamen giveaways were the prime subjects during the 30's. There were a number of buttons and tabs for the TV Mickey Mouse Club in the 50's and a few theme park buttons in the 50's-60's period. By the time Walt Disney productions celebrated its 50th year in 1973, pinback buttons had become a part of every promotion -- Grad Nite, America on Parade, Mickey and Donald's 50th birthdays, The Disney Channel, new theme parks, park souvenir buttons, film buttons and the much sought after Walt Disney World Costuming Division buttons. Collecting post 1980 buttons has achieved mania proportions on the West Coast. Prices commanded by authentic buttons only a few days old have been totally out of line with the eventual selling price when availability became known. The Disney organization has obliged collectors by issuing buttons in conjunction with every occasion, film, or promotional event.

The button boom has been around since 1984, but has failed to have much impact beyond the immediate areas of Disneyland and Walt Disney World, the source of most buttons and pins. Collecting is further complicated by the number of reproductions and "privately" minted products. There are probably as many phoneys as there are Disney made or authorized pinback subjects. Some are quite interesting and worth having. This book attempts to stick with official issues, but it is hard to nail down certain pieces. Some legit issues are only used for a day or two.

There is a tendency toward more cloisonne pins. A series of such pins

Joseph Dixon Crucible Co. was the leading producer of Disney
school supplies during the 30s. The company produced a wide
variety of regular No. 2 and colored pencils, pencil holders and fully
stocked pencil cases. The company also made composition books,
tablets, erasers and other school supplies.

196

was used for the Gift Giver Extraordinaire promotion at Disneyland in 1986, and continued as part of the 15th Anniversary celebration at Walt Disney World in 1987. Coca-Cola also issued 60 different pins for the 15th year event. The promotion was offered to Coke bottlers nationwide, but was used differently in virtually every market where it appeared. Many bottlers did not participate. The pins were framed in sets of 60 for major Coke customers and for sale to Disney employees. They also came in a set of 24, three different sets of 8, and individually. Anniversary celebrations, theme park events and attraction openings, ice shows, and character buttons for general retail sales are found at this classification. Buttons for EPCOT and Tokyo Disneyland are found at those classifications.

P1901	Oswald the Lucky Rabbit	25 - 250
P1902	Mickey Mouse Club Button	25 - 85
P1903	Sears Mickey Mouse Club Buttons	25 - 80
P1904	Theater Mickey Mouse Club Buttons, same as P1902, but w/names of various theaters, each	25 - 85
P1905	Mickey Mouse Club Button, waving	20 - 60
P1906	Same as P1905, but w/theater name, each	20 - 65
P1915	Mickey Mouse Club Button, orange	25 - 75
P1920	Fox Broadway MMC Button	35 - 140
P1921	Fox California MMC Button	35 - 140
P1922	Mickey Mouse Club, black on white	20 - 60
P1925	RKO Kiddie Kartoon Klub	50 - 150
P1928	Mickey Mouse Club Officer Buttons	Value ?
P1934	Western Theater Mickey Mouse	35 - 75
P1935	St. Louis Button, Mickey Mouse, 3/4"	25 - 65
P1936	Mickey Mouse, standing	25 - 60
P1937	Mickey Mouse, walking & waving	25 - 80
P1938	Mickey Mouse, full color	40 - 75
P1940	Police Department, Fire Department or Aviation Department Badges, each	75 - 275
P1945	Milk Promotion Buttons, cloth w/brass rim, Mickey (crude), Mickey (classic) different color backgrounds, Big Bad Wolf, Three Little Pigs, each	12 - 45
P1955	"For Better Health" Milk Button	60 - 250
P1956	Southern Dairies Ice Cream	50 - 200
P1960	Spingle-Bell-Chicko-K	30 - 120
P1963	Mickey Mouse Shoes Tab, Truitt Bros.	15 - 50
P1964	Mickey Mouse Undies	20 - 45
P1965	Mickey Mouse Hose (watch for pinkish repros)	20 - 60
P1966	Penney's Back-to-School	15 - 35
P1967	Mickey Mouse Sneakers, Converse	50 - 375
P1968	Mickey Mouse Soap	85 - 400

P1969	Mickey Mouse Emerson Radio	25 - 75
P1974	7th Birthday of Mickey Mouse, 1395	30 - 100
P1975	Mickey Santa at Merkel's Toyland	75 - 300
P1976	Donald Duck Jackets	60 - 200
P1977	Donald Duck Jellies	75 - 270
P1978	Icy-Frost Twins or Ducky Dubble Member	30 - 100
P1980	Mickey Mouse Good Teeth	30 - 90
P1981	Mickey on Skis, gloves & mittens	70 - 200
P1985	Mickey Mouse Globe Trotter & Follow My Adventures Buttons, various bakeries & dairies, each	20 - 45
P2010	Los Angeles Evening Herald & Express	30 - 75
P2011	Sunday Herald & Examiner	30 - 120
P2012	Mickey Mouse Evening Ledger Comics	40 - 130
P2013	Minnie Mouse Evening Ledger Comics	50 - 150
P2014	The Atlanta Georgian's Silver Anniversary, 1937	50 - 150
P2015	Boston Sunday Advertiser	30 - 70
P2025	Mickey Mouse, Kay Kamen	25 - 80
P2026	Who's Afraid of the Big Bad Wolf, Kamen	25 - 85
P2027	Donald Duck Wanna Fight, Kamen	100 - 400
P2029	Snow White & Seven Dwarfs, bakery & grocer employee	125 - 450
P2030	Snow White Jingle Club Member	10 - 35
P2031	Snow White Jingle Club, 3"	25 - 100
P2040	Walt Disney's Pinocchio	15 - 40
P2041	Pinocchio Good Teeth	85 - 225
P2042	Pinocchio on Victor Records	100 - 275
P2043	Jiminy Cricket Official Conscience Medal	25 - 60
P2045	Jiminy Cricket United Way	15 - 35
P2046	Jiminy Cricket "I'm No Fool About Safety" Tab	8 - 24
P2050	Dumbo D-X	20 - 40
P2051	Dumbo Song Book	40 - 125
P2064	Mickey Mouse Camera Tab	25 - 60
P2065	Donald Duck Peanut Butter, 10 different -- Mickey, Minnie, Donald, Pluto, Snow White, Dopey, Pinocchio, Dumbo, Bambi and Joe Carioca, each	15 - 45
P2080	Pinocchio at Hudson's	15 - 40
P2081	Peter Pan at Hudson's	15 - 40
P2082	Peter Pan, 3"	5 - 15
P2085	Mickey Mouse Club, KVOS-TV 12	8 - 24
P2086	TV Mickey Mouse Club Buttons & Tabs	2 - 12
P2106	Disneyland Flasher Badges, Mickey, Goofy or Tinker Bell, each	4 - 12
P2109	Donald Disneyland Flasher Badge	15 - 55

P2110	Fess Parker as Davy Crockett	10 - 30
P2114	Zorro, 7up, 1957	4 - 10
P2115	Disneyland Yearly Anniversary Pins , plastic or metal, 1956 to date, each	8 - 65
P2118	Cheerios Wiggle Picture Badge & 6 inserts, 1957	20 - 80
P2125	Golden Horseshoe Revue, 2 versions, each	15 - 40
P2128	Mod Mickey or Minnie's Yoo Hoo, unauthorized, each	5 - 20
P2135	Character Theme Park Souvenir 3" Buttons, each	2 - 6
P2140	Walt Disney World Yearly Anniversary Pins, plastic, 1972 to date, each	10 - 55
P2145	Disney On Parade	5 - 15
P2150	50 Happy Years, 1973	8 - 25
P2151	Fort Wilderness Campground Resort w/Mickey, 1973	5 - 15
P2152	I've Had Fun With Music	5 - 15
P2155	I Like Walt Disney Music	5 - 15
P2156	Liberty Square Medal	15 - 35
P2160	'74 Grad Nite	10 - 30
P2165	Disneyland Grad Nite '75, '76, ,'77 or '78, each	8 - 25
P2166	Snow White or any of the Seven Dwarfs, Benay-Albee, 1975, each	2 - 7
P2168	Mother's Day, 1978	5 - 15
P2169	Orange Bird Tab	3 - 9
P2170	Disneyland Grad Nite '79, '80, '81 or '82, each	5 - 12
P2174	Disneyland Grad Nite '83, '84, '85, '86, '87 or '88, each	5 - 10
P2175	Walt Disney World Grad Nite '84, '85, '86, '87 or '88, each	1 - 5
P2176	Grad Nite Pooh Bear Buttons	2 - 10
P2177	Mickey's Christmas Carol	4 - 10
P2178	Mickey Christmas Card Parade	10 - 35
P2185	Cervantes Ties	5 - 15
P2190	"A Different Glass Each Week"	5 - 15
P2191	Fl-84 Rangers	4 - 12
P2192	Music Festival Program Cloisonne Pin	3 - 9
P2193	Videopolis	1 - 2
P2203	Cake Happy Birthday Mickey, Disneyland or Walt Disney World, each	3 - 10
P2204	I Grew Up On Mickey Mouse	1 - 3
P2205	Mickey's Month, 1982 or '84, each	3 - 8
P2206	Happy Birthday Mickey -- phone	.50 - 1
P2208	Happy Birthday Mickey -- 56 years	5 - 15

P2225	Disneyland 100 Millions Smiles	10 - 25
P2226	Disneyland 200 Million	5 - 10
P2229	Disneyland 25, silver, 1"	4 - 10
P2230	Disneyland 25 Mickey or Minnie, each	5 - 15
P2232	I Was There -- Disneyland 25th Birthday Party	5 - 10
P2233	I'm 25 Today Too!	5 - 15
P2234	Family Reunions are all RELATIVE	5 - 15
P2235	Disneyland's My Home Town	5 - 15
P2237	Disneyland Anniversary Buttons, 26th thru 29th year, each	5 - 10
P2241	Disneyland 30th Year Souvenir Button	1 - 3
P2242	30th -- And the Best Has Yet To Come, 2" or 3", each	3 - 6
P2243	30th -- I'm A Winner	3 - 10
P2244	30th -- Cast Member	5 - 15
P2245	30th -- Official Birthday Party Button	4 - 8
P2246	30th -- Sword in the Stone	5 - 20
P2247	30th -- Parade Button	15 - 35
P2248	30th -- Cloisonne Lapel Button	5 - 15
P2249	30th -- Hollywood Bowl Concert	5 - 10
P2250	I Won a GM Car!	20 - 40
P2251	1986 Sword in the Stone	8 - 25
P2255	Disneyland 31st Birthday	2 - 6
P2260	Los Angeles Children's Museum Salutes Disneyland's 30th Anniversary Summer '85	5 - 10
P2261	Skyfest	2 - 8
P2262	Happy New Year, '86, Disneyland or WDW	2 - 5

Cloisonne Pins from the Gift Giver Extraordinaire (P2265-P2276)

P2265	Disneyland -- Mickey beating a drum	5 - 10
P2266	Main Street -- Mickey on an old time bike	2 - 4
P2267	Adventureland -- Goofy in safari hat	2 - 4
P2268	New Orleans Square -- Brer Fox playing a sax	5 - 25
P2269	New Orleans Square -- Mickey playing trumpet, gold lettering	5 - 15
P2270	Same as P2269, but w/red lettering	2 - 4
P2271	Bear Country -- Bear w/guitar	2 - 5
P2272	Frontierland -- Peg Leg Pete, w/pointed star	5 - 15
P2273	Same as P2272, but w/gold dots on star points to blunt them	2 - 4
P2274	Fantasyland -- Mickey as Sorcerer's Apprentice	2 - 4
P2275	Tomorrowland Donald, in space suit w/sharp point on lighting bolt	5 - 15
P2276	Same as P2275, but w/point of lighting bolt rounded	2 - 4
P2279	Tencennial Press Club	5 - 25
P2280	Walt Disney World -- Tencennial	2 - 5

P2281	Disneyland Circus Fantasy '86 or '87	3 - 10
P2284	Don't be late ... Disneyland	5 - 25
P2286	Disneyland '86 Spring or Fall Tour, each	5 - 25
P2287	Win A Car -- Grads Have More Fun At Grad Nite '86	3 - 15
P2288	Hands Across America -- May 25, 1986	5 - 28
P2290	Totally Minnie	2 - 4
P2291	Sword in the Stone	5 - 20
P2292	Captain EO, purple background	1 - 2
P2293	Captain EO, black background	1 - 2
P2294	Captain EO, cloisonne, black background, Disneyland or WDW	2 - 5
P2296	Captain EO, cloisonne, gold background	5 - 10
P2298	Captain EO, silver, hologram	5 - 20
P2300	Disneyland Comes to the Fashion Show Mall	5 - 15
P2301	Ogden Welcomes Mickey & Friends	5 - 15
P2302	Korean Festival Disneyland	5 - 15
P2305	Star Tours Aviator Wings, press giveaway	15 - 55
P2306	Star Tours, black background	2 - 10
P2307	Star Tours, logo only	2 - 5
P2308	Star Tours, w/Droids	2 - 5
P2309	Star Tours Logo Cloisonne	2 - 6
P2312	Grad Nite Cloisonne	3 - 9
P2313	Disneyland Hotel Fantasia Shop Mickey	2 - 8
P2314	Disneyland Hotel	1 - 2
P2400	Space Mountain, 4 versions, each	5 - 15
P2405	Big Thunder Mountain Railroad	5 - 15
P2410	New Fantasyland -- May 1983	8 - 20
P2411	New Fantasyland -- Sword in the Stone	10 - 25
P2412	Tour World Showcase Time Trial	3 - 15
P2413	Walt Disney World 14th Birthday	5 - 15
P2414	Sport Goofy Trophy, TWA, Adidas, Coca-Cola	5 - 15
P2416	WDW Golf Classic, 11 different	?
P2425	King Kamehameha is Koming	5 - 15
P2427	Crockett's Tavern	5 - 15
P2430	15 Years Happy Birthday Walt Disney World, light-up	8 - 25
P2431	15 Years Walt Disney World	2 - 8
P2432	15 Years Happy Birthday Cloisonne Pin	2 - 4
P2435	Liberty Square Cloisonne Pin	2 - 6
P2438	WDW Golf Classic Cloisonne Pin	5 - 20
P2439	Team Mickey's Athletic Club	1 - 4
P2442	Happy 53rd Birthday, Donald, June 9, 1987	5 - 20
P2443	Empress Lilly 10th Anniversary	5 - 12
P2444	The American Adventure Costume Pin	10 - 40

Costuming Division Cast Buttons Walt Disney World (P2450-P2455)

P2450	Maleficent -- You Want What Size!	100 - 200
P2451	Happiness is a New Spring Wardrobe!	100 - 200
P2452	Smile! It's a Nice Reflection on You!, round	95 - 200
P2453	When You're Lookin' Good, We're Lookin' Good!	85 - 175
P2454	Wardrobe Gets My Vote!	80 - 175
P2455	Snow White -- Season's Greetings, 3D Button	45 - 100
P2470	Salute to Georgia, Walt Disney World	5 - 15
P2471	Salute to Canada, Walt Disney World	5 - 15
P2475	WED and MAPO OPEN HOUSE	5 - 15
P2476	Festival Japan '80, '81 or '82, each	4 - 10
P2480	Festival Mexico	4 - 10
P2481	Saludos Puerto Rico, Walt Disney World	4 - 10
P2490	Thumper Easter Egg Hunt, 1983 or 1984	4 - 8
P2500	Disneyland Celebrates America	4 - 8
P2501	Sport Goofy	3 - 7
P2502	Sport Goofy,set of 4	10 - 25
P2509	The Sport Goofy Trophy -- Walt Disney World	10 - 20
P2510	20th Anniversary of New York World's Fair	5 - 10
P2515	Disneyland Convention Button, round or oval	3 - 8
P2516	Disneyland Convention Name Tag	2 - 4
P2517	"Ask Me About" Buttons, in shape of Mickey Mouse (many different) promoting events or features of Walt Disney World, each	5 - 20
P2540	Tour World Showcase Time Trials	3 - 10
P2575	Aspen Fantasia -- Winterland '83	5 - 10
P2576	Walt Disney Home Video	5 - 15
P2577	Find It in the Library Media Center	4 - 10
P2578	Mickey's Knights	2 - 6
P2579	Magic Kingdom Club, Donald	5 - 15
P2580	Magic Kingdom Club, Mickey	4 - 12
P2582	Donald -- I'm a Fire Safety Expert	5 - 15
P2584	Disney Summer Magic '85 -- Radio City	5 - 15
P2586	Goebel New Arrivals	2 - 6
P2587	I Love Walt Disney Films	2 - 6
P2588	WED/MAPO Halloween '85	10 - 25
P2589	Imagineering Open House 1986	5 - 15
P2590	One Stop Poster "Wise crack" series, each	1 - 2
P2595	One Stop Poster Made in USA series, each	1 - 2
P2600	Pinocchio, 3", movie	2 - 5
P2601	The Black Hole, 3", movie	2 - 6
P2602	The Black Hole, 2-1/2", movie flasher	5 - 10
P2604	101 Dalmatians, 3", movie	2 - 6
P2606	The Fox and the Hound, 3", movie	2 - 6
P2607	TRON, set of 3 movie, set	5 - 15

P2612	Splash, movie logo on blue	2 - 6
P2613	Splash, 2 scene flasher, movie	5 - 10
P2614	The Disney Store, opening Glendale store	2 - 6
P2615	Return to Oz, movie	2 - 6
P2616	The Black Cauldron, movie	2 - 6
P2618	Mickey Mouse Club	1 - 5
P2620	Snow White 50th Anniversary, 3"	5 - 10
P2621	Snow White and the Seven Dwarf set, wood grain borders, 8, each	2 - 6
P2622	McDonald's Employee Snow White Poster	5 - 12
P2624	6" Character Buttons, 15, each	2 - 3
P2700	The Disney Channel, Mickey satellite	15 - 60
P2701	The Disney Channel, blue logo on gray, 3", 2 versions, each	2 - 6
P2703	Same as P2701, only smaller, each	2 - 6
P2705	Mickey Launch Button, April 18, 1983	10 - 25
P2706	Same as P2705, only no date	10 - 25
P2707	Same as P2705, only plastic, not used	?
P2712	DTV, 2 versions, each	2 - 8
P2715	The Disney Channel, cloisonne pins, logo, Mickey cowboy, Mickey director, Tinker Bell, Donald 50th Birthday or Pinocchio, each	5 - 15
P2820	Disney Fan Buttons, 5 different, each	2 - 6
P2821	Same series as P2820, only Christmas, 3 different, each	2 - 5
P2822	Fan Buttons, plastic, 6 different, each	2 - 4
P2825	Ice Show Buttons, 14 different, each	2 - 4
P2830	Ice Show '86-87, Sport Goofy (2), Wuzzles, Gummi Bears w/ribbons, Snow White, each	2 - 5
P2850	Mouse Club Convention Buttons	5 - 15
P2854	5th Mouse Club Convention Pins -- Limited editions of 600 w/gold bags & 400 w/brown bags over Mickey's head -- 2 designs. Sold at 1987 convention.	5 - 10
P2870	Sam the Olympic Eagle Buttons, 24 different, each	2 - 5
P2890	WDW Village 10th Anniversary, 3/22/85	2 - 6
P2895	Howard Eldon, Ltd.	3 - 8
P2896	Fresno Bee, Disney designed	3 - 8
P2898	Golf Bag Tags, Walt Disney World, each	5 - 15

P3400 PLATES -- COLLECTORS'

Miniature collectors' plates have been available since the early days of Disneyland. Christmas plates began in 1973 and now different editions are marketed each year by Schmid, Grolier, and Disney theme parks. Grolier followed Schmid's Christmas series in 1979. Disney's own series premiered in 1985. Schmid closed the first Christmas series with 1982 and started over again in 1983. The Grolier plate illustrations are the same as used on each year's bisque figurine, bell and ornament. The Disney series is based on corporate Christmas cards issued 50 years previous. A 500 plate limited edition press giveaway was produced for the premiere of the "A Very Merry Christmas Parade" in 1977. Mother's Day plates began in 1974 and Schmid has produced many other special edition plates. Disney has produced special plates for America on Parade, Mickey's 50th Birthday, Mickey's Greatest Moments, the Disney Classics, Donald's 50th Birthday and other theme park merchandised subjects.

P3405	Fantasia, 50's Disneyland souvenir	50 - 200
P3420	Disneyland or Walt Disney World Miniatures,	
	each	1 - 8

Schmid Collector's Plates (P3450-P3555)

P3450	Christmas '73 "Sleigh Ride"	50 - 200
P3451	Christmas '74 "Decorating the Tree"	40 - 100
P3452	Christmas '75 "Caroling"	15 - 50
P3453	Christmas '76 "Building a Snowman"	10 - 30
P3454	Christmas '77 "Down the Chimney"	5 - 25
P3455	Christmas '78 "Night Before Christmas"	5 - 25
P3456	Christmas '79 "Santa Surprise"	5 - 20
P3457	Christmas '80 "Sleigh Ride"	5 - 20
P3458	Christmas '81 "Happy Holidays"	5 - 20
P3459	Christmas '82 "Winter Games"	5 - 20
P3460	Christmas '83 "Sneak Preview"	5 - 25
P3461	Christmas '84 "Command Performance"	3 - 15
P3500	Mother's Day '74 "Flowers for Mother"	8 - 40
P3501	Mother's Day '75 "Snow White and the Seven	
	Dwarfs"	10 - 30
P3502	Mother's Day '76 "Minnie Mouse and Friends"	8 - 20
P3503	Mother's Day '77 "Pluto's Pals"	5 - 15
P3504	Mother's Day '78 "Flowers for Bambi"	4 - 12
P3505	Mother's Day '79 "Happy Feet"	4 - 12
P3506	Mother's Day '80	4 - 12
P3507	Mother's Day '81	4 - 12
P3508	Mother's Day '82	4 - 12
P3524	Bi-Centennial	10 - 40
P3525	Valentine's Day '79 "Hands and Hearts"	8 - 20
P3526	Valentine's Day '80	5 - 15
P3527	Valentine's Day '81	5 - 15
P3530	Zodiac Plates, 12, each	5 - 20
P3542	Pinocchio 100th Birthday	4 - 12
P3546	Alice in Wonderland	4 - 12
P3547	Happy Birthday Pluto	4 - 12
P3550	Goofy Golden Jubilee	5 - 20

P3555   Four Seasons of Love Collection, 4, each   4 - 12

Grolier Disney Collection merchandise is sold entirely by mail. Limited edition pieces remain available until sold out. Resale on the collector's market is insufficient to base value ranges at this time. Items produced are listed for collector information only.

P3575   Grolier Christmas '79   --
P3576   Grolier Christmas '80   --
P3577   Grolier Christmas '81 (Only 6,000 produced vs.
        15,000 other years)   --
P3578   Grolier Christmas '82   --
P3579   Grolier Christmas '83   --
P3580   Grolier Christmas '84   --
P3581   Grolier Christmas '85   --
P3581B Grolier Christmas '85, bisque   --
P3600   Grolier Snow White Collection, 6   --
P3601   Grolier Pinocchio Collection, 6   --
P3603   Grolier Bambi Collection   --
P3604   Grolier Cinderella Collection   --
P3606   Grolier Peter Pan Collection   --
P3607   Grolier Miniature Alphabet Series, 26   --
P3690   Snow White and the Seven Dwarfs, Goebel,
        1980   8 - 45
P3695   Wedgewood Sleeping Beauty Castle (Disneyland)
        or Cinderella Castle (Walt Disney World), 1st
        edition, theme park series, each   15 - 50
P3696   2nd edition, Snow White and Dopey in
        Fantasyland   10 - 35
P3697   3rd edition, Mickey and Minnie on Main Street   10 - 30
P3710A Very Merry Christmas Parade, limited to 500   150 - 350
P3711   Mickey's Greatest Moments series, 6 -- Plane
        Crazy, Steamboat Willie, Brave Little Tailor,
        Sorcerer's Apprentice, Nifty Fifties (mistake
        plate), Nifty Nineties, or Mickey Mouse Club,
        each   4 - 15
P3712   Mickey and Minnie in Concert, bisque   8 - 20
P3713   Disney Classic Series, 6 -- Snow White,
        Pinocchio, Dumbo, Bambi, Alice in Wonderland
        or Peter Pan, each   4 - 12
P3720   Disneyland, 25 Years   15 - 40
P3721   Walt Disney World, 10 Years   20 - 40
P3722   Disneyland, 30 Years   20 - 40
P3723   Mickey's Greatest Moments Miniatures, each   2 - 5
P3724   Walt Disney World 15th Anniversary   20 - 35
P3725   Figment from EPCOT Center   4 - 10
P3726   Walt Disney (first sold at $75 then reduced
        to $35)   Still available

P3727	Disney Classics, Lady and the Tramp, 101 Dalmatians, The Aristocats, The Jungle Book, The Rescuers & The Fox and the Hound, each	4 - 8
P3730	Miniature Pewter Mickey Film Plates, theme park souvenirs, each	2 - 6
P3739	Snow White 50th Anniversary	15 - 30
P3740	Christmas Plates, 1985, 86 or 87, each	10 - 25

P3810 PLAYSETS

Playsets combine many small pieces into a themed set designed to result in hours of imaginary play. Items such as doctor's or nurse's kits, rocketship control panel, a science laboratory or entire miniature environments related to Disney characters, films or other productions. Plastic was the major factor in making playsets available in the early 50's. Playsets are usually found in various states of completeness.

P3855	Doctor, Nurse, or Make-up Kits, Hassenfeld, 1951-55, each	10 - 40
P3820	Davy Crockett Adventure Playset, Gardner	30 - 75
P3821	Davy Crockett at the Alamo, Marx	100 - 175
P3825	Walt Disney Television Playhouse, Marx	200 - 475
P3827	Professor Wonderful's Wonder-Lab, Gilbert	15 - 40
P3828	Disneyland Rocketship Control Board, Baxter	10 - 45
P3838	Sword in the Stone, Marx	125 - 250
P3850	Fold-away Disney Playworld, Intoport	10 - 40
P3851	Doctor or Nurse Kit, Carolina	5 - 20
P3853	Robin Hood Adventure, Kusan	15 - 30
P3854	Mickey Mouse Airlines, Kusan	15 - 30
P3855	Disneyland Castle, Kusan	15 - 30

P6200 POSTERS -- MOVIE

Movie poster collecting is a specialized area of Disneyana. Many collectors are oriented more toward films than toys or memorabilia. Posters were generic at first, but most animated shorts and all features had special posters. Features often had 2 or 3 different posters with each release until the 50's. Each feature film re-release has traditionally had new graphic treatments on all advertising materials, including posters in 2 or 3 sizes. As production of new animated short cartoons ground to a halt in the early 50's, generic posters were revived by RKO. This has been an active area of Disneyana interest and there is some affinity with cel collecting. Movie posters for animated feature films since 1955 sell for 25 - 80 each depending on the film. Live action film posters are valued at 5 - 20. The first generic Mickey Mouse posters (1928-30) bring several thousand dollars. Cartoon short posters from the 30's and 40's start at around 500 and are often priced from 1000 to 5000. Original release pre-war animated feature posters are the most valuable and are sometime priced above 1000. The other animated feature posters from 1945-52 can command 200 - 800 or more in Hollywood. Serigraph 8-color silkscreen reproductions of Disney cartoon short posters are produced by Circle Fine Art Corp. (Chicago) for sale at art galleries and theme park Disneyana shops for 20 each. Springbok division of Hallmark Cards, Inc. reproduced the Two-Gun Mickey poster around 1975, valued at 5 - 15.

P7250 PRINTING SETS

Fulton Specialty and Marks Bros. produced the first rubber stamp printing sets in 1933-34. Fulton continued till 1942 and produced many highly collectible sets. The George Borgfeldt Corp. was licensed for printing sets exclusively for 1949-50. Multi-Print of Milan, Italy made an exceptional series of printing sets on a foreign license in the 70's. These were imported and sold by major department stores and Disney theme parks.

P7255	Mickey Mouse Printing and Coloring Set, Marks Bros.	250 - 500
P7256	Mickey Mouse Print Shop, Fulton, 3 sizes	40 - 175
P7257	Mickey Mouse Picture Printing Set, Fulton, 3 sizes	100 - 250
P7258	Bad Wolf/3 Pig Artistamp Picture Set, Fulton, 2 sizes	85 - 200
P7259	Donald Duck Art Stamp Picture Set, Fulton, 3 sizes	45 - 150
P7260	Snow White and the Seven Dwarfs Art Stamp Picture Set, Fulton, 3 sizes	25 - 120
P7261	Pinocchio Art Stamp Picture Set, Fulton, large size	80 - 200
P7275	Sword in the Stone Printer Set, Colorforms	20 - 45
P7280	Italian Multi-Print Sets, 2 sizes, Snow White, Winnie the Pooh, Dumbo, The Jungle Book and Carousel (main characters), each	10 - 45
P7285	Mickey's Printing Set, Straco	2 - 6
P7286	Mickey Mouse Rubber Stamp Set	2 - 6

P7300 PRINTS -- ART AND FRAMED PICTURES

The first framed pictures, Reliance by Bates Art Industries, were reproduced "cel like" on the back of glass. Courvoisier Galleries released the first art prints in 1940. Henry A. Citroen sold an extensive line of luminous pictures in white frames from 1944-46. The New York Graphic Society followed with prints from *Snow White* and *Bambi* in 1947. Disneyland marketing department artist Charles Boyer did a Walt

Disney take-off painting of Norman Rockwell's "Self Portrait" for the cover of an employee magazine in 1978. Many recipients requested frameable copies, and Boyer did a signed/numbered edition of 1,800. These were sold to employees for $4 each. Its success led to many other Boyer limited edition lithographs. Another Rainbow has produced a series of Carl Barks signed lithographs. Disney artist John Hench signed a 750 limited edition of the 25th and 50th Mickey Mouse birthday paintings he created. An employee drawing was held for the right to purchase a portfolio of the two prints for $50 each in 1978. Hench also did a 60th birthday painting that was sold to employees in 1988 for $10.

P7305	Reliance Glass Pictures, Three Little Pigs, Red Riding Hood & Big Bad Wolf (8 different) or Mickey, Minnie, Horace & Clarabelle (? different), Bates Art Industries, each	35 - 250

Courvoisier Galleries (P7310-P7317)
(came framed or in mailing envelope)

P7310	Pinocchio, w/Jiminy Cricket on foot	20 - 60
P7311	Geppetto, creating Pinocchio	20 - 60
P7312	Pinocchio, Jiminy Cricket, Figaro & Cleo	20 - 60
P7313	Pinocchio, Geppetto and Figaro, on raft	20 - 60
P7314	Mickey & Pluto	25 - 70
P7315	Donald & Better Self	25 - 70
P7316	Bunnies, in bed	20 - 40
P7317	Snow White w/Forest Animals	25 - 50
P7320	Citroen Luminous Pictures -- Mickey; Minnie; Donald; Goofy; Donald & Mickey; Bambi; Thumper; Dopey; Thumper & girlfriend; Snow White & forest animals; Doc & Grumpy; Wynken, Blynken & Nod; and others, each	5 - 15
P7324	New York Graphic Society, Snow White (2 different) or Bambi (2 different), each	10 - 35
P7349	"Self Portrait", Boyer	300 - 700
P7350	"Partners", Boyer	125 - 350
P7351	"The Band", Boyer	35 - 80
P7352	"New Fantasyland", Boyer	45 - 100
P7353	"Tokyo Disneyland", Boyer	50 - 180
P7354	"Disneyland 30th Year", Boyer	15 - 30
F2110	John Hench Mickey 50th Birthday Portfolio	500 - 1,000

P7800 PULL TOYS

Many manufacturers made push or pull toys as part of their line. Several specialized. The leading producers of classic Disney pull toys were Fisher-Price (see F7600) and the N. N. Hill Brass Company. Other manufacturers are noted with item.

N. N. Hill Brass Co. was licensed to produce Disney character pull toys, telephones and banks from 1933 to 1942. A bell ringer was a major feature on all N. N. Hill Brass toys.

P7808	Mickey Wood Car, Borgfeldt	350 - 850
P7815	Pluto, pulling twin revolving Mickeys,1934	225 - 500
P7816	Revolving Mickeys, 4 wheels,1934	150 - 425
P7817	Mickey, 2 wheels, w/handle,1934	150 - 375
P7820	Tanglefoot, pulling large fixed Mickey,1935	110 - 250
P7821	Tanglefoot, pulling small revolving Mickey, 1935	145 - 300
P7822	Horace, pulling 2 bell wheels,1935	115 - 225
P7823	Long bill Donald, pulling 2 bell wheels,1935	135 - 300
P7825	Mickey Wheelbarrow, Toy Kraft, 1935	115 - 225
P7826	Mickey Kite Pull Cart, w/handle,1935	95 - 200
P7827	Running Mickey Wagon, Toy Kraft, 1935	105 - 225
P7828	Mickey Horse Cart, Toy Kraft, 1935	115 - 245
P7829	Mickey House or Tent Wagon, Toy Kraft, 1935	95 - 200
P7835	Mickey or Donald, 2 wheels w/revolving Mickeys,1936	165 - 375
P7837	Horace or Pluto, pulling small Mickey, 2 wheels, 1936	150 - 325
P7839	Medium bill Donald, 2 bell wheels,1936	150 - 300
P7840	Mickey's Head or Full Figure Hobby Horses, 1936	95 - 200
P7842	Mickey on Belly, 4 wheels, pull toy,1936	80 - 140
P7943	Bank Pull Toy	80 - 140
P7944	Large Mickey, on 2 bell wheels	90 - 195
P7950	Toy Kraft Mickey or Donald, 2 horse cart, 1936	115 - 225
P7952	Wagon, Mickey w/Pluto or w/elephant, 1936	115 - 225
P7960	Large Elmer Elephant, 2 wheels,1938	75 - 155
P7961	2 Ice Skating Mickeys, on bell cart,1938	125 - 260
P7962	Donald, pulling 2 revolving Donalds, 2 wheels, 1938	130 - 260
P7963	Snow White & Prince, on bell cart,1938	130 - 275
P7964	Seven Dwarfs, pulling Snow White,1938	130 - 275
P7965	Dopey & Doc, pulling Snow White,1938	130 - 275
P7966	Seven Dwarfs, pulling 2 wheels bell ringer, 1938	130 - 275
P7967	Dopey & Doc, pulling cart w/small Snow White & Dopey atop 2 wheels, bell ringer, 1938	125 - 255
P7970	Ferdinand & Matador Bell Cart,1940	120 - 275
P7971	Pinocchio & Figaro,1940	125 - 255
P7972	Pinocchio & Cleo,1940	80 - 185
P7985	Lady and the Tramp Pull Toy, Eldon, 1955	25 - 55
P7986	Strombeck-Becker Wooden Pull Toys, each	20 - 45

R1000 RADIOS, PHONOGRAPHS AND TAPE PLAYERS

Emerson radios and phonographs were produced from 1933-40. RCA made Alice in Wonderland, Snow White and Mickey Mouse 45 rpm players in 1951. GE clock radios give the initial appearance of being made in the 50's, but records indicate they were produced in 1970-71. There may be other collectible radios or phonographs. Noblitt-Sparks is recorded as a late 30's maker; however, the author hasn't run across one yet. This company may also have been making the Emerson products. Radios since the 60's are much smaller and have been produced largely of plastic in Japan and Taiwan. A reproduction of the Emerson Mickey "carved" radio was made in the 70's.

R1005	Mickey, brown "carved" radio, 1933-39	650 - 1,400
R1006	Mickey, white or black radio w/aluminum plate over grill cloth	500 - 1,100
R1008	Mickey Phonograph, Emerson	850 - 1,700
R1010	Snow White Radio, white, box shaped	350 - 800
R1011	Snow White Radio, brown, rectangular, "carved" figures	450 - 900
R1025	Alice in Wonderland Phonograph, 45 rpm, RCA	65 - 145
R1026	Snow White Phonograph, 45 rpm, RCA	65 - 145
R1027	Mickey Mouse Phonograph, 45 rpm, RCA	65 - 145
R1028	Donald Duck Electric Phonograph, Spears	150 - 300
R1040	Show 'n Tell Phonograph/Viewers, GE	10 - 30
R1045	Mickey, Donald or Pooh Phonographs, character arms	25 - 55
R1055	Character Transistor Radios, each	5 - 35

R3000 RECORDS -- PHONOGRAPH

Disney recorded music, film soundtracks, storyteller, educational, theme park and other recordings is a vast collecting area into itself. There are picture discs, albums with "pop-up" scenes, albums combined with books and all the different formats of recording technology from 78 rpm to digital compact disc. There isn't space to list each individual recording, but the material presented is representative. Recording and distribution rights were sold to major labels until 1955. The Walt Disney Music Co. began in 1956 to produce soundtracks and records from the Mickey Mouse Club, releasing titles on Disneyland and Buena Vista Record labels. Exceptions have been promotional albums such as "The Greatest Hits of Walt Disney" and the fantastic Ovation Records Anthology of Classic Disney Art and Music, including a 52-page book on the history of Disney recorded music. (A 7" promotional preview of this album was made). Records have also been packaged with dolls, watches and other products. The *Pete's Dragon* soundtrack was released on Capitol

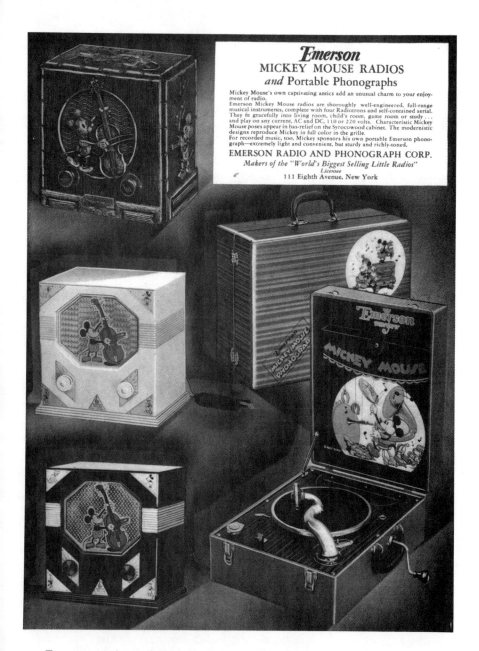

Emerson radio and phonographs in 1934. The company would later produce Snow White radios in two different versions.

Records. Other more recent titles have been released on outside labels.

R3005	Mickey Mouse or Silly Symphony	
	Picture Discs, 1933-38, RCA, each	300 - 650

RCA Victor Record Albums (R3013-R3049)

R3013	Snow White, three 78 rpm records in	
	illustrated envelope	40 - 110
R3014	Pinocchio, illustrated 78 rpm album	25 - 75
R3016	Pinocchio, 78 rpm	15 - 65
R3020	Dumbo, 78 rpm	15 - 65
R3022	Bambi	10 - 40
R3023	Bambi, 78 rpm	4 - 24
R3024	Snow White, 78 rpm in hardcover album	15 - 65
R3025	Snow White, 45 rpm, different cover	5 - 25
R3026	Peter and the Wolf, 78 rpm	3 - 20
R3028	Three Little Pigs	6 - 30
R3030	Johnny Appleseed, 78 or 45 rpm, Decca	6 - 30
R3031	Ichabod and Mr. Toad, 78 or 45 rpm, Decca	3 - 20
R3032	Johnny Appleseed	6 - 30
R3033	Pecos Bill	6 - 35
R3035	Cinderella, 78 or 45 rpm	5 - 25
R3036	Treasure Island	5 - 18
R3039	Peter Pan	5 - 25
R3045	Lady and the Tramp	5 - 20
R3048	20,000 Leagues Under the Sea, 78 or 45 rpm	5 - 25
R3049	Davy Crockett	5 - 18

Capitol Records (R3050-R3069)

R3050	Mickey and the Beanstalk, 78 rpm	10 - 25
R3052	Uncle Remus, 78 rpm	8 - 20
R3055	Little Toot, 78 rpm	6 - 18
R3056	The Sorcerer's Apprentice, 78 rpm	10 - 25
R3057	Three Little Pigs, 78 rpm	10 - 25
R3058	Mickey Mouse Birthday Party, 78 rpm	10 - 25
R3060	So Dear To My Heart, 78 rpm	8 - 25
R3062	Robin Hood, 78 rpm	8 - 20
R3065	Lady and the Tramp, 45 rpm	5 - 15
R3069	Davy Crockett	5 - 18

Decca Records (R3070-R3079)

R3070	Snow White, 78, 45, or 33-1/3 rpm	10 - 25
R3071	Pinocchio, 78 rpm	10 - 40
R3072	Saludos Amigos, 78 rpm	8 - 25
R3073	The Three Caballeros, 78 rpm	8 - 20
R3076	Songs from Lady and the Tramp, 33-1/3 rpm	8 - 20
R3079	Davy Crockett	6 - 18
R3080	Alice in Wonderland Premium Records, 2	5 - 20

RCA Victor (1933-55), Capitol (1947-55) and Decca (1947-55) were the major licensees to produce Disney music on phonograph records prior to Walt Disneys formation of his own Disneyland label in 1955.

Columbia Records (R3085-R3099)

R3085	The Whale Who Wanted to Sing at the Met, 78 rpm	7-40
R3088	Bongo, 78 rpm	5-25
R3094	Ballad of Davy Crockett, 78 rpm	5-15
R3095	Davy Crockett, Indian Fighter, 45 rpm	5-15
R3096	Davy Crockett Goes to Congress, 45 rpm	5-15
R3097	Davy Crockett at the Alamo, 45 rpm	5-15
R3099	Songs from the Magic Kingdom	3-12

R3200 Little Golden Records

Little Golden Records were produced by Simon & Schuster in 78 and eventually 45 rpm. Some 33-1/3 speed records were produced in the 50's, but none Disney. Disney titles began with a separate numbering system, but were merged with the regular one somewhere between 100-200, even though the identifying "D" was retained as a preface. Mitch Miller and the Sandpipers were the talent on the first 100 or so records. Only records in jackets are considered collectible. Most sell in the 2 - 7 range.

R3200	Theme park series	5-20
R3200	Sleeping Beauty titles	4-10

R3500 Disneyland and Buena Vista Records, Disney's own labels, produced a small number of 78 rpm records. They did a number of 45 rpm singles, but put a major production effort in the long playing 33-1/3 speed which was fast becoming the standard of children's records when the label went into business in the mid-50's. Ads in the 1956 issues of *Mickey Mouse Club* magazine show attractively designed covers for the major Disney classics featuring the original film soundtracks. Soon thereafter, the record and book versions appeared. Around 1963 a short series of "Pop-up Panorama Storybook" albums were issued. New 45 rpm storybook albums came along in the 60's and have become a regular product category for each new film. Cassette tape versions of the same storybooks were added in the 70's. Compact discs were first issued in 1987.

R3501	Mickey Mouse Club, 45 or 78 rpm, each	2 - 8
R3502	Bongo, 78 rpm, Disneyland	3-10
R3525	Annette titles	8-25
R3549	Wheaties Mickey Mouse Club Package Back Records, each	3-10
	Disneyland On Records (see D5140)	
R3550	33-1/3 LP Albums, 50's	4-15
R3551	Other 45 rpm records or albums, 50's or 60's	3-10
R3552	Adventures In Music series, 45 rpm, RCA	4 - 12
R3556	Fantasia, 3 record set w/program, Disneyland, 1st ed.	25 - 75
R3556A	VISTA, 2nd ed.	15 - 35

R3557	Small World, theme song N.Y. World's Fair souvenir record in mailer, 1963	5-15
R3600	LP Albums, 60's (except pop-up)	2-8
R3620	Pop-up albums w/4 complete pop-up scenes. Titles nclude Dumbo and Sword in the Stone, each	20-50
R3700	LP Albums, 70's and 80's	2-5
R3701	45 rpm records or albums, 70's or 80's	2-4

The Disney labels have also released albums for many of their theme park attractions. Most remain available, but some were withdrawn due to attraction or other changes.

R3900	Theme park albums in current release	1-7
R3950	Withdrawn theme park records	8-25
R4000	Premium albums	2-15
R4050	Special anniversary albums	2-15
R4075	Picture discs, Snow White, Pinocchio, Cinderella, Lady and the Tramp, Mary Poppins, Fox and the Hound, or Mickey's Christmas Carol, each	1-6
R4090	America on Parade	15-50
R4091	Walt Disney World Electric Water Pageant, 1973	10-35
R4092	Disney's Main Street Electrical Parade	1-3
R4093	A Musical Souvenir of Walt Disney World's Magic Kingdom	1-7
R4200	Ronco's The Greatest Hits of Walt Disney, w/uncut cutouts & song sheets	12-35
R4200	Record & jacket only	2-8
R4210	The Magical Music of Walt Disney w/book	20-50
R4211	Promotional sampler for R4210	2-10
R4215	Show 'n Tell Record & Filmstrip, GE, each	2-10
R4220	Fantasia, compact disc	5-25

R5000 RINGS

The earliest Mickey ring on record was made by Cohn & Rosenberger in 1931. Brier Mfg. distributed rings in the mid to late 30's. Ostby & Barton sterling silver rings were sold beginning in 1947 and also packaged with some Ingersoll watches of the same period. There have been a number of premium rings and the theme parks prompted a proliferation of souvenir rings.

R5005	Mickey, Cohn & Rosenberger	25-85
R5010	Mickey, Donald or Dopey, Brier	25-75
R5020	Mickey, Donald, Pluto, Bongo or Bambi, pastel or uminous background, oval or square, each	10-35
R5025	Donald Duck "Living Toy" Ring, Kellogg's PEP, 1949	15-40

R5026	Weather Bird Pinocchio Ring	20 - 100
R5032	Hardy Boys Ring, International Shoe, premium	10 - 25
R5038	Snow White Ring, 1972	2 - 10
R5041	Sword in the Stone Ring, hard plastic	10 - 20
R5042	Sword in the Stone Ring, soft plastic	10 - 25
R5043	Sugar Jets, series of 8 character rings -- Mickey, Minnie, Donald, Pluto, Dumbo, Snow White, Pinocchio & Peter Pan, flexible plastic, each	10 - 25
R5051	Mickey Mouse Club, flexible plastic	6 - 18
R5100	Theme Park Character Souvenirs, cloisonne	1 - 10
R5101	Theme Parks Logo Souvenirs	1 - 8
R5102	Same as R5100 only silver	2 - 20
R5103	Character Ring, souvenir, metal	1 - 4
R5110	Sam the Olympic Eagle, plastic	1 - 2

Also see J2000 JEWELRY

R6000 ROCKING HORSES, BOUNCE, SPRING ACTION AND OTHER PLAY EQUIPMENT

The Mengel Co. created several different ways to rock and ride Mickey and Snow White. Pontiac Spring and Bumper Co. developed four different characters to bounce on. There were also Fantasia unicorns, Mickey seesaws, Mickey slides and other outdoor play equipment.

R6004	Mickey, large head hobby horse, Borgfeldt	260 - 700
R6005	Mickey, rocking horse, Mengel (A repro version is being sold by The Disney Stores)	250 - 500
R6006	Mickey, shoofly rocker, Mengel	300 - 600
R6007	Mickey, riding swing, Mengel	300 - 600
R6008	Mickey, folding 8' slide, Mengel	125 - 300
R6010	Spring Action Bounce Toy -- Mickey, Donald, Pluto or Dopey, Pontiac Spring	150 - 300
R6009	Mickey, riding scooter, Mengel	300 - 600
R6010	Donald, seesaw	150 - 300
R6017	Donald, shoofly rocker	125 - 275
R6018	Snow White and Prince, shoofly rocker	135 - 300
B6050	Fantasia Unicorn, outdoor bounce toy, 70's	10 - 50

R9000 RUGS, TAPESTRIES AND MATS

Mickey Mouse area rugs and tapestries have been made since 1935. If the piece is velvety, it is likely to be from the 30's. Beware of newer, yet dirty, carpets being sold as old. Character carpets, some marked "Made in Belgium", come as large as 6' x 9'. Most, however, are around 2-1/2' x 4'. They were imported by Quetta Carpet Ltd. There have been other area rug licensees for brief periods since 1971, which have

The Mickey Mouse rocking horse produced by the Mengel Company of St. Louis from 1935 to 1939 continues to be so popular it has been reproduced for sale at Disney theme park shops and the Disney Stores throughout the U.S. The modern quality of the new version makes it easy to spot.

produced inexpensive photo rugs. Value on the 30's velvet-like examples range from 75 - 350. Newer area rugs sell for 10 - 45. Photo rugs are seen in the 5 - 10 range.

S1000 SALT AND PEPPER SHAKERS

There were some 30's Mickey china salt and peppers made in Germany and Japan. Plastic Novelties was authorized to make them in 1935 and a J. L. Wright metal set -- Sneezy and Dopey -- was made in 1938. The largest producer was Leeds China. Goebel included a few sets in its line (see G5500). Dan Brechner made a number of sets and Disney theme parks have sold souvenir sets.

S1015	Mickey, bone china salt & pepper in holder	75 - 250
S1025	Sneezy/Dopey, pair, metal, J. L. Wright	20 - 60
S1040	Mickey/Minnie, Leeds	10 - 22
S1041	Donald/Donald, Leeds	8 - 20
S1042	Dumbo/Dumbo, 2-1/2", Leeds	8 - 20
S1043	Dumbo/Dumbo, 4", Leeds	15 - 30
S1044	Pluto/Pluto, Leeds	8 - 20
S1045	Thumper/Thumper, Leeds	8 - 20
S1060	Mickey/Mickey, Brechner	8 - 20
S1061	Donald/Donald, Brechner	5 - 15
S1062	Ludwig Von Drake/Donald, Brechner	8 - 22
S1063	Mickey/Minnie, on bench, Brechner	12 - 25
S1064	Snow White/Dopey, Enesco	15 - 35
S1075	Dwarf Heads	5 - 12
S1100	Mickey/Minnie Heads, glass jar	4 - 8
S1110	Mickey Salad Maker, ceramic pie-eyes	4 - 10

S1500 SAND BOX TOYS, SAND PAILS AND LITHO METAL SHOVELS

Ohio Art Company was the major producer of Disney lithographed material toys in the 30's. Sand pails, shovels, watering cans and sand sifters were made in a variety of sizes picturing Mickey, Minnie, Donald, Pluto, Three Little Pigs, Snow White and the Seven Dwarfs. Many Ohio Art pieces in the late 30's are dated. J. Chein & Co. made litho metal sand pails in the 50's and 60's. Eldon Mfg. Company made plastic sets starting in 1955. The slightest rust has dramatic negative impact on value.

Ohio Art Company (S1510-S1545)

S1510	Ohio Art Sand Sets, includes sprinkling can, small bucket & litho shovel w/Disney characters, plus sand mold & scoop, in box	200 - 500
S1511	Same as S1510, but no sprinkling can	175 - 425

S1512	Same as S1510, but includes sand elevator	260 - 650
S1513	Same as S1510, but includes sand sifter	210 - 500
S1520	Litho Shovels, single piece litho metal, 2 sizes	25 - 120
S1521	Litho Shovels, wooden handle	65 - 175
S1522	Litho Snow Shovels	155 - 325
S1525	Sand Pails, 3" to 3-1/2" tall, each	18 - 55
S1526	Sand Pails, 4" tall, each	30 - 75
S1527	Sand Pails, 5" tall, each	45 - 100
S1528	Sand Pails, 8" to 10", each	65 - 150
S1529	Sand Pails, 12" or more	150 - 350
S1535	Sand Sifter, 6" diameter	25 - 60
S1536	Sand Sifter, 7-1/2" diameter	25 - 55
S1540	Sprinkling Cans, 3" tall, each	25 - 60
S1541	Sprinkling Cans, 4" - 4-1/2" tall, each	30 - 85
S1542	Sprinkling Cans, 6" tall or larger	40 - 135
S1545	Sand Sifter Set, w/scoop & molds	65 - 145
S1650	Chein Sand Pails	10 - 35
S1700	Eldon Sand Mold Sets, each	5 - 18

S2000 SCHOOL SUPPLIES

Walt Disney once recalled the first time he was ever paid for the use of Mickey Mouse on merchandise. He was in New York, and an unknown man sought him out at his hotel and gave Walt $300 cash to use his characters on pencil tablets. The first actual licenses were issued to the Powers Paper Company and American Lithographic Co. in 1931. Disney characters have appeared on school supplies almost continuously ever since.

S2005	Powers Paper Binders, Composition Books, Tablets, Stationery & Drawing Tablets, copyright by Walt Disney, values vary widely depending on completeness, condition, amount of writing & graphics, each	25 - 100
S2060	Powers Paper, main characters, copyright Walt Disney Enterprises see S2005), each	15 - 85
S2090	Powers, Snow White characters (see S2005), each	15 - 65
S2112	Pinocchio character, each	10 - 45
S2120	Mickey Mouse Ice Cream Cone Ruler	20 - 70
S2122	Tablets, w/Walt Disney Comics and Stories cover art, each	10 - 30
S2128	Tablets, Win a Trip to Disneyland, each	8 - 20
S2130	Pencil Tablet, w/trading cards, each	8 - 20
S2131	Mickey Mouse Club Scribble Pads, each	5 - 10
S2133	Davy Crockett or Zorro, each	10 - 22

S2135	Tablets, Notebook Filler Paper, Folders or Book Covers, 60's, 70's or 80's, each	1 - 10
S2140	School Bags, 40's or 50's	5 - 20
S2141	School Bags, 60's, 70's or 80's	1 - 10

S2300 SCRAPBOOKS AND PHOTO ALBUMS

Krueger did early scrapbooks largely featuring tipped on plates. Whitman did a great Mickey/Minnie scrapbook in 1936, a Snow White version with the original movie poster art in 1938, and one from Pinocchio. There were a couple different Mickey Mouse Club scrapbook designs in 1956 and a 1977 version for the New Mickey Mouse Club. Photo albums were produced in the 40's in conjunction with the TV MMC. Theme parks produced a series of vinyl photo albums filled with photo scenes of each land.

S2303	Three Little Pigs Scrapbook	10 - 55
S2304	Three Little Pigs, Krueger	20 - 75
S2305	Mickey/Minnie	25 - 65
S2307	Snow White and the Seven Dwarfs	20 - 60
S2310	Pinocchio, Whitman #634	25 - 60
S2313	Comic Art Scrapbooks, each	8 - 20
S2315	Mickey Mouse Club Designs, 50's, #1863 & others	8 - 20
S2316	New Mickey Mouse Club, 1977	3 - 8
S2350	Photo Albums, General Products, each	2 - 8
S2365	Theme Park Photo Albums w/photos, each	2 - 8

S3000 EVAN K. SHAW COMPANY

Evan K. Shaw was the successor to or perhaps always owned the American Pottery Company. The company also purchased the Vernon Kiln Company or just some of its molds. Exactly how all this took place, or when, is the subject of conflicting data. Labeled pieces found indicate ceramic figures once sold as American Pottery were later advertised and marked "Shaw." The initial figures are listed at American Pottery (see A5000). The exclusively Shaw pieces seem to start with The Three Caballeros (1945-46) even though the record shows the license to be in the name of American Pottery Co. at 527 W. 7th Street, Los Angeles from 1943-50 and in the name of Evan K. Shaw at the same address for the years 1945-55. Lady and the Tramp figures were the last Disney ones produced by the company.

Shaw figures were also sold as Metlox Poppytrail Pottery. American Pottery was licensed two years before Shaw, and dual licenses existed for a few years in the 40's. The reason could be a company name change, Shaw was simply a distributor for several makers, a Shaw buy out of American, a separate business division, or perhaps another reason lost

221

in the records.

A record of the ceramic pieces sold by Shaw, however, is complete. In fact, the workshop inventory of Disney figures was stored when all licensing rights expired. This stock was sold in 1986 and made available to collectors. It included the miniature figures produced near the end of Shaw's license and rarely seen prior to this discovery. A very special "thank you" goes to Bob Molinari for help regarding American Pottery and Evan K. Shaw. Bob Molinari is the owner of Fantasies Come True, an exclusively Disneyana shop, 8012 Melrose Ave., Los Angeles, CA 90046. The code numbers have been revised in this section to reflect the additions and corrections made. High end prices are mainly obtainable on the West Coast where ceramic collecting is very popular and where earthquake damage has placed a premium on mint specimen originals with tags.

S3001	Snow White and the Seven Dwarfs, 5" to 8", set	500 - 1,200
S3002	Bambi or Faline (9 versions produced in two general sizes, approximately 7" and 10" -- see S3061 for miniatures and fourth size figures), -- large approximate 10", each	40 - 150
S3003	-- medium approximate 7", each	40 - 150
S3004	Thumper or Thumper's Girl Friend, large 4"	20 - 40
S3005	-- medium 2-1/2"	30 - 60
S3006	Flower, large 4"	20 - 45
S3007	Flower, medium 2-1/2"	20 - 45
S3008	Mickey or Minnie, 7"	60 - 150
S3009	-- often marked "Mexico", 4"	30 - 90
S3010	Donald, Jose or Panchito, each	75 - 200
S3014	Dumbo, standing or sitting up, each	40 - 120
S3015	Stork or Crow from Dumbo, 1946, each	50 - 155
S3016	Little Toot	200 - 400
S3017	Large Thumper Planter	100 - 250
S3018	Large Flower Planter	100 - 250
S3019	Pottie	400 - 1,500
S3020	Pinocchio or Jiminy Cricket, each	150 - 400
S3022	Figaro, 2 running, 1 seated, each	50 - 200
S3026	Pluto, 4 different poses, each	20 - 150
S3029	Small versions were made of many Dumbo, Three Caballeros, Bambi, Pinocchio and main character figures. Some are marked "Made in Mexico", some not. While more scarce, they lack color and detail. Some collectors feel they are worth more, others feel they are not as valuable as art. The buyer can be his own judge on these.	
S3030	Owl, 2-1/2"	50 - 150

S3032	Brer Rabbit Planter	100 - 400
S3033	Planters, Bambi, Thumper, or Flower, on log, each	75 - 250
S3034	Planters, Donald in boat or Pluto in doghouse, each	50 - 200
S3036	Large Bambi Planter	100 - 250
S3037	Planters, Donald beehive or Minnie w/buggy, each	50 - 200
S3039	Stag, Adult Bambi	90 - 500
S3040	Cinderella in rags	100 - 400
S3041	Cinderella or Prince, dressed for the ball, each	75 - 300
S3044	Bruno, sitting or prone (repainted from Pluto mold)	50 - 150
S3046	Gus or Jaq, each	35 - 125
S3048	Bluebirds, Mama Mouse or Baby Mouse, each	50 - 150
S3051	Alice In Wonderland	175 - 450
S3052	Tweedledee or Tweedledum, each	150 - 300
S3054	Walrus	150 - 300
S3055	March Hare, White Rabbit or Mad Hatter, each	75 - 200
S3058	Dormouse	50 - 150
S3059	*Fantasia* and *Dumbo* figures from Vernon Kilns molds were sold as American Pottery. The absence of Vernon Kilns marks and glaze on the bottom usually indicates an American Pottery piece. Elephants, hippos and Dumbo figures have been seen. They are currently selling for 20% to 40% below prices for Vernon Kilns (see V3000).	

Confusion exists between the medium Shaw figures identified in this volume as S3003, S3005, S3007, S3009, and the miniature series produced in 1955-56. These were made as Poppytrail Pottery figures by Metlox Manufacturing Company, Manhattan Beach, CA. The line was called "Walt Disney's World of Enchantment in Ceramics." In addition to the figures listed below, there was a fire plug and ceramic dog house. There were also a few figures produced in a fourth size between the medium and the miniatures.

S3060	Teapots, 4 different, each	100 - 285
S3061	Snow White and the Seven Dwarfs, set	200 - 600
S3062	Peter Pan, sitting or standing, each	50 - 150
S3064	Tinker Bell or Mermaid, each	50 - 300
S3066	Wendy, Michael, or Nana, each	40 - 100
S3069	Lady or Tramp, each	20 - 65
S3071	Peg	50 - 100
S3072	Jock, Trusty, Dachshund, or Limey, each	25 - 70
S3076	Si, Am or Scamp Pup, each	50 - 100
S3077	Pup#1, Pup#2 or Pup#3, each	20 - 60
S3078	Bambi, w/butterfly	30 - 90

S3079	Bambi, standing or prone, each	30 - 80
S3081	Thumper, Flower w/flower, or Flower w/o flower, each	20 - 50
S3084	Dumbo or Timothy, each	40 - 150
S3086	Pinocchio, Figaro, or Jiminy Cricket, each	40 - 150
S3089	Mickey or Donald, 2 sizes, each	30 - 80
S3092	Pluto	40 - 120
S3093	Huey, Louie or Dewey, each	20 - 40
S3096	Three Little Pigs, 3, each	20 - 40
S3099	Stormy, standing or prone, each	10 - 30

S3500 SILVER CUPS, PLATES, BOWLS, SILVERWARE AND FLATWARE

Silver products were popular baby gifts in the 30's. Mickey Mouse, Snow White and Pinocchio silverware was available from 1931-42 and in 1947-48. The Wm. Rogers spoon offered by *Post-O* cereal is one of the most common. Davy Crockett and Mickey Mouse Club cutlery sets were produced in the 50's. Mary Poppins pieces were made in the 60's and Disney main character flatware was introduced and has remained available 1970 to present. The 1931 William Rogers & Son (later International Silver Co.) eating utensils were sold with the Borgfeldt lollypop hands wooden Mickey Mouse figure. By 1934 the company was still using some Borgfeldt pieces (such as small wood Mickey in row boat), but had begun to create a special line of pull toys (perhaps made for them by N. N. Hill Brass Co.). Sets were also gift boxed for older children. Oneida and Silvercraft of California were other 40's makers. All pieces are silverplate.

1847 Rogers Bros. (William Rogers & Son, succeeded (by International Silver Co. S3505-S3599)

S3505	Borgfeldt Doll w/spoon & fork	800 - 1,800
S3510	Mickey Row Boat w/cup	700 - 1,500
S3511	Three Pigs items on wooden cut-outs, each	80 - 150
S3512	Cup or Eating Utensils on pull toy	200 - 800
S3540	Character Silver Sets, boxed	160 - 500
S3550	Mickey or Minnie Baby Spoon or Fork, Cereal Spoon, Child's Knife, Fork or Spoon, each	5 - 12
S3575	Three Pigs Baby Spoon or Fork, each	5 - 15
S3576	Three Pigs Youth Knife, Fork or Spoon, each	5 - 15
S3577	Mickey Napkin Rings, each	10 - 40
S3578	Mickey or other Character Silver Cup	40 - 110
S3580	Silver Porringer, Cereal Bowl or Baby Plate, each	35 - 90
S3590	Snow White Baby Spoon or Fork, each	8 - 20
S3591	Snow White Child's Knife, Fork or Spoon, each	8 - 20
S3599	Pinocchio Child's Knife, Fork or Spoon, each	5 - 15

International Silver Co., a licensee from 1931 to 1941, sold silver plated eating utensils, plates, bowls and cups. Deluxe packaging included a wood toy. The spoon is the most common piece. It was also available from Post-O cereal for 10¢ and one boxtop.

S3600	Snow White Silver Cup, Cartier	50 - 150
S3610	Silvercraft of California Sets	75 - 200
S3611	Cup, SOC	15 - 75
S3612	Fork, Spoon or Baby Spoon, SOC, each	5 - 15
S3613	Napkin Ring, SOC	10 - 25
S3625	Disneyland Souvenir Sugar Spoon ©1954	25 - 65
S3630	Davy Crockett Fork or Spoon, Flatware, each	5 - 15
S3635	Mickey Mouse Club Cutlery Set, Plastic Metal	10 - 25
S3636	Individual pieces from S3635, each	2 - 5
S3650	Mary Poppins Sugar Spoon, International Silver, 1964	5 - 15

S5000 SOAP AND BUBBLE BATH

Figural soap of Borgfeldt import was advertised in the Dec 1931 *Good Housekeeping* magazine. It was made by D. H. & Co. of London, England. There were two other soap licensees beginning in 1932, but the figural products of the Lightfoot Schultz Co. (1934-42) are the best known to collectors. The colorful boxes are also prized. Bar soap with transfer pictures was made by Pictorial Products, Inc. in 1934. Monogram added shampoo to bar soap sets in the 40's. Colgate-Palmolive-Peet Co. introduced Soaky soap bars in the 50's and liquid Soaky bubble bath in figural plastic containers around 1968.

S5003	Mickey or Minnie, figural, D. H. & Co., each	80 - 250
S5015	Mickey Mouse Toilet Soap, Pictorial Products	40 - 95

Lightfoot Schultz Co. (S5020-S5075)

S5020	Boxed Sets, Mickey, Donald, Pluto or Elmer Elephant in various combinations, each multi-character box	37 - 200
S5030	Same characters as S5020, individually boxed	30 - 85
S5031	Same as 5020, individual unboxed soap, each	10 - 45
S5045	Snow White and the Seven Dwarfs Set, in book box	65 - 150
S5052	Individual Boxed Soaps from S5045, each	10 - 25
S5053	Individual Unboxed Soaps from S5045	5 - 10
S5054	Same soap as in 5045, only 1968 reissue in clear plastic top package instead of book	25 - 75
S5060	Ferdinand the Bull, 2 versions, boxed	10 - 25
S5061	Same as 5060, unboxed	5 - 15
S5062	Pinocchio Book Boxed Set -- Pinocchio, Jiminy Cricket, Geppetto, Honest John, and Cleo, on rope, set	70 - 175
S5063	Same as S5062 in individual boxes, each	10 - 50
S5068	Large size Pinocchio or Jiminy Cricket, boxed	15 - 75
S5075	Same as S5062 or S5068, w/o boxes	5 - 18
S5080	Molded Full Figure, Kerk Guild, each	5 - 15

S5081	Same as S5080, boxed set, Donald, Mickey and Pluto	25 - 85
S5082	Bath Ball, Donald, Mickey or Pluto, head only, Kerk Guild, each	15 - 35
S5090	Monogram Character Soap Sets, 2 to 6 bars w/ or w/o shampoo, each set	15 - 60
S5091	Individual bars or bottles from S5090, each	4 - 12
S5094	Alice in Wonderland Soap Collection	25 - 75
S6020	Soaky Soap Bar Dispenser, Picture and Bars	10 - 40
S6021	Character Wrapper Bars, 6 different, each	3 - 9
S6030	Soaky Figural Bottles, Snow White, Dopey, Mickey, Donald, Bambi & others, each	5 - 15
S6045	Avon Mickey or Pluto, each	5 - 15
S6050	Theme Park Souvenir Soap Sets	5 - 20

S8500 STOVES

The Metal Ware Corp. (Two Rivers, WI) 1936-37 made Mickey Mouse stoves in two models. The regular toy store original sold for 50¢. The electrified version retailed for a dollar. Current values are 65 - 170.

T2000 TEA SETS

The first children's tea sets were china (see C6100 CHINAWARE). Ohio Art introduced litho tin sets in 1933. Beetleware (one of the first plastics) sets came along in 1934. Larger tea sets contained enough place setting for six or eight children (or dolls). Small metal sets included a teapot, cream, sugar, cups and saucers and serving tray. Large metal sets include extra place settings plus dinner plates and a larger tray.

Ohio Art Company (T2030-T2045) high value is

	for boxed sets	80 - 225
T2030	Mickey/Minnie Tea Set for 2	75 - 280
T2031	Mickey/Minnie Tea Set for 6	135 - 450
T2035	3 Pigs Tea Set for 2 or 3	125 - 330
T2036	3 Pigs Tea Set for 4 or 6	150 - 400
T2038	Snow White Tea Set for 2 or 3	125 - 350
T2039	Snow White Tea Set for 4 or 6	150 - 425
T2041	Donald/Clara Picnic Tea Set for 2 or 3	110 - 250
T2042	Donald/Clara Picnic Tea Set for 4 or 6	125 - 325
T2044	Pinocchio Tea Set for 2	155 - 375
T2045	Pinocchio Tea Set for 6	200 - 475
T2060	Mickey/Minnie/Donald/Pluto Tea Set, Chein, 1952	50 - 150
T2070	Snow White Plastic Pot & Cups, Chein, 1968	15 - 50
T2075	Mickey/Goofy/Pluto w/plastic Pot & Cups	15 - 50
T2080	Worcester Illustrated Plastic Sets, each	10 - 35

| T2090 | Alice In Wonderland, china, theme park souvenir, 80's | 5 - 8 |
| T2150 | Litho Tin English Sets sold in Canada, each | 25 - 75 |

T6400 TOOTHBRUSH HOLDERS

George Borgfeldt & Co. (NYC) 1931-41 was the importer of Japanese porcelain bisque toothbrush holders. There were single figure Mickey or Minnie figural designs for a single toothbrush and various characters or group designs to accommodate multiple toothbrushes. (see F6000 FIGURES -- PORCELAIN BISQUE for individual figural listing) Miller Studios, Inc. (New Philadelphia, OH) 1975-76 also produced toothbrush holders.

T6405	Mickey, w/hanky to Pluto's nose	225 - 500
T6406	Mickey & Minnie on couch, Pluto at feet	180 - 425
T6407	Mickey & Minnie standing	100 - 225
T6410	Three Pigs, Practical laying bricks	65 - 145
T6411	Three Pigs, at brick piano	65 - 145
T6412	Three Pigs Band	65 - 145
T6414	Long bill Donald, at water fountain or pillar	600 - 1,250
T6415	Long bill Donald, profile	200 - 450
T6416	Twin long bill Donalds	225 - 500
T6418	Donald, arms around Mickey & Minnie	150 - 395
T6420	Dumbo	200 - 450

T6500 TOPS

George Borgfeldt & Co. sold tin little musical tops made by Fritz Bueschel circa 1933-39. These came in several different sizes ranging from 6-1/2" to 14" in diameter. Chein made similar tops periodically in the 50's and 60's and from 1972-84. Kidco, Inc. made unique figural tops (1981-82).

T6510	Bueschel Spinning Toys, various sizes, each	75 - 225
T6530	Chein Musical Tops, various sizes, 50's, each	35 - 75
T6535	Chein Musical Tops, various sizes, 1968-84	15 - 55
T6560	Kidco Figural Tops, Mickey, Donald, Goofy or Pluto, each	10 - 25

T7900 TOYS -- BATTERY OPERATED MECHANICAL

The most collectible Disney battery operated toys are the largely metal ones made in this country and Japan from the 50's to mid-60's. This, unfortunately, is the period where available records are sparse. Since these are relatively recent toys many are still to be found. Batteries were

used in toys found at other classifications.
Also *see* T9000 TRAINS AND HANDCARS

T7950	Mickey Drummer	300 - 900
T7955	Mickey Magician, light-up eyes	450 - 1,200
T7956	Mickey or Donald, convertible cars, each	15 - 35
T7958	Pluto, lantern	50 - 200
T7960	Walking Pluto	75 - 250
T7965	Fire Truck w/Donald climbing ladder	800 - 2,000
T7970	Character Talking Bus	125 - 400
T7980	Mickey Drum Major, walker, plastic	20 - 50

T9000 TRAINS AND HANDCARS

The Lionel Corporation was on the brink of bankruptcy when it acquired a license to make Mickey/Minnie handcars on July 19, 1934; a little over two months after being placed in receivership. On the strength of the license, it was permitted to borrow additional short term money. The loan was paid back two months early and the company was returned to its management on Jan 21, 1935 after repaying all its creditors. The headline on the Kay Kamen ad reproducing some of the many newspaper articles on the subject read "Red to Black on a Handcar -- Mickey Mouse Pulls That Way". The Circus train and Santa handcar were added in 1935; other handcars in 1936. Louis Marx and Mar-Line made several trains and a Mickey/Donald handcar. Pride Lines, Ltd. hand crafted a streetcar for the tenth anniversary of Walt Disney World in 1981 and has originated and reproduced many rail pieces since.

Schuco made two models of the Disneyland-Alweg monorail system. The larger set featured a red monorail with two center cars. The smaller set had less "track" and a blue monorail train with only one center car. These sets, licensed and produced in Germany, were imported and sold at Disneyland in 1962-63 for around $30.

Pride Lines Ltd was licensed in 1982 to make character trolley cars and banks. They also reproduced Lionel handcars before creating handcars and trains of their own design..

The Lionel Corporation (T9005-T9020)

T9005	Mickey/Minnie Handcar, color variations exist	300 - 650
T9006	Santa/Mickey Handcar	400 - 950
T9007	Mickey Mouse Circus Train Set, complete in box	3,500 - 7,000
T9008	Same as 9007, but train only	1,000 - 2,500
T9010	Mickey Freight or Passenger Train, each	500 - 1,000
T9015	Donald/Pluto Handcar	400 - 850
T9020	Bi-Centennial Train, diesel locomotive, caboose & 13 character box cars	400 - 1,000
T9025	Mickey Mouse Meteor, Mar-Lines	200 - 650

T9027	Mickey Mouse Train on base, Marx	165 - 385
T9028	Disneyville Train Set w/cardboard accessories	150 - 350
	Mickey Mouse Express (see W7000 WIND-UP TOYS)	
T9030	Mickey/Donald Handcar & Base, Marx	250 - 850
T9031	Same as T9030, handcar only	45 - 135
T9045	Disneyland Train, metal locomotive, Marx	15 - 55
T9046	Casey Jr. Disneyland Train, plastic locomotive, Marx	10 - 45
T9047	Blue Monorail Set, Schuco	300 - 750
T9048	Red Monorail Set, Schuco	450 - 1,000

Pride Lines, Ltd. has produced many electric motorized streetcars and handcars. They are listed here with the original retail price for each unit.

T9081   Streetcars -- Walt Disney World Tencennial ($275), Minnie Mouse -- green ($275), Minnie Mouse -- ivory ($275), Mickey Mouse -- orange ($275), Donald's 50th Birthday -- limited to 1,000 ($350) and Disneyland 30th Year -- limited to 750 ($395).

T9095   Handcars -- Mickey/Minnie Lionel repro ($250), Donald/Pluto Lionel repro ($250), Mickey Fantasia ($250), Uncle Scrooge "Gold Mobile" ($250) and Donald's 50th Birthday -- limited to 1,000 ($295).

Commemorative pieces were limited and are no longer produced. Resale experience is limited, but the Tencennial Streetcar realized over twice its selling price at one auction.

V3000 VERNON KILNS CERAMICS

Vernon Potteries, Ltd. (LA) was a Disney licensee from Oct 10, 1940 to July 22, 1942 when they assigned all rights, inventory and molds to American Pottery Company. In that short time the company distinguished itself as a major contributor to Disneyana. Thirty-six of the forty-two figurines, all eight bowls and vases, plus all the company's Disney china patterns were based on *Fantasia*. The figures are museum quality art. Each figure has a number incised in the unglazed cavity, plus ink markings -- "Disney Copyright 1940 (or 41) Vernon Kilns U.S.A." The last digit(s) in the Tomart number is (are) identical to the number incised on Vernon Kilns figures, bowls and vases.

V3001-V3006	Satyrs, 4-1/2", each different	55 - 120
V3007-V3012	Sprites, standing, each different	65 - 140
V3008	Reclining Sprite	80 - 200
V3013	Unicorn, black w/yellow horn	80 - 195
V3014	Sitting Unicorn, 5"	130 - 250
V3015	Rearing Unicorn, 6"	145 - 295
V3016	Donkey Unicorn, 5-1/2"	155 - 310

V3017	Reclining Centaurette, 5-1/2"	200 - 450
V3018	Centaurette, 7-1/2"	300 - 600
V3019	Baby Pegasus, black, 4-1/2"	80 - 195
V3020	White Pegasus, head turned, 5"	80 - 195
V3021	White Pegasus, 5-1/2"	80 - 195
V3022	Centaurette, 7-1/2"	300 - 600
V3023	Nubian Centaurette, 8"	250 - 550
V3024	Nubian Centaurette, 7-1/2"	235 - 525
V3025	Elephant, 5"	150 - 300
V3026	Elephant, trunk raised	170 - 345
V3027	Elephant, dancing, 5-1/2"	160 - 320
V3028	Ostrich, 6"	350 - 700
V3029	Ostrich, 8"	350 - 700
V3030	Ostrich, 9"	400 - 800
V3031	Centaur, 10"	500 - 1,000
V3032	Hippo, arm outstretched, 5-1/2"	200 - 450
V3033	Hippo	150 - 325
V3034	Hippo, 5"	150 - 325
V3035-V3036	Hop Low Mushroom Salt & Pepper Set	75 - 115
V3037	Baby Weems	225 - 500
V3038	Timothy Mouse	95 - 185
V3039	Crow	450 - 950
V3040	Dumbo, falling on his ear	50 - 100
V3041	Dumbo, standing	65 - 120
V3042	Mr. Stork	600 - 1,100

(Higher values on bowls and vases are for hand painted rather than solid colors)

V3120	Mushroom Bowl	55 - 125
V3121	Goldfish Bowl	120 - 250
V3122	Winged Nymph Bowl	75 - 175
V3123	Winged Nymph Vase	100 - 200
V3124	Satyr Bowl	75 - 165
V3125	Sprite Bowl	90 - 155
V3126	Goddess Vase	100 - 350
V3127	Pegasus Vase	200 - 400

There were two basic designs to Vernon Kilns china dinnerware plate patterns -- a border and a full plate design. The teapot, cream and sugar and salt and pepper are particularly attractive pieces in the set. Asking prices on dinnerware are 30 - 50 per large plate up to several hundred for a teapot, cream and sugar set in the most sought after patterns. The author has firsthand knowledge of only one dinnerware sale -- four dinner plates for 30 each and a complete service for 8 for 1500.

W1900 WALT DISNEY WORLD

"The Florida Project" was planned, designed and implemented under tight security to avoid an onrush of land speculators like those who choked off Disneyland. On Oct 25, 1965 Walt Disney announced the company had purchased nearly 44 square miles of orange groves and swamp land near Orlando, Florida. Walt died a year later, but Walt Disney World opened as scheduled on Oct 1, 1971. On Oct 25, 1971 Roy Disney formally dedicated the new venture to his brother, the entire Disney organization, and all in the world who seek "a Magic Kingdom where the young at heart of all ages can laugh and play and learn -- together." In the first 10 years over $750 million was spent on construction. In addition to the Magic Kingdom, the original complex included three Disney hotel resorts -- the Contemporary, Polynesian and Golf Resort (since renamed the Disney Inn). The original plan also included the Asian, Persian and Venetian hotels (never built); Fort Wilderness Campgrounds; Treasure Island (a zoo and aviary since renamed Discovery Island); River Country swimming resort and the city of Lake Buena Vista with major hotels, shopping center, condominiums, "treehouses", offices, recreation and restaurants. The Grand Floridian Beach Resort Hotel opened in 1988 on the site planned for the Asian Resort Hotel.

EPCOT Center is also on the property, as is the Disney/MGM Studios Theme Park, Pleasure Island and Typhoon Lagoon separate gated attractions. Each segment of Walt Disney World generates an ever changing flow of souvenirs and collectibles. Even operating supplies are intriguing as they change from one promotion to the next. Much of the merchandise is listed at various classifications throughout Tomart's Disneyana. The items listed here are an example of the items exclusively connected with the "World" and its operation.

Walt Disney World's Magic Kingdom has been slow to expand since the opening of EPCOT Center. Special events have been the main focus. The Gift Giver promotion was moved from Disneyland for the park's 15th year celebration and the 15-year logo was merchandised through-out the park. Mickey's Birthdayland was created for Mickey's 60th birthday in 1988 and was widely merchandised.

W1905	Preview Edition, souvenir book	5-25
W1910	The Story of Walt Disney World, commemor- ative edition	5-15
W1911	A Pictorial Souvenir of Walt Disney World, 1972-76	5-15
W1914	Liberty Square Declaration of Independence, given to children who joined fife & drum corps for Liberty ceremony	10 - 35
W1915	Convention Pop-up Brochure	5-15
W1916	Haunted Mansion Souvenir Tombstone	4-12
W1920	Hotel Newspapers, 1971 or 1972, each	3-10
W1921	Hotel Newspapers, 1973-79, each	2 - 6
W1922	Hotel Newspapers, 1980-84, each	2 - 4
W1923	Hotel Newspapers, 1985-87, each	1 - 3

W1930	GAF Complementary Guidebooks, each	2-10
W1931	Kodak Sponsored Guidebooks, each	1-5
W1940	Expanded Guidebooks for Hotel Guests, each	2-10
W1950	Operating Supplies, such as paper or plastic bags, cups, plates, food wraps or containers, film processing envelopes, hotel supplies, or other disposables, each	1-5
W1951	Operating Supplies, 15th year, each	1-3
W1952	Illustrated Dixie Crystal Sugar Bags, each	1-2
W1953	Fun Meal Box	1-2
W1960	Miscellaneous Informational Folders or Booklets, each	1-3
W1970	Walt Disney World - A Pictorial Souvenir Booklet, 1977-82	1-5
W1971	Combination Walt Disney World/EPCOT Center Souvenir Booklets	1-4
W1975	Dial Guide to Walt Disney World, 1980	1-3
W1978	Wet Paint Sign	1-5
W1980	Pirates of the Caribbean Purse	2-4
W1981	Walt Disney World The First Decade	5-12
W1983	Steve Birnbaum Walt Disney World Guide, revised yearly since 1983	1-2
W1984	Sport Goofy Trophy Souvenir Program	1-5
W1985	Walt Disney World Information Kits	1-5
W1990	Walt Disney World Magic Magic Kingdom Map, 1971	8-20
W1991	Second Map Design, shows completed Tomorrowland, 1977	5-15
W1992	Third Map Design, includes Big Thunder, 1979	2-8
W2000	*Eyes & Ears* and Other Employee Newsletters, each	2-5
W2010	Employee Relations Information Books	5-15
W2020	Employee Relations Policy Instruction Books	5-15
W2030	15th Year History Book	5-15
W2031	"I'm a Winner" Sticker	1-2

W4100 WASHING MACHINES AND WASHTUBS

Ohio Art made litho tin laundry sets (consisting of a washtub, scrub board and clothes rack) for the Three Little Pigs and Mickey/ Minnie (smaller). The company's litho tin washing machine reportedly did a nice job on doll clothes. Precision Specialties made plastic washing machines and Modere Toys made a Donald litho automatic washer.

W4110	Laundry Sets, complete in box, Ohio Art	180 - 350
W4111	Three Little Pigs Tub & Scrub Board only	35 - 95
W4112	Mickey/Minnie Tub & Scrub Board only	50 - 120

W4115	Litho Tin Washing Machine, Ohio Art, 1935	150 - 350
W4125	Snow White or Minnie Plastic Washing Machine, Precision	25 - 55
W4130	Donald Automatic Washer	20 - 50

W4200 WATCHES

There have been well over 400 Disney character and theme park watches produced ... many in very limited editions for use as awards or special events. The variety of watches produced accelerated rapidly in 1971. Specialized collecting interest grew with the variety of time pieces. Still, the older watches maintain the greatest value. There were over 6 million of the first Mickey Mouse wristwatches made. You'll find one for sale at any good size antique toy or advertising show. Every collector wants one because it was the first. Yet few are willing to spend much on a limited edition theme park watch which is much rarer. Prices on watches vary more than other types of Disneyana. It's important the watch be working. Original boxes are more important for watches because many collectors only collect watches in the original boxes. The bands are often replaced or missing. Dirt on the face, face damage or loose hands also hurt value.

Ingersoll-Waterbury Company (W4203-W4230)
W4203	Mickey Mouse Pocket Watch	100 - 450
W4204	Mickey Mouse Wristwatch, metal band	85 - 275
W4205	Mickey Wristwatch, leather band w/metal Mickeys	85 - 285
W4207	Sterling Advertising Fob	150 - 400
W4210	Three Little Pigs & Wolf Pocket Watch & Fob	450 - 875
W4211	Three Little Pigs & Wolf Wristwatch	250 - 600
W4217	Mickey Lapel Watch, w/decal on back	200 - 450
W4218	Same as W4217, Donald is main figure	250 - 800
W4224	Rectangular Mickey Wristwatch, w/revolving Mickey second hand	100 - 225
W4225	Same as W4224, but deluxe version w/Mickey & Donald charms on band	150 - 350
W4226	Same as W4224, but regular second hand	50 - 150
W4230	Donald Duck Pocket Watch, w/Mickey decal on reverse	200 - 450

Ingersoll/U.S. Time (W4240-W4299)
W4240	Mickey, rectangular pupil eyes, 1946	55 - 125
W4241	Donald, rectangular, 1946	130 - 295
W4242	Snow White or Daisy, rectangular	130 - 250
W4242A	Snow White, round	250 - 350
W4243	Little Pig or Louie, rectangular	200 - 400
W4245	Mickey, head only, Kelton/U.S. Time	195 - 450

W4246	Mickey, round, two sizes, 1947	30 - 90
W4248	Donald, round, adult, 1947	40 - 120
W4249	In 1948 Ingersoll offered 10 different character watches w/luminous hand dials. This 20th birthday watch promotion featured Mickey, Donald, Daisy, Pluto, Bongo, Pinocchio, Jiminy Cricket, Dopey, Joe Carioca & Bambi, each	80 - 325
W4260	Mickey's 20th Birthday Watch & Pen, in cake box	300 - 600
W4261	In 1949 the same series was reoffered in special boxes that included a ballpoint pen w/Mickey or Donald decal, boxed, each	200 - 575
W4270	Danny, 1949	225 - 500
W4275	Cinderella	15 - 60
W4275A	Cinderella Wristwatch, in plastic slipper, in box	200 - 500
W7276	Alice in Wonderland	15 - 60
W4276A	Alice in Wonderland, in box w/plastic tea cup	300 - 600
W4280	Davy Crockett Wristwatch, on powder horn, in box	150 - 450
W4282	Zorro Wristwatch, name only, in hat box	150 - 350
W4283	Zorro, watch only	50 - 100
W4285	Cinderella, Snow White and Alice in Wonderland Wristwatches, w/ceramic or plastic statuettes of namesake, w/name only on watch dial, each	60 - 155
W4288	Same as W4285, except figures are plastic & image appears on each watch	60 - 155
W4299	Mickey Mouse or Donald Duck Wristwatch, no image, name only	25 - 75
W4300	Mickey Mouse, electric, 1970, Timex	150 - 300
W4301	Mickey Mouse, wind, Timex	35 - 150

Elgin National Industries/Bradley Time (W4325 - W4600)

Elgin and Bradley Time continued innovative packaging and added a lot of product excitement by reintroducing pocket watches, pendant and lapel watches, animated and digital wristwatches, plus special edition watches. The number of different watches produced since 1972 far exceed the number of Ingersoll/U.S. Time/Timex watches produced from 1933-1971. Some general price categories are provided as an introduction to the post-1971 time pieces. Individual watches are priced as information warrants.

General Guidelines

W4325	Child's Character Wristwatch, regular	15 - 95
W4350	Special Event Wristwatch	20 - 85

The Ingersoll-Waterbury Company produced the first Mickey Mouse watch in 1933. Over 6 million of the original watch were eventually produced. The second version of the wristwatch came

with a leather band. Some form of a Mickey Mouse watch has been for sale ever since. The company name was changed to U.S. Time in the mid-40s and to Timex later on. They remained the watch licensee until 1971.

W4375	Regular & Railroad Pocket Watches, each	15 - 85
W4390	Special Event Pocket Watches, each	45 - 135
W4400	Numbered Special Editions, each	30 - 150
W4425	Same as W4400, but precious metal, each	300 - 2,500
W4426	Golf Classic and other Presentation Watches	?
W4500	Animated Children's Wristwatches, each	20 - 120
W4600	Children's Plastic Play Watches, each	2 - 10

Post-1971 Watches Identified

W4302	1960's Round Dial, 1" in diameter, Mickey is holding a hat, Seiko, plastic case	--
W4303	1967-69 Round Dial, 1" in diameter w/sweep second hand, labeled "Disneyland" above figure. Made in Japan by Hamilton (Vantage) and sold only at Disneyland. There was also an electric version, and one w/a clear plastic back. The first 500 had white gloves on Mickey.	--
W4304	1968-71 Round Dial, 1" in diameter, labeled "Ingersoll/ c. WDP". Black numbers, numeral 5 on foot, some versions do not have the Ingersoll name, #160101	--
W4310	Winnie the Pooh & Honey Pot, 1969	45 - 75
W4311	1969-71 Round Dial, 17 jewel, made by Windert for sale at Disneyland, "Disneyland" above figure. Also two versions w/3/4" dial, one w/yellow point at end of its second hand, #10035/1762	--
W4315	Snow White & Dopey, 1970, heads only	35 - 70
W4316	Cinderella, bust w/castle, 1970	35 - 70
W4317	Alice in Wonderland, head in pink flowers, 1970	35 - 70
W4317	Walt Disney World Open, 1971, limited edition, electric, Helbros #408	--
W4320	Skindiver, standing Mickey, 1971, Bradley #6418	35 - 75
W4322	Pinocchio, 1971	18 - 40
W4323	Minnie Mouse, wearing hat, facing right, 1971, Timex, 1" and 3/4" version	35 - 125
W4326	Winnie the Pooh & Balloon, Winnie the Pooh w/honey	35 - 75
W4328	Mickey, small size wristwatch, numeral 6 on foot, 1972, Bradley #6801	--
W4329	Mickey, small size wristwatch, smaller Mickey figure, 1972, Bradley #6811	--
W4330	Mickey, walking, old style, shoe touches numeral 7, 1972, Bradley	20 - 45
W4333	Mickey, calendar (date), 1972, Helbros	--

238

W4334	Mickey, calendar (day-date), 1972, Helbros	30 - 65
W4335	Mickey, calendar (date), self-winding,1972, Helbros	--
W4336	Mickey, calendar (day-date), self-winding, 1972, Helbros #1-633/65392	20 - 75
W4337	Mickey, 17 jewel, 1972, Helbros	25 - 55
W4338	Mickey, electric calendar, 1972, Helbros	25 - 55
W4340	Mickey, pendant, 1972, Bradley #6826	--
W4345	Walt Disney World Open, w/Mickey, 1972, Elgin, limited edition	--
W4346	Skindiver, standing Mickey, silver face, 1972, Bradley #6824	20 - 75
W4347	Minnie Mouse, facing left, 1972, Bradley #6809	20 - 55
W4348	Minnie Mouse, wearing bow, facing right, 1972, Bradley #6822	15 - 45
W4349	Minnie Mouse, pendant watch, 1972, Bradley	25 - 75
W4351	Donald Duck, 1972, Bradley #6825	15 - 40
W4352	Cinderella, 1972, Bradley #6810	15 - 40
W4353	Alice in Wonderland, 1972, Bradley #6818	15 - 40
W4354	Goofy, 1972, Bradley	30 - 70
W4355	Winnie the Pooh, 1972, Bradley #6806	15 - 40
W4360	Goofy, 1972, Helbros, counterclockwise numerals	275 - 750
W4361	Minnie Mouse, 1972, 17 jewel, Helbros	25 - 55
W4364	Mickey, skindiver, walking old-style Mickey, 1973	20 - 60
W4365	Mickey, digital, rectangular face, 1973, #6848	25 - 75
W4366	Old-style Mickey, walking, shoe does not touch numeral 7, stem adjacent to 4, 1973, #6990	15 - 40
W4367	Old-style Mickey, walking, shoe does not touch numeral 7, stem adjacent to 3, 1973, #6808	15 - 40
W4368	Mickey Bubble Case, #6870, Mickey bubble pendant, #6870, 1973	20 - 50
W4369	Mickey Mouse Bubble Case Wristwatch	20 - 60
W4374	Mickey Walt Disney World Open, 1973, Elgin, limited edition	--
W4376	Mickey Disney 50th Anniversary, 1973, individually numbered, #6868	40 - 125
W4380	Mary Poppins, 1973, Bradley #6880	25 - 75
W4381	Walt Disney World Open, 1974, Helbros #3101/67931-S, limited edition	--
W4382	Mickey Mouse Time Teacher, blue dial, small MM head, 1974	20 - 45
W4383	Mickey Mouse, digital, round face, 1974	15 - 30

W4384 Winnie the Pooh ,digital, 1974	15 - 30
W4385 Winnie the Pooh Time Teacher, 1974, Bradley	15 - 40
W4386 Robin Hood, 1974, Bradley #6931	20 - 50
W4389 Walt Disney World Golf Classic, 1975, Elgin, limited edition	--
W3291 Mickey Mouse Club, 1975, #6646	20 - 45
W4392 Bicentennial, labelled "July 4, 1776", Mickey in Colonial garb, 1975, #6642	45 - 100
W4393 Bicentennial Pocket Watch, 1975	45 - 100
W4395 Oval Watch, old-style Mickey, 1975, #6691	25 - 60
W4398 Walt Disney World Golf Classic, 1976, Elgin, limited edition, #6641GC	--
W4401 Mickey Accutron, 1976, Bulova #6001/ T1113417	50 - 250
W4403 Redesigned Mickey from 1972 watch, larger figure, 1976, men's-#6305, ladies'-#6307	15 - 45
W4404 Minnie Mouse, wearing bow, facing right, no polka dots on skirt, 1976, Bradley #6303	15 - 50
W4405 Minnie Mouse Golf Classic Wristwatch, 1976, Elgin	--
W4408 Winnie the Pooh, 1976, Sears, 7-Jewel, revised design Pooh w/honey	20 - 65
W4409 Walt Disney World Golf Classic, 1977, 3 versions, limited edition	--
W4410 Elliott the Dragon, 1977, Bradley	15 - 45
W4412 Penny, 1977, Bradley #6676	15 - 45
W4415 Mickey, baseball, 1978, #6699	20 - 50
W4416 Mickey, football, 1978, #6701	20 - 50
W4417 Mickey, tennis, 1978, #6700	20 - 50
W4418 Mickey, basketball, 1978, #6702	20 - 50
W4420 Mickey Watch, same as 1976, but w/clear lucite case, 1978, #6317	20 - 60
W4421 Mickey Watch, same as 1976, but 7 jewels, 1978, #6695	20 - 50
W4422 Walking old-style Mickey, 7 jewels 1-1/4" face, silver bkgd., 1978	20 - 50
W4424 Mickey, moving head, 1978	20 - 55
W4428 Mickey's 50th Birthday, 1" face, round, old-style Mickey, 1978, #6506	40 - 125
W4429 Mickey's 50th Birthday, 7/8" face, round, old-style Mickey, 1978, #6507	20 - 45
W4430 Mickey's 50th Birthday, rectangular face, old-style Mickey, 1978, #6505	20 - 45
W4431 Mickey and Minnie, 1978, Bradley #6504	20 - 60
W4432 Mickey and Minnie, tennis, 1978, Bradley #6957	20 - 60

PRIDE LINES LTD.

Collectibles

Early in 1981 Walt Disney Productions licensed Pride Lines Ltd. of New York. Pride Lines was to produce a product line of high quality, nostalgia-oriented Disney collectibles. The very first Disneyana product by Pride Lines was a Mickey Mouse Mechanical Coin Bank, followed by the "Tencennial" Streetcar commemorating Walt Disney World's 10th Anniversary.

1982 saw a Minnie Mouse Coin Bank and the second in the streetcar series "Minnie and her Friends". For Christmas of 1982 Pride Lines produced its first handcar "Santa's Little Helper". Many of these early products have escalated in value due to the demand by collectors of high quality, antique-oriented, American-made Mickey Mouse memorabilia of relatively low production quantities.

Through the years Pride Lines has *reproduced* a collectors treasure or two, such as the "Mickey in the Chair" figurine of the early 1930's and the Mickey and Minnie Handcar also of the early 1930's. But, in general, the Disneyana products by Pride Lines are all unique and original, designed to coincide with a specific Walt Disney Company promotion. Most of these products are dated, some commemorative items are numbered, but *all* are produced with the same high quality and integrity by the craftsmen at Pride Lines.

1981 - 1983

PRIDE LINES LTD.

651 W. Hoffman Ave. Lindenhurst, N.Y 11757

[516] 225-0033

1986

1983

1983 – 1985

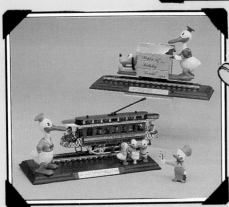

1984

1989

1987

1988

1987

1988

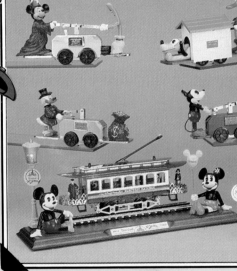

1988

1985

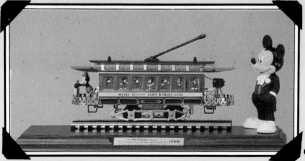

1988

© THE WALT DISNEY CO.

One of Kay Kamen's earliest achievements upon becoming the sole representative for Disney licensing in 1933 was the creation of a dairy and bakery division. These signs came from the years 1934 and 1938 demonstrating some of the colorful point-of-purchase material the Kamen art department produced to support local dairy and bakery licensees.

W4433	WDW Golf Classic, '78 National Team Championship	--
W4435	Winnie the Pooh, 1978, Sears	20 - 40
W4436	WDW Golf Classic, '79 National Team Championship	--
W4440	Animated eyes, stopwatch/counter functions, day/date display, 1980, Alba quartz, Japan, #Y728-4000 42	15 - 40
W4441	Mickey Mouse, jogger, rotating Mickey, 1980, Bradley #1255DFE4	20 - 55
W4442	"Supersize" Mickey, 1980, Bradley #1137CFR3, also available in small dial size and tank shape	25 - 70
W4443	Mickey LCD quartz, 1" face, 1980, Bradley #1094ZFE4	15 - 40
W4445	Mickey Mouse, soccer, moving foot, 1980, Bradley #1168DFE2	20 - 55
W4447	Mickey and Minnie, disco, moving heads & rim, black face, 1980, Bradley #1073DFW5	20 - 75
W4449	Mickey, oval bangle, silver, 1980, Bradley #1029F4S4, also available in round version	20 - 40
W4452	Mickey, square bangle, silver, 1980, Bradley #1120F4SF	20 - 40
W4453	WDW Golf Classic, '80 National Team Championship, Elgin	--
W4454	WDW Golf Classic, 1980 Pro-Am, Elgin	--
W4455	Mickey Tank Watch, 1980, Bradley #1138EFE2	20 - 40
W4458	1980-81 Digital Mickey, w/blinking eyes, day/date, Alba #Y744-5080	15 - 35
W4460	Disneyland 25th Anniversary, 1980, Elgin #6207 (rare - only 334 made)	150 - 500
W4461	Minnie Mouse, moving head, 3/4" face, 1980, Bradley #1570BFR4	20 - 60
W4462	Herbie Goes Bananas, 1980, Lucerne	20 - 40
W4463	Fox and the Hound, 1980, Bradley	20 - 40
W4469	Mickey, gold figure in relief, 7 jewels, stars for numbers, 1981, Bradley #0185-10300	25 - 60
W4470	WDW Golf Classic, '81 National Team Championship, Elgin	--
W4471	WDW Golf Classic Tencennial, 1981, Elgin	--
W4473	William Tell Mickey Alarm, Mickey shoots arrows at falling apples game; digital Mickey & Minnie musical alarm, Alba #Y758-5000, plays theme from "Mickey Mouse Club", Minnie's eyes wink, 1981	15 - 45

W4474	Mickey & Minnie "Valentine" Digital Musical Alarm, Alba #Y755-5000, Mickey throws kisses to Minnie, plays "Holidaya" and "Cuckoo Waltz", 1981	15 - 45
W4475	Mickey & Minnie Tennis Digital Musical Alarm & Game, Alba #Y757-5010, plays "Jambalaya" and "De Camptown Race", 1981	15 - 45
W4476	WDW Tencennial Watch, Accutron, 1981, Bulova #92154/10610 (limited edition), women's pendant version, (very limited edition)	85 - 300
W4478	Snow White, digital, 1981, Alba, musical alarm, plays "It's a Small World"	15 - 35
W4479	Chip & Dale, digital, 1981, Alba	15 - 35
W4480	Chip & Dale, 1981, Alba, green face	15 - 45
W4482	WDW Golf Classic, 1982, Elgin, quartz	--
W4485	Mickey Mouse LCD, quartz 7/8" face, 1982, Bradley #1192XFE4, Mickey is "holding" the display	15 - 25
W4486	Western Mickey, twirling lariat, western-tooled plastic band, 1982, Bradley #1233DFD4	20 - 45
W4487	Mickey & Pluto LCD, quartz, 1" face, MM is holding the display, 1982, Bradley #1191YFE4	15 - 30
W4488	Mickey & Pluto, standard movement, 7/8" face, MM is holding a bone, Pluto has a "wagging" head, 1982, Bradley #1078DFE4	20 - 55
W4489	TRON, 1982, Bradley	15 - 30
W4490	WDW Pro-Am 1982 Golf Classic, Elgin, quartz, EPCOT symbol	--
W4491	WDW Pro-Am 1982 Golf Classic, Elgin, quartz, EPCOT symbol, women's	--
W4492	Minnie Mouse LCD quartz, 1982, Bradley #1581XFR4	15 - 35
W4494	Sport Goofy, tennis, 1982, Bradley #1844DFE4	15 - 40
W4495	Sport Goofy, golf, 1982, Bradley #18430DFE4	15 - 40
W4496	Sport Goofy, soccer, 1982, Bradley #1845DFE4	15 - 40
W4501	EPCOT Center/Figment, 1982, Bradley, digital LCD, 5 function quartz, white or black band	12 - 35
W4502	EPCOT Center/Figment w/rainbow, 1982, Bradley #1396BFW4, white or black band	12 - 35
W4503	EPCOT Center, 1982, rectangular black face, gold logo & lettering, quartz movement, black leather band, Elgin #1373SB	20 - 65
W4504	EPCOT Center, same as above, women's, 1982, Elgin #1372SB	20 - 65

W4505	EPCOT Center, round brushed gold 1" face, w/black logo & lettering, stainless steel link band w/gold trim, quartz movement, 1982, Elgin #1378S4Y6	25 - 75
W4506	EPCOT Center, same as above, 3/4" face, women's, 1982, Elgin #1377S4Y4	25 - 75
W4507	EPCOT Center, quartz, round gold face w/silver Spaceship Earth, gold monorail & planters, 1-1/4" face, silver link band w/gold trim, 1982, Bradley #1384S4Y6	25 - 85
W4508	EPCOT Center, same as above, 15/16" face, women's, 1982, Bradley #1383S4Y6	25 - 85
W4509	EPCOT Center, quartz movement, gold 1-1/8" round face w/gold raised EPCOT Center logo, black leather band, 1982, Accutron	90 - 225
W4510	EPCOT Center, same as above, 3/4" face, women's, 1982, Accutron	90 - 225
W4511	50th Anniversary/MM Watch, old-style Mickey, 7/8" face, gold face, men's or ladies' version, "50 Years of Time with Mickey" inscribed on back, 1983, Bradley	40 - 125
W4512	WDW Golf Classic, quartz, 1983, Elgin	--
W4513	"The Mickey Mouse Classic Collection ", gold casing, 1-1/8" face, calendar/date, brown leather band (limited edition of 2000), 1983, Japan	25 - 75
W4514	Disney Channel Premium, Mickey as Sorcerer's Apprentice, digital, 1984	20 - 45
W4515	Baume & Mercier 14k Gold Mickey Mouse Watch, Mickey head from cartoon opening, 1-1/8" face, gold mesh band, 1984	1,700 - 3,500
W4516	Baume & Mercier 14k Gold Mickey Mouse Watch, ladies' style, Mickey head from cartoon opening, 5/8" face, gold mesh band, 1984	1,700 - 3,500
W4517	WDW Golf Classic, quartz, 1984, Elgin	--
W4519	Mickey, runner pop-up LCD, square red plastic case, 1-1/8" face, red plastic band, figure of Mickey against yellow circle background, pop-up button on face, 1984, Bradley	15 - 25
W4520	Donald Duck 50th Birthday Watch, 7/8" round face, inscribed on back: "Birthday Commemorative Edition, Donald Duck (1984)," Bradley #1603AFB3	20 - 50

W4521	Donald Duck 50th Birthday Watch, 1-1/8" round gold face, labeled on back: "Birthday Commemorative Edition, Donald Duck (1984)," Bradley #1605TBE6	35 - 100
W4522	Donald Duck 50th Birthday Watch, quartz, 13/16" round gold face, ladies', 1984, Bradley #1604SBE6	35 - 100
W4523	Donald Duck 50th Birthday Watch, Donald Duck Orange Juice promotion, 1984	5 - 20
W4525	Disneyland, gold relief of Sleeping Beauty Castle on gold face, gold band, 1-1/8" face, quartz, 1984, Seiko	30 - 90
W4526	Disneyland, 7/8", same as above, ladies' style, 1984, Seiko	30 - 90
W4527	Cinderella, quartz, LCD, 3/4" white face w/castle & Cinderella picture, light blue plastic band, 1984, Bradley	12 - 25
W4528	Disney Summer Magic 1985, Mickey against NYC skyline, Walt Disney Speciality Products	12 - 20
W4530	Disneyland 30th Anniversary, quartz, 1-1/8" white face w/rainbow-colored 30th Anniversary castle logo, 1985, Bradley	25 - 75
W4531	Disneyland 30th Anniversary, quartz, same as above, ladies', 3/4" face, 1985, Bradley	25 - 75
W4522	Disneyland 30th Anniversary, quartz, 1-1/8" gold face w/embossed Mouse ears logo, "Disneyland Thirty Years, 1955-1985", Gift-Giver machine prize, 1985, Bradley	100 - 265
W4523	Disneyland 30th Anniversary, quartz, 3/4" face, same as above, ladies' style, 1985, Bradley	100 - 265
W4524	Disneyland 30th Anniversary, quartz, gold face w/Disneyland castle logo in relief, "Disneyland" (in black letters), "30th year" (in gold relief), 1-1/8" face, 1985, Bradley	30 - 90
W4525	Disneyland 30th Anniversary, quartz, 3/4" face, same as above, ladies' style, 1985, Bradley	30 - 90
W4526	Black Cauldron, silver case, black band, 1" face, 1985, premium, Frito-Lay/"Chee-tos"	15 - 30

Lorus division of Seiko became the exclusive licensee in 1986 and showed 52 different character watches in their 1987 retail catalog.

W4528	Walt Disney World 15th Anniversary, quartz, gold face, 1-1/8" w/15th Anniversary logo, 1986, Lorus	25 - 60

W4529 Walt Disney World 15th Anniversary, quartz,
      3/4" face, same as above, ladies' style, 1986,
      Lorus   25 - 60
W4530 Captain EO/The Disney Channel Promo
      Watch, 1986, TDC promotion   12 - 25
W4531 Star Tours Inaugural Flight, January 1987,
      Disneyland, Ballanda Corp.   12 - 25
W4532 Snow White Golden Anniversary, 1987, Lorus   15 - 30

Tokyo Disneyland has also produced special watches not identical to Lorus designs sold in the U.S. Most notable of these are the press and VIP presentation watches connected to special events and the opening of new attractions. Values are 20 - 60 for commemorative products, to several hundred for the presentation watches.

W6400 WEATHER HOUSES AND VANES

The Weatherman (Chicago) 1946-53 made a plastic weather forecaster valued at 20 - 60. Always be sure the blue rooster is on top before buying. A plastic wind direction, rain and temperature unit was sold in the 70's. Value 2 - 10.

W7000 WIND-UP TOYS

Wind-up toys combine art and engineering to provoke curiosity and fascination. They are as intriguing today as they were the day they were removed from the original box. Values are naturally higher if the toy is in good working condition. Some of the earliest Disney wind-up toys were made of celluloid in Japan and imported by George Borgfeldt & Co. There were undetermined variations of these delicate toys made until 1942. There were also celluloid toys made after the War, but these had pupil rather than pie-cut eyes. Borgfeldt imported Schuco wind-ups from Germany around 1932-35. Later versions of Schuco Donald Ducks and other toys were post-war imports. Louis Marx introduced U.S. made litho tin toys in late 1937 and made wind-ups (some plastic) until the 50's. In the late 40's the Marx Import Division added litho tin wind-ups made in Japan under the name Linemar. Other makers made plastic or tin wind-ups till the mid-50's. Linemar litho tin wind-ups were made until 1961 at least. Small plastic wind-up figures made by TOMY (Japan) began turning up as theme park souvenirs around 1978. Five fingered Mickey with teeth litho tin wind-ups by English and German makers (c. 1929-31) W7002-W7020. Some were imported by Borgfeldt, some not.

W7002 Mickey Mouse Slate Dancer   3,500 - 8,000
W7004 Mickey & Minnie on motorcycle   4,500 - 10,000
W7005 Mickey Mouse Musical Band   2,000 - 4,800
W7007 Mickey Walker   2,500 - 4,500

Early celluloid and litho tin toys are some of the most desirable Disneyana collectibles.

W7008	Mickey Walker w/moving eyes	6,000 - 14,000
W7010	Mickey & Minnie Organ Grinder	2,000 - 5,000
W7012	Mickey Mouse Paddle Boat	1,800 - 5,000
W7014	Minnie pushing Felix the Cat in carriage	2,500 - 5,000
W7015	Mickey Mouse w/Felix the Cat in basket	2,000 - 4,000
W7017	Mickey & Felix lighting cigars	2,000 - 4,500
W7020	Mickey Mouse Drummer, c. 1930-31	900 - 2,000

Celluloid Wind-ups made in Japan (W7025-W7085)

W7025	Horace Horsecollar pulling Mickey	4,500 - 15,000
W7028	Mickey on celluloid Pluto w/wooden rockers	1,000 - 2,200
W7030	Pluto pulling Mickey in cart	450 - 1,400
W7031	Mickey walking Pluto	975 - 2,000
W7034	Mickey driving 3-wheel cart w/mouse	675 - 1,700
W7035	Standing Mickey Whirligig	1,300 - 3,500
W7037	Mickey Tricycle Whirligig	1,250 - 3,000
W7038	Mickey on tricycle	750 - 1,700
W7039	Mickey Trapeze I	325 - 500
W7040	Mickey Trapeze II	375 - 500
W7042	Mickey/Minnie Swing, facing each other	475 - 1,100
W7043	Mickey Walker, 6"	1,300 - 2,800
W7045	Three Little Pigs Trapeze	300 - 900
W7046	Mickey/Minnie Trapeze, both to front	600 - 1,300
W7047	Balloon Man w/toys, one is Mickey	325 - 750
W7050	Mickey on wooden rocking horse	750 - 1,800
W7052	Mickey Whirligig w/dangle characters	950 - 3,000
W7070	Long bill Donald Walker, 4-1/2"	475 - 1,100
W7071	Long bill Donald Walker, 3"	450 - 1,000
W7074	Mickey & Donald Trapeze	600 - 1,400
W7075	Long bill Donald on elephant	1,500 - 3,500
W7078	Pluto pulling long bill Donald in cart	400 - 875
W7079	Long bill Donald on tricycle	675 - 1,600
W7082	Long bill Donald Whirligig	1,200 - 3,000
W7085	Long bill Donald Whirligig w/characters	1,475 - 3,500
W7100	Tumbling Mickey, Schuco	150 - 375
W7102	Three Little Pigs playing fife, fiddle or drum, Schuco, each	225 - 550
W7103	Walking-squawking long bill Donald, Schuco, 1st version, all metal	600 - 1,200
W7110	Mickey Mouse Speedway Car, complete set	2,500 - 5,000
W7111	Individual Mickey or Donald cars for W7110, each	150 - 300
W7115	Composition Donald Walker, 1938, Borgfeldt	200 - 495
W7118	Dopey Walker, 1938, Marx	150 - 365
W7119	Ferdinand the Bull, 1939, Marx	65 - 225

Louis Marx & Company, Inc. was the leading producer of Disney tin wind-up toys from 1936 until the early 50's when focus shifted to plastic designs and tin toys from the companys import division (Linemar). These intricate litho tin mechanical toys cost only $1 or $2 and could entertain a child for hours. Today, plastic is cheaper, but the high cost of TV advertising makes the actual cost of producing the toy irrelevant.

W7120	Composition Pinocchio Walker, 1940, Borgfeldt	200 - 450
W7121	Ferdinand and Matador	275 - 650
W7122	Pinocchio Walker, 1939, Marx	125 - 345
W7123	Pinocchio the Acrobat, 1939	125 - 295
W7124	Wise Pluto, 1940, Marx	115 - 250
W7125	Roll Over Pluto, 1940, Marx	100 - 225
W7126	Roll Over Figaro, 1941, Marx	100 - 225
W7127	Bouncing Dumbo, 1941, Marx	120 - 235
W7130	Donald Duck w/plastic bill, Schuco	150 - 295
W7133	Tail wind Pluto, Marx	110 - 235
W7134	Goofy the Gardener, Marx	155 - 395
W7135	Donald Duck (and Goofy) Duet, 1946, Marx	130 - 400
W7136	Mickey Mouse Express, 1949, Marx	150 - 375
W7138	Mickey, Donald or Pluto Gym Toy Acrobat, eyes, Linemar, each	125 - 225
W7141	Walt Disney's Rocking Chair, celluloid Donald w/pupil eyes on litho tin Dumbo rocker. Activated by pulling string anchored by solid plastic Pluto, Linemar	250 - 500
W7144	Merry-go-round w/4 celluloid figures	165 - 385
W7145	Disney Parade Roadster, Marx	125 - 275
W7146	Pecos Bill Ridin' Widowmaker, Marx, plastic	95 - 225
W7148	Donald Duck & his nephews, Marx, plastic	125 - 275
W7149	Donald the Skier, Marx, plastic	200 - 450
W7150	Donald the Drummer, plastic w/metal drum, 2 sizes,Marx	100 - 275
W7160	Donald Duck, Mavco	75 - 155
W7161	Donald Duck the Gay Caballero, Mavco	75 - 155
W7162	Mickey Mouse Scooter Jockey, Mavco	85 - 155
W7165	Mickey the Musician (xylophone), no key came in the center, plastic, Marx	85 - 150
W7170	Fuzzy Walking Donald	95 - 170
W7175	Mickey w/rotating wire tail, plastic, Marx	50 - 125
W7176	Pluto w/rotating wire tail, plastic, Marx	55 - 125
W7178	Mickey w/rotating wire tail, metal, Linemar	85 - 175
W7180	Mickey's Disney Jalopy, Linemar	120 - 235
W7185	Dancing Cinderella & Prince, Irwin	40 - 95
W7188	Mechanical Donald w/rotating tail	60 - 125
W7189	Mechanical Goofy w/rotating tail	60 - 125
W7190	Mechanical Pluto w/rotating tail	60 - 125
W7191	Pluto pulling cart, Linemar	175 - 425
W7192	Mickey riding rocking horse Pluto, Linemar	350 - 700
W7194	Partying Pluto, Linemar	75 - 165
W7195	Climbing Fireman Donald, Linemar	135 - 350
W7196	Stretchy Pluto, Linemar	100 - 250
W7197	Mickey on roller skates, Linemar	450 - 900

W7200	Minnie on rocker, knitting, Linemar	110 - 245
W7204	Mickey, Pluto or Goofy on unicycle, Linemar, each	125 - 325
W7206	Big Bad Wolf Jumper, Linemar	160 - 345
W7207	Jumping Three Little Pigs, Linemar, each	160 - 335
W7214	Mickey or Donald Crazy Car, Linemar, metal figures, each	85 - 195
W7216	Mickey or Donald Crazy Car, Linemar, plastic figures, each	80 - 185
W7220	Donald Drummer, metal, Linemar	200 - 425
W7225	Remote squeeze action Donald, Pluto, Jiminy Cricket or Bambi, not wind-up, Linemar, each	55 - 165
W7245	Disneyland Ferris Wheel, Chein	110 - 250
W7246	Disneyland Roller Coaster, w/ both cars, Chein	135 - 325
W7248	Pinocchio, Toy Soldier or Ludwig Von Drake Walker, 1961, Linemar, each	80 - 195

W8000 WORLD WAR II

The bombing of Pearl Harbor had an immediate and lasting impact on the newly formed Walt Disney Productions. Hundreds of soldiers took over part of the studio for preparations. Over 1,200 military Insignias were designed gratis and regular projects were pushed aside to make training films. Cartoons and animated shorts took a new slant to support the war effort. Disney artists also designed uncounted posters, program covers for events, even holders for ration stamp books. Kids bought insignia iron-on transfers while their dads lit cigarettes with matches from Pepsi- Cola's matchbook cover series using many of the same Disney designs. There was even a trading card series. Magazine articles offer some good insight on what was going on at the studio during this period. A couple of special war publications were attempted, but were abandoned.

W8010	Insignia Designs, on transfers, matchbook covers, or trading cards, each item	1 - 6
W8015	Plate, 63rd Signal-BN-Assoc. Reunion	5 - 25
W8050	Posters, providing troop information, USO activities or a message for defense plant workers, each	5 - 50
W8075	"What is Propaganda?", booklet	4 - 20
W8076	"Winter Draws On", booklet on de-icing featuring Gremlin type Spandules"	4 - 20
W8100	Programs, with war support art, each	10 - 45
W8150	Ration Book Holder	8 - 25
W8175	Magazine Articles	2 - 10

W8200	House Organs or other World War II items	1-75
W8300	Dispatch From Disney (Vol 1, No. 1), 1943. Only issue of magazine type booklet created by the artists left at the studio to those in the service. Covers people, projects, Walt and plans for the future.	100-250

Y5000 YO-YOS

Products in this class have been made of wood, plastic and one Mickey Mouse Club version with litho tin circles inserted into a plastic housing. Value of any of these versions is around 3 - 15.

Z5000 ZORRO

Zorro offered adventure, excitement, mystery and a great identity for our own alter-egos when he first burst upon the TV screen Oct 10, 1957. He was a highly merchandised character too -- from paint sets and puzzles to an assortment of weapons and disguises such as hats, capes, masks and dry cleaning bag costumes. The program aired for two years on ABC-TV, on Walt Disney Presents, for years in syndication and on The Disney Channel in the mid-80's.

Z5010	Hat & Mask, Bailey	10 - 25
Z5011	Hat & Mask, Hatters	10 - 28
Z5012	Polo Shirt Pack w/mask & cardboard stand-up	40 - 75
Z5013	Costume & Mask, Ben Cooper	8 - 20
Z5015	Whip Set w/mask, whip, ring & lariat, Shimmel	40 - 95
Z5018	Action Set w/hat, mask, whip, lariat, pistol, 2 fencing foils & sheath knife, Marx, set	85 - 200
Z5020	Cap Pistol, Marx	20 - 65
Z5022	Target Set, 2 guns, 4 darts & target, Lido	25 - 70
Z5023	Target set, 1 gun, 3 suction cup darts, shoot guard in window, city gates open and Zorro rears up on horse, Knickerbocker	75-150
Z5024	Target Game & Water Pistol, Knickerbocker Plastic Co.	30 - 75
Z5030	Plastic Figures, Zorro on horse, Lido, 3 sizes	50 - 150
Z5034	Large Plastic Zorro on horse w/all accessories, Marx	85 - 200
Z5035	Tray or Jigsaw Puzzles, Jaymar, each	5-15
Z5036	Bookends, pair	30 - 75
Z5040	Oil Painting by Numbers, Hassenfeld	20 - 50
Z5045	Magic Paint w/water pictures, Whitman, each	3 -10
Z5060	Magic Slate Game, Strathmore	5 - 20
Z5070	School Tablet, Westab	4 - 15
Z5075	Lunch Box w/thermos, Aladdin	20 - 55

Z5080	Dry Cleaning Bag Costume, paper, Emery	10 - 30
Z5090	Coloring & Storybooks, Whitman, each	5 - 20
Z5097	Pocket Flashlight, unmasked Zorro	8 - 25
Z5098	2 in 1 Bean Bag Toss Game	35 - 75
Z5100	Zorro Game, Whitman	10 - 45

WHERE TO
BUY AND SELL

Hall Brothers of Kansas City used Mickey Mouse on Hallmark cards from 1931 to 1955 and was also licensed from 1972 to 1984. The very earliest cards are marked Hall Brothers. The Hallmark name began appearing in 1934. The company also produced the highly collectible Walt Disney Studio Christmas cards for a number of years.

WHERE TO BUY AND SELL

Everything is out there somewhere. Thousands of Disney items are found each year. Collectors find duplications or sometimes decide to sell their collections.

The best way to find items you're searching for is to contact as many dealers and collectors as possible. Ask what they have for sale or for specific items. Let them know your interest and get back in touch in a month or two.

Subscribe to the mail auctions. Watch the prices realized, where available, to determine the bids necessary to acquire items in a mail auction. Mailing a bid is usually not enough to capture a choice item. Call on the closing day to determine where your bid stands and decide if you wish to bid higher. A 10% raise over the highest bid is usually required.

The dealers and collectors listed have paid for the representation. They are some of the most active people in the buying and selling of Disneyana.

Sellers are advised to contact the individual collectors if they wish to sell an item or two at "retail." Collections can best be sold without delay to a dealer. Naturally this would be at a price where the dealer could make money.

A substantial collection might also be sold through ads in collector publications or at major toy shows.

Collector and dealer advertisers are largely known to the author. The publication reserved the right to reject any individuals with a questionable reputation. The publisher, however, cannot be responsible for any transactions between readers and advertisers. If a conflict arises, however, Tomart will contact the dealer or collector in an attempt to resolve the matter. Please contact Tomart Publications, P.O. Box 292102, Dayton, OH 45429 in the event of a problem.

The Mouse Man Ink

What you are about to read will lead you to one of the finest sources of Disney collectibles in the world.

The Mouse Man Ink publishes 6 new mail order catalogs a year with over 500 vintage Disneyana items per catalog to select from. All items have catalog numbers to match numbers in each of Tomart's DISNEYANA catalog and price guides.

Each item is accurately graded and dated to assure you of its condition prior to purchase. Each of my catalogs reflect the average current retail values of Disneyana in the United States. Each catalog carries all lines of Disney collectibles from animation art, books, toys, watches, clocks, comics, movie posters, lobby cards, figures, games, magazines, plates, china, sheet music, pinback buttons to Disneyland and Walt Disney World collectibles and more.

To get in on this action just send $1.00 for my latest catalog or $5.00 for an annual subscription of 6 catalogs to:

The Mouse Man Ink
P.O. Box 3195
Wakefield, Massachusetts 01880

This is the finest hour
for all Disneyana collectors in the world.

100% Disneyana

268

MOUSE MANIA II
- specialize in Disneyland.
Send lrg 50¢ SASE for catalog.
"Updated regularly."
Mouse Mania II
Rick Marcelino
7272 Florey St.
San Diego, CA 92122
(619) 457-2214

Buying -- Selling -- Trading
DISNEYANA
Especially vintage Disney: mint
in the box watches, wind-ups,
ephemera. Mail us your want list
or call (718) 456-5636 Also buying all other character collectibles
Rose Consoli
60-54 68th Road
Queens, NY 11385

FOR SALE: Disney buttons, pins,
plates, figurines, posters, PVCs,
books. Many unusual "special
event" items. Over 300 different
buttons, pins. $2 for illustrated
catalog. $5 overseas.
Halo
Box 2271-T
Anaheim, CA 92814

30's Disney Wanted.
Any and all. Write listing condi-
tion and price wanted.
Rebecca Trissel
4376 U.S. 127 South
Greenville, OH 45331
Not available by phone.

Buy -- Sell -- Trade
Disneyana Pins, buttons, coins,
paper & much more. LSASE for
list.
Ron Inouye
P.O. Box 3302
Gardena, CA 90247

Disney collector - seller, prefers
the early and unusual. Find a
treasure to buy or trade for, send
refundable $1 with LSASE.
Linda Kazee
P.O. Box 281
Galloway, OH 43119

Sheet music from Disney movies,
cartoons, television, and theme
parks wanted -- new as well as
old. Please send title, condition,
and price to:
Steve Pepper
4595 E. Huntington
Fresno, CA 93702

SELL OR BUY DISNEYANA
• Grolier • Schmid • Applause
• Crystal • Posters • Buttons
• Statues • Music Boxes • Stamps
• Anri • Plus much more. 260
page catalog $5.00
H & B Stern
No. Mission Road
"Porcelain Treasures"
Rd #2,
Wappingers, NY 12590
(914) 227-5848

ANIMATION ART

Lady and the Tramp (1955), set of 2 cels from "Bella Notte" sequence

Hare-Um, Scare-Um (1939), cel of early,
formative version of Bugs Bunny

WALT DISNEY
MGM
WARNER BROS.
Hanna-Barbera
Lantz
Fleischer
Ralph Bakshi
Paul Terry

Cels, Animation & Storyboard Drawings
Background Paintings, Promotional Art
from
Feature Films, Short Cartoons, and Television

CARTOONS & COMICS
P.O. Box 1694, Burbank, CA   91507

Please write or telephone for a free catalog

Bought and Sold

Fantasia (1940), cels of Ostrich and Elephant Ballerinas from "Dance of the Hours"

Snow White and the Seven Dwarfs (1937), storyboard painting of the Dwarfs' cottage

Mickey Mouse (c. 1941), storyboard painting by Milt Kahl

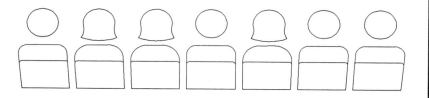
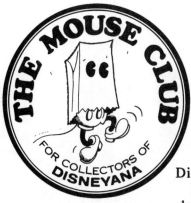

Greetings
Young America

Walt Disney

"Mickey may be the leader of the club, but **Tomart's Illustated DISNEYANA Catalog & Price Guides** are the leader of the definitive guidebooks on Disneyana"
-- Collector's Showcase Magazine

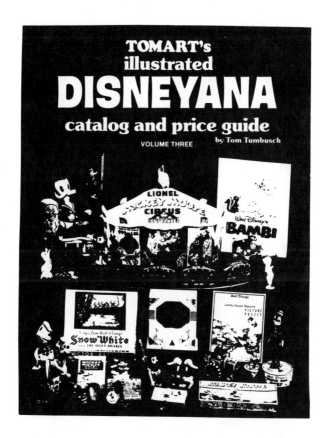

TOMART's
illustrated
DISNEYANA
catalog and price guide
VOLUME THREE by Tom Tumbusch

The Condensed Edition of Tomart's *illustrated DISNEYANA catalog and price guide* is the ideal reference for readers with an occasional need to research a popular Disney collectible. The four volume series is for avid collectors and dealers who need a definitive source to the entire field.

There are two major differences between the Condensed Edition and the larger books. The four volume series has photographic representation for most listings and inclusion of more unusual items not found or collected as frequently as those listed in the Condensed Edition.

Over 20,000 items are pictures ... 80 pages in dazzling full color. Value estimates are provided for over 40,000 Disney items. Each book in the 592 page series is crammed with valuable information.

Tomart's DISNEYANA series has become the "Bible" of Disneyana collecting. Photos of character design changes and other illustrations are used along with hundreds of dates and other facts to precisely identify any Disneyana item.

TOMART's
illustrated
DISNEYANA
catalog and price guide
VOLUME FOUR — SUPPLEMENT EDITION   by Tom Tumbusch

Each volume is 8-1/2" x 11", 144 pages, soft bound with wrap around laminated color cover. The classification system is the same as the one used in this Condensed Edition; however, there are approximately three times as many categories reported.

Volume Four contains a list of all known manufacturers licensed to use Disney characters from late 1929 to 1987. The years licensed and the products authorized are also listed.

In Tomart's DISNEYANA four volume series you will find three ways to identify any item of interest -- 1) The Disney Time Line presented in this volume, but more fully illustrated in the full size edition; 2) a photo of the item, one of over 20,000 shown in color or b&w; and 3) a manufacturer listing giving the products licensed and the years produced.

Disneyana is highly prized by over 50,000 people in the U.S. alone. No other source serves the entire field like the four volume series of Tomart's DISNEYANA.

Photocopy ONLY - Do not remove from book

ORDER FORM
Tomart Publications Book Dept.
P.O. Box 292192
Dayton, OH 45429

Enclosed is my check or money order in the amount of $_____ for the following publications:

Tomart's illustrated DISNEYANA catalog and price guide

____ Complete illustrated set -- Vol. 1--4 @ $95   _____

____ Vol. One ISBN: 0-914293-01-X only @ $24.95   _____

____ Vol. Two ISBN: 0-914293-02-8 only @ $24.95   _____

____ Vol.Three ISBN: 0-914293-03-6 only @ $24.95   _____

____ Vol. Four ISBN: 0-914293-04-4 only @ $24.95   _____

____ Condensed Edition ISBN: 0-914293-05-2 @ $19.98_____

Sub-total   _____

Ohio residents add 6-1/2% sales tax   _____

Shipping (for complete set of Vols 1--4 add $4;
          individual books add $1.95 per book)   _____
          (Outside U.S.A. extra)

Total enclosed   _____

☐ Check if books are to be autographed

Name _____

Street Address_____

City, State, Zip _____

Photocopy ONLY - Do not remove from book

Early History
of the
Character Merchandise Division

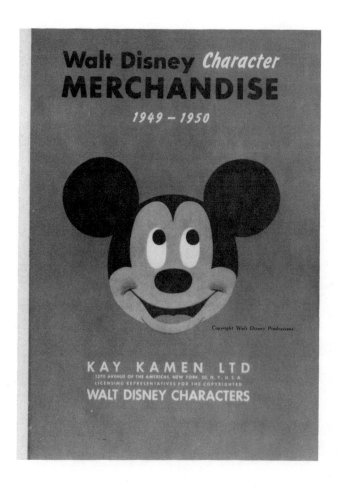

Kay Kamen and Walt Disney circa 1934

Roy Disney signed an exclusive licensing agreement with George Borgfeldt and Company in 1930. He and Walt initially viewed merchandise as a publicity tool. As the demand for licenses grew, the time it involved was distracting to film making. So Borgfeldt was signed to manufacture or sub-license a wide variety of toys, dolls, games and figures for sale in North America.

William Levy was given similar rights for the rest of the world. Working from the offices he established in London, Levy had immediate success in signing up manufacturers. Borgfeldt was much slower in getting Mickey merchandise to market and the quality of products they developed largely displeased Roy and Walt Disney.

Dissatisfaction with Borgfeldt resulted in several emergency measures to help meet demand for Mickey merchandise. Charlotte Clark, a Los Angeles seamstress, was granted a direct license to produce dolls in various sizes. Bullocks Wilshire department store was given permission to have celluloid toys, dolls, marionettes, and perhaps other products manufactured to be sold in conjunction with their name. Eventually rights were granted to the McCall Corporation to sell patterns for the Charlotte Clark doll.

The records Levy kept in London never made it to the Disney Archives, but for whatever reasons his initial success was not sustained.

Merchandising Mickey Mouse was an unrelenting problem when Walt Disney received a phone call from Herman "Kay" Kamen, a Kansas City advertising executive, in 1932. Kamen related his ideas and Disney was candid about the problems they had encountered. Walt agreed to meet with him the next time he was in California. Kay Kamen bought a ticket on the next train to California and appeared at the Hyperion Avenue studio a day and a half later.

Walt was surprised to see him so soon, but he grabbed Roy and the three men discussed Kamen's plans, the current contracts, and how they might work together. Kamen returned to the Studio at a later date with detailed plans. The immediate decision was to retain him as the Disney's representative in charge of character merchandise.

When the exclusive agreements with Borgfeldt and Levy ran out in 1933 Kay Kamen, Ltd. Incorporated was formed to act as the sole licensing representative for Disney character licensing worldwide.

Kay Kamen was a master salesman. He was born in Baltimore in 1892 which made him around 40 years old when he contacted Walt Disney. He became a hat salesman in 1918 and learned retailing. Exactly when he settled in Kansas City is undetermined, but the Kamen-Blair advertising agency was formed there in 1926.

Handsome he wasn't, but he always dressed sharp and cultivated a commanding presence. Those who knew Kamen clearly remember how polite, charming, and attentive he was.

He was a generous man. He went to bat for employees when they needed his help and slipped them extra money in a pinch. He paid the family of one valued employee full salary while he served during World

War and peace in the 1937 offices of the Kay Kamen staff art department. (Top photo-front) Henry Bausili (Back row, l to r) Lou Cunette, Fritz Mochow, Lou Lispi, John Stanley and Clarence Allen. (Bottom photo-front row) Henry Bausili, Lou Lispi and John Stanley (Back row) Lou Cunette and Fritz Mochow

War II. Favored bellboys around the country received $100 Christmas tips. There were benefits, of course. Kamen knew the worth of trusted employees. And can you imagine the reception he received in hotel lobbies around the country where he customarily arranged to meet customers and prospects?

The heart of Kay Kamen's sales pitch was a share in success ... a share in the established stature of Mickey Mouse and the unspoken promise of elegance which the persona of Kay Kamen generated.

Lou Lispi, named Kamen's art director in the early 40's, described the way his boss invited prospective licensees to participate in Mickey's success.

"An appointment would be made and Kay would personally greet the prospect in the hotel lobby where he had established a suite stocked with presentation materials. Everyone would get to know each other and perhaps have a drink in the bar. The group would return to the room where Kay would make his presentation.

"He would start out by giving a history of the Studio ... talk about Walt Disney ... and the newest Mickey Mouse film scheduled to appear in the area. He would explain the film in detail. Then he would take what he was saying about Mickey Mouse and transfer the film action and Mickey Mouse's character traits into merchandising ideas. Then he would say, 'When you see the picture - the animation and wonderful story, the action and the humor of the

Kay Kamen artists Nick Petti, Bob Brackman (instructor) and Lou Lispi at an Art Student's League of New York event in 1936.

285

Jim Forbes, Lou Lispi, Tom DeStasio, Jim Tanaka and visitor at the New York Toy Fair in the early 50's. A visitor had the option of a drawing of Mickey, Donald or himself.

gag sequences - you come out of the theater fascinated with what you saw. Then you walk into a store and pick up the Mickey Mouse you viewed on the screen - and hold it and play with it - it's an entirely different feeling - a very, very good merchandising feeling you'd get no other way.'

"I prepared layouts of the product ideas Kay was presenting. Each pastel or watercolor sketch was prepared and mounted on black paper in a newspaper size portfolio."

"He described each one in detail and then talked to them about the profits, the terms of his contract and costs. Just as the financial details were sinking in, he would tell the prospect what he would do for them. 'I will make up point-of-sale material for you. And I will share in your advertising and point of purchase material costs.'

"If I was there he'd have me explain just how we would do it. 'I will have my Art Department work out the product and package designs,' Kay would add, 'you'll have the exclusive right to make this merchandise. Nobody could make this but you.' In the end the prospect or customer was swayed by two major factors - 1) his business was going to be connected with Walt Disney's motion picture company, and 2) he was going to have sales volume greater than he ever had before. Kamen always translated Mickey Mouse into more profits for the prospect.

"He would complete his pitch with examples of the Mickey Mouse merchandise success story. Ingersoll was one of his favorite case histories on the tremendous selling power of Mickey Mouse."

There was no standardized licensing agreement before the Kamen organization was established. Borgfeldt and Levy tended to talk minimal fees and varied royalty arrangements ... whatever they felt the market would bear. There was little or no control on art or design which resulted in constant friction between the Studio and its licensees.

These problems were given top priority. A standard up front fee based on expected sales was established. Separate royalties were set for print uses, music, and dimensional products.

The only way to control the art quality was to create a staff of merchandise artists which would use Studio model sheets and other materials as guides in creating product design, packaging, and point-of-sale materials.

Roy Disney was involved in hiring early staff members. Virtually all the artists hired in the early years came from Kansas City. The Disney brothers had Kansas City ties ... as did Kay Kamen. The connection, however, wasn't the ad agency or family friendships. The link was the Kansas City Art Institute. Professors often recommended outstanding students to the Disneys. Once a few were hired, they recommended friends. New York and separation from family proved to be a problem for most and turnover was a problem with the Kansas City boys in the 30's.

William Levy, Walt Disney and Kay Kamen with U.S. Time Mickey Mouse
watch circa 1946.

Snow White and Pinocchio provided new opportunities for character
licensing, but the outbreak of World War II nearly destroyed it all. Long
time associations were severed due to material shortages. Many established licensees never returned. Staff members were drafted and, at one
point, there was only one artist.

Wood was available, but little else. Kay Kamen turned his attention to
licensing food products. Donald Duck Orange Juice was the first. Coffee,
mustard, rice and many other products followed.

Some material remained restricted until 1947 and the character
licensing operating was still regaining its strength when Kay Kamen,
along with his wife Kate, was killed in a plane crash in the Azores,
October 28, 1949.

Kay Kamen probably contributed more to the Mickey Mouse phenomenon than we'll ever know. His financial contribution to Walt
Disney's company is a matter of record ... a $30 million increase in the
retail sales of Mickey Mouse merchandise (1933-1937). It was an
irreplaceable loss and the complexion of character merchandising began
to change immediately.

O.B. Johnston joined the studio in 1934 and became the character
merchandise liaison to the Kamen organization in the early 40's. Upon

288

The New York staff with Guy Williams (Zorro) in 1957. (Front row) Phil Sammeth, Pete Smith, Guy Williams and Vince Jefferds. (Back row) Jim Tanaka, Tom DeStasio, Al Konetzni, Malcolm Decker, Lou Lispi, Tom McQuillan and Irving Handlesman.

Kamen's death it was Johnston's job to convert the Kay Kamen organization to a division of Walt Disney Productions. The office was to remain in New York, but the Studio was to have greater influence than before. The transition from management by a benevolent entrepreneur to corporate climbers proved to be a difficult period. Many licensees used to the personal support Kamen provided all the way to major buyers were disenchanted with managers who didn't have the decision making power Kamen did. Some key employees quit.

The first two division managers Johnston hired didn't last. The third was Vince Jefferds who came from TSS Seedman, a Long Island based department store chain. Jefferds, remembered more out of respect than affection, instituted many cost cutting measures. He converted artists Al Konetzni and Tom De Stasio to salesmen so they could develop concept sketches in meetings or over lunch. He tried to use more existing art from the Studio and encouraged licensees to develop the art themselves, subject to approval by the art director of the merchandise division.

In an attempt to control character quality ever tightening specifications and standards were created. Character model sheets were developed for licensee reference, but problems persisted with "unofficial" Disney art and there is a real question if such policies made or lost money for the company.

Johnston's major contribution was developing a program to permit merchandise for animated features to be manufactured and on sale in time for the film's release. Previously there was a lag of several months. This actually began in 1949. The most successful advance licensee participation was for *Lady and the Tramp* in 1955.

H.G. "Pete" Smith joined the division as a sales representative in 1950. He eventually became assistant manager and took over the New York office as Director of U.S. Licensing when Vince Jefferds moved to the Studio in 1960.

Together they guided the character merchandise division into the 1980's.

Walt Disney's last visit to the New York Merchandise Licensing office in 1965. (l to r) Lou Lispi, Pete Smith, Walt Disney, Al Konetzni, Jean Besterman and Joe Pellagrino.

Index

INDEX

This subject index provides a cross reference for the Condensed Edition of Tomart's Disneyana series. Entries found in this book are identified by the letter C in the index listing. As a convenience to owners of the larger four volume set a V1, V2, V3 or V4 notation has been provided. Information in the Condensed Edition is the latest available and supersedes all previously published data.

Baby Needs (other than playthings) - B1000-V1

Baby Rattles - B1200-V1

Baby Utensils - Silver (See Silver Cups, Plates, Bowls, Silverware & Flatware - S3500-V3 & C)

Badges (See Pinback Buttons, Pins & Badges - P1900-V2, 3, 4 & C)

Bags - Shopping (See Shopping Bags - S3450-V4; Household Goods, Products & Misc. - H6000-V2 & 4)

Baking Dishes (See Cookware & Kitchen Sets - C9150-V1)

Ball Point Pens (See Pens, Pencils & Pencil Boxes - P1300-V2 & C)

Ballantine Books (See Books—Paperback, Pocket Size - B3800-V1, 4 & C)

Balloons - B1300-V1

Balls - B1250-V1

Banjos (See Musical Instruments - M9500-V2 & 4)

Banks - B1350-V1, 4 & C

Banners (See Pennants - P1200-V2 & 4)

Bantam Books (See Books—Paperback, Pocket Size - B3800-V1, 4 & C)

Barrettes & Hair Ornaments - B1550-V1

Baseball Bats, Balls, Gloves (See Sporting Goods - S5600-V3)

Basketballs (See Sporting Goods - S5600-V3)

Bath Sponges (See Sponge Toys - S5500-V3)

Bathing Suits (See Apparel - A8000-V1 & 4)

Beachballs (See Inflatables - I5000-V2)

Bean Bag Games (See Games—Skill - G3200-V2, 4 & C)

Beds (See Furniture - F9700-V2)

Bedspreads (See Sheets, Pillows, Bedspreads & Drapes - S3400-V3)

Beetleware (See Dinnerware - Plastic - D3000-V1)

Bells - B1600-V1

Belts & Buckles - B1700-V1 (Also see Jewelry (except Rings) - J2000-V2, 4 & C)

Benches (See Furniture - F9700-V2)

Better Little Books (See Books—Big Little Books, Big Big Books, Better Little Books, Wee Little Books and Penny Books - B2600-V1, 4 & C)

Beverages (See Donald Duck Products - D8000-V2 & C; Food & Drink Products - F8500-V2 & 4)

Bibo & Lang Books (See Books—Story - B5200-V1, 4 & C)

Bibs (See Baby Needs (other than playthings) - B1000-V1)

Bicycles (See Wheel Goods—Bicycles, Wagons, Scooters, Etc. - W6500-V3)

Big Big Books (See Books—Big Little Books, Big Big Books, Better Little Books, Wee Little Books and Penny Books - B2600-V1, 4 & C)

Big Golden Books (See Books—Golden Books—Little, Big, Giant and Tiny - B3400-V1, 4 & C)

Big Little Books (See Books—Big Little Books, Big Big Books, Better Little Books, Wee Little Books and Penny Books - B2600-V1, 4 & C)

Big Tell-A-Tale Books (See Books—Story - B5200-V1, 4 & C)

Billfolds (See Wallets & Billfolds - W1500-V3)

Binders (See School Supplies - S2000-V3 & C)

Bingo Games (See Games—Other - G3500-V2 & C)

Binoculars - B1760-V1

Birthday Cards (See Cards—Greeting - C2000-V1 & 4)

Birthday Party Kits (See Party Supplies & Hats - P0600-V2)

Bisque Figures (See Figures—Porcelain Bisque - F6000-V2, 4 & C)

Blackboards & Slates - B1780-V1

Blankets (See Baby Needs (other than playthings) - B1000-V1; Sheets, Pillows, Bedspreads & Drapes - S3400-V3 & 4)

Blocks - B1800-V1 (Also see Alphabets & Numbers - A3900-V1)

Blotters - B1850-V1 & 4

Blouses (See Apparel - A8000-V1 & 4)

Blue Ribbon Books (See Books—Pop-up & Mechanical - B3900-V1 & 4; Books—Story - B5200-V1, 4 & C)

Board Games (See Games—Board - G1001-V2, 4 & C)

Boats - B1875-V1 (Also see Cars, Trucks & Airplanes - C3500-V1)

Book Bags (See School Supplies - S2000-V3 & C)

Book Plates & Bookmarks - B1900-V1 & 4

Bookends - B1880-V1

Books - B2500-V1 & C

Books - Art & Animation - B2501-V1, 4 & C

Books - Big Little Books, Big Big Books, Better Little Books, Wee Little Books and Penny Books - B2600-V1, 4 & C

Books - Coloring, Painting & Activity - B2775-V1, 4 & C

Books - Comics (See Comic Books—Newsstand - C7000-V1, 4 & C)

Books - Cut or Punch Out - B3100-V1, 4 & C

Books - Dell Fast Action - B3290-V1 & C

Books - Golden Books - Little, Big, Giant and Tiny - B3400-V1, 4 & C

Books - Linen Like - B3300-V1, 4 & C

Books - Music (See Sheet Music, Folios & Music Books - S3100-V3 & 4)

Books - Others - B6200-V1, 4 & C

Books - Paperback, Pocket Size - B3800-V1, 4 & C

Books - Pop-up & Mechanical - B3900-V1, 4 & C

Books - Reference - B4500-V1, 4 & C

Books - Scrapbooks (See Scrapbooks & Photo Albums - S2300-V3, 4 & C)

Books - Stamps & Sticker - B4700-V1, 4 & C (Also see Stickers & Sticker Books - S7000-V3 & 4)

Books - Story - B5200-V1, 4 & C

Books - Whitman Novels - B6150-V1 & C

Books & Magazines - Sponsored - B4000-V1, 4 & C

Booties (See Baby Needs (other than playthings) - B1000-V1)

Boots (See Footwear—Slippers, Socks, Shoes, Etc. - F8600-V2 & 4)

Bottle Caps (See Donald Duck Products - D8000-V2 & C; Food & Drink Products - F8500-V2 & 4; Household Goods, Products & Misc - H6000-V2 & 4)

Bottle Warmers (See Baby Needs (other than playthings) - B1000-V1)

Bottles (See Donald Duck Products - D8000-V2 & C; Food & Drink Products - F8500-V2 & 4; Household Goods, Products & Misc - H6000-V2 & 4; Milk Bottles & Collars - M6200-V2 & C)

Bow & Arrow Sets (See Games—Skill - G3200-V2, 4 & C)

Bowling Games (See Games—Skill - G3200-V2, 4 & C; Sponge Toys - S5500-V3)

Bowls (See Chinaware - C6100-V1, 4 & C; Dinnerware—Plastic - D3000-V1; Silver Cups, Plates, Bowls, Silverware & Flatware - S3500-V3 & C)

Boxes (See Tin Boxes & Containers - T4000-V3)

Boxing Gloves (See Sporting Goods - S5600-V3)

Bracelets (See Charms & Charm Bracelets - C6000-V1; Jewelry (except Rings) - J2000-V2, 4 & C)

Braytons Laguna Pottery - B6900-V1 (Also see Figures—Ceramic - F3300-V2 & C)

Bread Cards & Premiums - B7100-V1 & 4

Bread Wrappers & End Seals - B7200-V1 & 4

Briefcases (See Luggage, Briefcases, Tote Bags, Etc. - L8500-V2)

Brochures (See Auction Catalogs - A9000-V1 & 4; Books—Reference - B4500-V1, 4 & C; Disneyland - D5000-V1 & 4; EPCOT Center - #6000-V2 & 4; Euro Disneyland - E8000-V4; Merchandise Catalogs - M3900-V2 & 4; Tokyo Disneyland - T5000-V3 & 4; Walt Disney World - W1900-V3 & 4)

Brooches (See Jewelry (except Rings) - J2000-V2, 4 & C)

Brushes (See Hair Brushes, Combs & Accessories - H1700-V2)

Bubble Bath (See Soap & Bubble Bath - S5000-V3 & C)

Bubble Buster, Bubble Pipes & Bubble Makers - B8300-V1 & C

Bubble Gum Cards (See Gum Cards, Gum Wrappers & Trading Cards - G9100-V2 & 4)

Bubble Makers (See Bubble Buster, Bubble Pipes & Bubble Makers - B8300-V1 & C)

Bubble Pipes (See Bubble Buster, Bubble Pipes & Bubble Makers - B8300-V1 & C)

Buckets (See Sand Box Toys, Sand Pails & Litho Metal Shovels - S1500-V3 & C)

Buckles (See Belts & Buckles - B1700-V1; Jewelry (except Rings) - J2000-V2, 4 & C)

Bulbs - Christmas Decoration (See Christmas Tree Ornaments & Decorations - C6400-V1)

Bulbs - Light (See Christmas Lights & Shields - C6300-V1 & 4; Lamps, Lampshades & Nightlights - L1000-V2, 4 & C)

Bumper Stickers - B8700-V1

Buses (See Cars, Trucks & Airplanes - C3500-V1)

Business Cards - B8850-V1

Buttons - Clothing - B8900-V1

Buttons & Badges - Pinback (See Pinback Buttons, Pins & Badges - P1900-V2, 3, 4 & C)

Cake Pans (See Household Goods, Products & Misc. - H6000-V2 & 4)

Calculators - C0800-V1

Calendars - C1000-V1 & 4

Cameras - C1200-V1 & 4

Candles - C1400-V1

Candy, Candy Boxes & Wrappers - C1500-V1

Candy Dishes (See Chinaware - C6100-V1, 4 & C)

Candy Machines (See Candy, Candy Boxes & Wrappers - C1500-V1; Gum Ball/Candy Machines - G8900-V2)

Candy Tins (See Tin Boxes & Containers - T4000-V3)

Canes - C1560-V1 & 4

Caps (See Apparel - A8000-V1 & 4; Hats & Caps - H3000-V2 & 4)

Card Games (See Games—Card - G2000-V2, 4 & C)

Cardboard Figures (See Advertising Signs - A3000-V1 & 4; Figures—Cardboard - F2500-V2 & C)

Cards - Greeting - C2000-V1 & 4

Cards - Gum (See Gum Cards, Gum Wrappers & Trading Cards - G9100-V2 & 4)

Cards - Playing (See Games—Cards - G2000-V2, 4 & C)

Cards - Postcards (See Postcards - P6000-V3 & 4)

Carpet Sweepers (See Sweepers - S9800-V3)

Cars, Trucks & Airplanes - C3500-V1

Casting Sets & Figures - C5000-V1, 4 & C

Catalogs (See Auction Catalogs - A9000-V1 & 4; Books—Reference - B4500-V1, 4 & C; Merchandise Catalogs - M3900-V2, 4 & C)

Ceiling Globe (See Lamps, Lampshades & Nightlights - L1000-V2, 4 & C)

Celluloid Figures & Toys (See Figures—Celluloid - F3000-V2, 4 & C)

Cels (See Animation Cels & Backgrounds - A7000-V1, 4 & C)

Ceramics (See American Pottery Company - A5000-V1, 4 & C; Braytons Laguna Pottery - B6900-V1; Figures—Ceramic - F3300-V2 & C; Goebel - G5500-V2, 4 & C; Hagen-Renaker Ceramics - H1000-V2 & C; Leeds China Company - L2500-V2 & C; Evan K. Shaw - S3000-V3, 4 & C; Vernon Kilns Ceramics - V3000-V3, 4 & C)

Cereal Bowls (See Chinaware - C6100-V1, 4 & C; Dinnerware—Plastic - D3000-V1; Silver Cups, Plates, Bowls, Silverware & Flatware - S3500-V3 & C)

Cereal Box Premiums - C5400-V1

Cereal Packages & Cutouts - C5500-V1 & 4

Certificates (See Awards & Certificates - A9500-V1 & 4)

Chairs (See Furniture - F9700-V2)

Chalkboards (See Blackboards & Slates - B1780-V1)

Charms & Charm Bracelets - C6000-V1

Chests (See Furniture - F9700-V2)

Chinaware - C6100-V1, 4 & C

Chord Organs (See Musical Instruments - M9500-V2 & 4)

Christmas Cards - Corporate - C6200-V1 & 4

Christmas Cards - Other (See Cards—Greeting - C2000-V1 & 4)

Christmas Lights & Shields - C6300-V1, 4 & C

Christmas - Misc - C6510-V4

Christmas Premiums - C6335-V1

Christmas Tree Ornaments & Decorations - C6400-V1

Clay & Play Dough Sets - C6575-V1

Clocks - C6600-V1, 4 & C

Clothes Hangers - C6750-V1 & 4

Clothes Racks (See Furniture - F9700-V2)

Clothing (See Apparel - A8000-V1 & 4)

Coasters (See Ashtrays & Coasters - A8850-V1 & 4)

Coats (See Apparel - A8000-V1 & 4)

Cocomalt Books (See Books—Story - B5200-V1, 4 & C)

Coffee Cups (See Mugs - M8500-V2)

Coins & Medallions - C6800-V1 & 4

Collars, Milk Bottles (See Milk Bottles & Collars - M6200-V2 & C)

Collectors Plates (See Plates—Collectors - P3400-V3, 4 & C)

Cologne (See Perfume, Cosmetics & Toiletries - P1500-V2; Soap & Bubble Bath - S5000-V3 & C)

Colorforms - C6925-V1 (Also see Books—Others - B6200-V1, 4 & C)

Coloring Books (See Books—Coloring, Painting & Activity - B2775-V1, 4 & C)

Coloring Sets (See Crayon & Coloring Sets - C9400-V1, 4 & C)

Combs & Comb Holders (See Hair Brushes, Combs & Accessories - H1700-V2)

Comforts (See Sheets, Pillows, Bedspreads & Drapes - S3400-V3)

Comic Art - Original (See Original Comic Art - O5000-V2 & C)

Comic Book Subscription Premiums, Promotions & Acknowledgements - C7950-V1, 4 & C

Comic Books - Premium & Giveaway - C8000-V1, 4 & C

Comic Books & Digests - Newsstand - C7000-V1, 4 & C

Comic Strips (See Newspaper Comic Strips - N3000-V2 & 4)

Compacts - C8700-V1

Composition Books (See School Supplies - S2000-V3 & C)

Composition Figures (See Figures—Composition - F4700-V2 & C)

Construction Sets - C8800-V1 & 4

Containers (See Banks - B1350-V1, 4 & C; Candy, Candy Boxes & Wrappers - C1500-V1; Chinaware - C6100-V1, 4 & C; Cookie Boxes & Premiums - C8900-V1 & 4; Cookie Jars - C9000-V1, 4 & C; Fishing Tackle & Kits - F7750-V2; Flower Vases & Planters - F7900-V2 & 4; Gum Ball/Candy Machines - G8900-V2; Household Goods, Products & Misc. - H6000-V2 & 4; Lamps, Lampshades & Nightlights - L1000-V2, 4 & C; Leeds China Company - L2500-V2 & C; Lunch Boxes & Kits - L9000-V2 & C; Matches & Match Safes - M3200-V4 & C; Music Boxes - M9000-V2 & 4; Pens, Pencils & Pencil Boxes - P1300-V2 & C; Salt & Pepper Shakers - S1000-V3 & C; Sand Box Toys, Sand Pails & Litho Metal Shovels - S1500-V3 & C; Soap & Bubble Bath - S5000-V3 & C; Tin Boxes & Containers - T4000-V3; Tool Boxes & Sets - T6000-V3; Toothbrush Holders - T6400-V3 & C; Vernon Kilns Ceramics - V3000-V3, 4 & C; Washing Machines & Washtubs - W4100-V3 & C)

Cookie & Biscuit Cutters - C8925-V1

Cookie Boxes & Premiums - C8900-V1 & 4

Cookie Jars - C9000-V1, 4 & C

Cookware & Kitchen Sets - C9150-V1

Copper Tapping Kits (See Craft Sets - C9350-V1, 4 & C)

Cosmetics (See Perfume, Cosmetics & Toiletries - P1500-V2)

Costumes & Play Outfits - C9200-V1 & 4

Courvoisier Galleries (See Animation Cels & Backgrounds - A7000-V1, 4 & C; Prints—Art & Framed Pictures - P7300-V3, 4 & C)

Coveralls (See Apparel - A8000-V1 & 4)

Cozy Corner Books (See Books—Story - B5200-V1, 4 & C)

Craft Sets - C9350-V1, 4 & C

Crayon & Coloring Sets - C9400-V1, 4 & C

Creamers (See Pitchers - P3000-V3)

Creepers (See Apparel - A8000-V1 & 4)

Crib Accessories (See Baby Needs (other than playthings) - B1000-V1)

Cribs (See Furniture - F9700-V2)

Cricket Noise Makers - C9750-V1 & 4

Cross-Stitch Kits (See Sewing, Needlework, Embroidery, Etc. - S2800-V3)

Cufflinks (See Jewelry (except Rings) - J2000-V2, 4 & C)

Cups (See Mugs - M8500-V2; Silver Cups, Plates, Bowls, Silverware & Flatware - S3500-V3 & C)

Cups & Saucers (See Chinaware - C6100-V1, 4 & C; Dinnerware—Plastic - D3000-V1)

Curtains & Draperies - C9800-V1

Cut-Out Books (See Books—Cut or Punch Out - B3100-V1, 4 & C; Books - Others - B6200-V1, 4 & C)

Cut-Out Dolls (See Books—Golden Books—Little, Big, Giant and Tiny - B3400-V1, 4 & C; Dolls—Paper - D7800-V2, 4 & C)

Cutlery - Silver (See Silver Cups, Plates, Bowls, Silverware & Flatware - S3500-V3 & C)

Decals - D2000-V1 & 4 (Also see Bumper Stickers - B8700-V1)

Decoplaques (See Craft Sets - C9350-V1, 4 & C)

Decorations - Christmas (See Christmas Tree Ornaments & Decorations - C6400-V1)

Decorations - Wall Plaque (See Wall Decorations - W1000-V3; Tiles - T3500-V3)

Del Rey Books (See Books—Paperback, Pocket Size - B3800-V1, 4 & C)

Dell Books (See Books—Cut or Punch Out - B3100-V1, 4 & C; Books—Paperback, Pocket Size - B3800-V1, 4 & C; Books—Story - B5200-V1, 4 & C; Comic Books & Digests—Newsstand - C7000-V1, 4 & C)

Dell Figures (See Figures—Dell - F4850-V2)

Dental Floss (See Household Goods, Products & Misc. - H6000-V2 & 4)

Desk & Chair Sets (See Furniture - F9700-V2)

Diapers & Accessories (See Baby Needs other than playthings) - B1000-V1)

Dinnerware - China (See Chinaware - C6100-V1, 47 & C)

Dinnerware - Plastic - D3000-V1

Dishes (See Baby Needs (other than playthings) - B1000-V1; Chinaware - C6100-V1, 4 & C; Cookware & Kitchen Sets - C9150-V1; Dinnerware—Plastic - D3000-V1; Glasses—Drinking - G4000-V2 & C; Mugs - M8500-V2; Pitchers - P3000-V3; Silver Cups, Plates, Bowls, Silverware & Flatware - S3500-V3 & C; Tea Sets - T2000-V3 & C)

Disney Channel, The - D3400-V1

Disney Dollars - D3575-V4 & C

Disney Fun Pals (See Disneykins - D4000-V1, 4 & C)

Disney Magazine (See Books & Magazines—Sponsored - B4000-V1, 4 & C)

Disney Newsreel (See Employee Publications - E5000-V2 & 4)

Disney on Parade - D3700-V1

Disney Times (See Employee Publications - E5000-V2 & 4)

Disneykings (See Disneykins - D4000-V1, 4 & C)

Disneykins - D4000-V1, 4 & C

Disneyland - D5000-V1, 4 & C

Disneyland Line (See Employee Publications - E5000-V2 & 4)

Disneyland Magazine & Fun to Know - D6070-V1

Displays (See Animated & Other Store Displays - A5500-V1 & 4)

Doctor Kits (See Playsets - P3810-V3 & C)

Doll Houses - D6075-V1

Dolls - D6100-V1, 2, 4 & C

Dolls - Paper - D7800-V2, 4 & C

Dominos (See Games—Other - G3500-V2 & C)

Donald Duck Products - D8000-V2 & C

Door Stops (See Household Goods, Products & Misc. - H6000-V2 & 4)

Doubleday (See Books—Reference - B4500-V1, 4 & C; Books—Story - B5200-V1, 4 & C)

Draperies (See Curtains & Draperies - C9800-V1; Sheets, Pillows, Bedspreads & Drapes - S3400-V3)

Drawing Sets & Materials - D8500-V2, 4 & C

Dresses (See Apparel - A8000-V1 & 4)

Drinking Straws (See Straws & Pumps - S9000-V3)

Drums - D9000-V2 (Also see Musical Instruments - M9500-V2 & 4)

Dungarees (See Apparel - A8000-V1 & 4)

Dusters (See Apparel - A8000-V1 & 4)

Ears (See Mickey Mouse Ears - M5000-V2 & 4)

Earthenware Figures (See Figures—Ceramic - F3300-V2 & C)

Easter Egg Dye - Transfer & Decoration Sets - E1500-V2 & 4

Electric Games (See Games—Electric & Electronic - G2900-V2, 4 & C)

Electronic Games (See Games—Electric & Electronic - G2900-V2, 4 & C)

Embroidery (See Craft Sets - C9350-V1, 4 & C; Sewing, Needlework, Embroidery, Etc. - S2800-V3)

Employee Publications - E5000-V2 & 4

End Tables (See Furniture - F9700-V2)

Enesco (See Figures—Ceramic - F3300-V2 & C)

EPCOT Center - E6000-V2 & 4

Erasers (See Drawing Sets & Materials - D8500-V2, 4 & C)

Euro-Disneyland - E8000-V4

Eyes & Ears (See Employee Publications - E5000-V2 & 4)

Fabric - F0500-V2

Facial Tissues (See Household Goods, Products & Misc. - H6000-V2 & 4)

Fan Cards - F1000-V2 & C

Fans - F1500-V2

Feeding Sets (See Baby Needs (other than playthings) - B1000-V1; Dinnerware—Plastic - D3000-V1)

50th Birthday - Donald Duck - F1900-V2

50th Birthday - Mickey Mouse - F2000-V2 & 4

Figure Painting Kits (See Craft Sets - C9350-V1 & 4)

Figures - Bisque (See Figures—Porcelain Bisque - F6000-V2, 4 & C)

Figures - Cardboard - F2500-V2 & C

Figures - Celluloid - F3000-V2, 4 & C

Figures - Ceramic - F3300-V2 & C (Also See American Pottery Company - A5000-V1 & 4; Braytons Laguna Pottering - B6900-V1; Goebel - G5500-V2, 4 & C; Leeds China Company - L2500-V2 & C; Evan K. Shaw Co. - S3000-V3, 4 & C; Vernon Kilns Ceramics - V3000-V3, 4 & C)

Figures - Composition - F4700-V2 & C

Figures - Dell - F4850-V2

Figures - Lead (See Casting Sets & Figures - C5000-V1 & 4)

Figures - Marx (See Disneykins - D4000-V1, 4 & C; Figures—Plastic - F5500-V2, 4 & C)

Figures - Others - F7300-V2

Figures - Pewter - F5000-V2

Figures - Plastic - F5500-V2, 4 & C (Also see Disneykins - D4000-V1, 4 & C)

Figures - Porcelain (See Figures—Porcelain Bisque - F6000-V2, 4 & C; National Porcelain Co. - N2500-V2 & C)

Figures - Porcelain Bisque - F6000-V2, 4 & C

Figures - Rubber - F7000-V2, 4 & C

Figures - Vending Machine Injected Molded - F4900-V2

Figures - Wood - F7200-V2 & C

Film Promotion Materials, Misc. - F7450-V4

Film Rental & Sales Catalogs - F7580-V2

Films, Slides & Viewers - F7500-V2, 4 & C

Fire Engines (See Cars, Trucks & Airplanes - C3500-V1)

Fisher-Price Toys - F7600-V2 & C (Also see Pull Toys - P7800-V3 & C)
Fishing Tackle & Kits - F7750-V2
Flashlights - F7800-V2
Flip Movies - F8200-V2
Flour & Feed Sacks - F7885-V2
Flower Seeds (See Seeds & Bulbs - S2500-V3)
Flower Vases & Planters - F7900-V2 & 4 (Also see Chinaware - C6100-V1, 4 & C; Leeds China Company - L2500-V2 & C)
Foam blocks **& Puzzles** (See Sponge Toys - S5500-V3)
Folios - Music (See Sheet Music, Folios & Music Books - S3100-V3 & 4)
Food & Drink Products - F8500-V2 & 4 (Also see Donald Duck Products - D8000-V2 & C)
Food Warmers (See Baby Needs (other than playthings) - B1000-V1)
Footballs (See Sporting Goods - S5600-V3)
Footwear - Slippers, Socks, Shoes, Etc. - F8600-V2 & 4
Foreign Language Books (See Books—Others - B6200-V1, 4 & C)
Fountain Pens (See Pens, Pencils & Pencil Boxes - P1300-V2 & C)
Friction Toys - F9000-V2 & 4
Frisbees (See America on Parade - A4000-V1 & 4; Sporting Goods - S5600-V3)
Fun to Know (See Disneyland Magazine & Fun to Know - D6070-V1)
Furniture - F9700-V2
Games - G1000-V2 & C
Games - Board - G1001-V2, 4 & C
Games - Cards - G2000-V2, 4 & C
Games - Educational - G2500-V2 & C (Also see Alphabets & Numbers - A3900-V1)
Games - Electric & Electronic - G2900-V2, 4 & C
Games - Other - G3500-V2 & C
Games - Puzzle - G3000-V2, 4 & C
Games - Skill - G3200-V2, 4 & C
Garden City Books (See Books—Story - B5200-V1, 4 & C)
Giant Golden Book (See Books—Golden Books—Little, Big, Giant and Tiny - B3400-V1, 4 & C)
Gift Wrap (See Wrapping Paper, Ribbon & Tape - W8600-V3)
Glass Bottles (See Milk Bottles & Collars - M6200-V2 & C)
Glass Pictures (See Prints—Art & Framed Pictures - P7300-V3, 4 & C)
Glasses - Drinking - G4000-V2 & C
Glasses - Eye & Sun - G4900-V2
Globe of the World - G4980-V2 & C
Gloves & Mittens - G5000-V2
Glue (See Household Goods, Products & Misc. - H6000-V2 & 4)
Goebel - G5500-V2, 4 & C
Gold Key Books (See Comic Books & Digests—Newsstand - C7000-V1, 4 & C)
Golden Books (See Books—Golden Books—Little, Big, Giant and Tiny - B3400-V1, 4 & C)
Golden Library of Knowledge (See Books—Golden Books—Little, Big, **Giant and Tiny** - B3400-V1, 4 & C)
Golden Melody Books (See Books—Pop-up & Mechanical - B3900-V1, 4 & C)
Golden Press Books (See Books—Art & Animation - B2501-V1, 4 & C; Books—Golden Books—Little, Big, Giant and Tiny - B3400-V1, 4 & C)

Golden Star Library (See Books—Big Little Books, Big Big Books, Better Little Books, Wee Little Books & Penny Books - B2600-V1, 4 & C)

Good Housekeeping Childrens Pages - G6000-V2 & 4

Greeting Cards (See Cards—Greeting - C2000-V1 & 4)

Grolier (See Christmas Tree Ornaments & Decorations - C6400-V1; Figures—Porcelain Bisque - F6000-V2, 4 & C; Music Boxes - M9000-V2 & 4; Plates—Collectors - P3400-V3, 4 & C)

Grooming Sets (See Hair Brushes, Combs & Accessories - H1700-V2; Baby Needs (other than playthings) - B1000-V1)

Grosset & Dunlap Books (See Books—Reference - B4500-V1, 4 & C; Books—Story - B5200-V1, 4 & C)

Guidebooks (See America on Parade - A4000-V1; Disneyland - D5000-V1, 4 & C; EPCOT Center - E6000-V2 & 4; 50th Birthday—Mickey Mouse - F2000-V2 & 4; Tokyo Disneyland - T5000-V3 & 4; Walt Disney World - W1900-V3 & 4)

Guitars (See Musical Instruments - M9500-V2 & 4)

Gum Ball/Candy Machines - G8900-V2

Gum Ball Machine Prizes (See Charms & Charm Bracelets - C6000-V1)

Gum Cards, Gum Wrappers & Trading Cards - G9100-V2 & 4

Guns, Swords & Other Play Weapons - G9700-V2 & 4Hagen-Renaker Ceramics - H1000-V2 & CHair Brushes, Combs & Accessories - H1700-V2 (Also see Baby Needs (other than playthings) - B1000-V1)

Hair Ornaments (See Barrettes & Hair Ornaments - B1550-V1)

Hallmark Books (See Books—Pop-up & Mechanical - B3900-V1, 4 & C)

Hallmark Ornaments (See Christmas Tree Ornaments & Decorations - C6400-V1)

Halloween Outfits (See Costumes & Play Outfits - C9200-V1 & 4)

Handbags (See Purses & Handbags - P8500-V3; Jewelry (except Rings) - J2000-V2 & 4)

Handcars (See Trains & Handcars - T9000-V3, 4 & C)

Handkerchiefs & Hanky Books - H2100-V2

Harmonica (See Musical Instruments - M9500-V2 & 4)

Harmony Books (See Books—Reference - B4500-V1, 4 & C)

Harper Books (See Books—Story - B5200-V1, 4 & C)

Hassocks (See Furniture - F9700-V2)

Hats & Caps - H3000-V2 & 4 (Also see Baby Needs (other than playthings) - B1000-V1)

Hawthorne Books (See Books—Reference - B4500-V1, 4 & C)

Heath Books (See Books—Story - B5200-V1, 4 & C)

High Chairs (See Baby Needs (other than playthings) - B1000-V1)

Hingees (See Figures—Cardboard - F2500-V2 & C)

Hobby Horses (See Rocking Horses, Bounce, Spring Action & Other Play Equipment - R6000-V3, 4 & C)

Holt Books (See Books—Reference - B4500-V1, 4 & C)

Home Foundry (See Casting Sets & Figures - C5000-V2 & 4)

Home Movie Title Cards - H5975-V4

Horns (See Musical Instruments - M9500-V2 & 4)

Hot Dishes (See Baby Needs (other than playthings) - B1000-V1)

Housecoats (See Apparel - A8000-V1 & 4)

Household Goods, Products & Misc. - H6000-V2 & 4

Houses (See Doll Houses - D6075-V1; Play Houses, Tents, Etc. - P3800-V3)

Houseshoes (See Footwear—Slippers, Socks, Shoes, Etc. - F8600-V2 & 4)
Hummels (See Goebel - G5500-V2, 4 & C)
Ice Cream & Related Products - I1500-V2
Ice Shows - I2000-V2
Ice Skates (See Skates - S4000-V3)
Infant Needs (See Baby Needs (other than playthings) - B1000-V1)
Inflatable Furniture (See Furniture - F9700-V2)
Inflatables - I5000-V2
Ink Blotters (See Blotters - B1850-V1 & 4)
Ink Pens (See Pens, Pencils & Pencil Boxes - P1300-V2 & C)
Insignias (See Books—Stamps & Stickers - B4700-V1 & 4; Pens, Pencils & Pencil Boxes - P1300-V2 & C; World War II - W8000-V3 & 4)
Instruments (See Musical Instruments - M9500-V2 & 4)
Iron-on Appliques & Transfers - I6000-V2
Jack-in-the-Boxes - J1000-V2
Jackets (See Apparel - A8000-V1 & 4)
Jackknives (See Knives, Pocket - K5000-V2, 4 & C)
Jam Jars (See Banks - B1350-V1, 4 & C)
Jeans (See Apparel - A8000-V1 & 4)
Jewelry (except Rings) - J2000-V2, 4 & C
Jewelry Boxes (See Music Boxes - M9000-V2 & 4)
Jewelry Making (See Craft Sets - C9350-V1, 4 & C)
Jigsaw Puzzles (See Puzzles & Puzzle Sets—Jigsaw, Tray, Wood & Others - P9000-V3 & 4)
Joinies (See Figures—Cardboard - F2500-V2 & C)
KK Publications (See Books—Story - B5200-V1, 4 & C)
Kaleidoscopes - K1000-V2
Key Chains & Cases - K2000-V2 & 4
Key Rings (See Jewelry (except Rings) - J2000-V2, 4 & C)
Kitchen Sets (See Cookware & Kitchen Sets - C9150-V1; Stoves - S8500-V3 & C)
Kites - K3000-V2
Kits - Model (See Model Kits - M6500-V2 & C)
Knickerbocker (See Dolls - D6100-V1, 2, 4 & C; Figures—Composition - F4700-V2 & C)
Knives, Pocket - K5000-V2, 4 & C
Labels (See Patches & Labels - P0800-V2 & 4)
Lace Locks (See Baby Needs (other than playthings) - B1000-V1)
Lamps, Lampshades & Nightlights - L1000-V2, 4 & C
Lanterns, Magic & Lantern Slides - L2000-V2 & 4
Lap Trays (See Trays - T9200-V3 & 4)
Lapel Pins (See Jewelry (except Rings) - J2000- V2 & 4)
Lapel Watch (See Watches - W4200-V3, 4 & C)
Laundry Sets (See Washing Machines & Washtubs - W4100-V3 & C)
Lawn Decorations (See Household Goods, Products & Misc. - H6000-V2 & 4)
  Lead Figures (See Casting Sets & Figures - C5000-V1, 4 & C)
  Lead Foundries (See Casting Sets & Figures - C5000-V1, 4 & C)
Leathercraft (See Craft Sets - C9350-V1, 4 & C)
Leeds China Company - L2500-V2 & C (Also see Cookie Jars - C9000-V1, 4 & C; Flower Vases & Planters - F7900-V2 & 4; Salt & Pepper Shakers - S1000-V3 & C)
Letterheads - L4000-V2 & 4
License Plates - L4600-V2 & 4

Mickey Mouse Clubs - M4500-V2 & C
Mickey Mouse Ears - M5000-V2 & 4
Mickey Mouse Fan Club - M5100-V4
Mickey Mouse Magazines - M5400-V2 & C
Mickey Mouse Weekly - M5500-V2
Military Insignias (See Books—Stamps & Stickers - B4700-V1 & 4; Pens, Pencils and Pencil Boxes - P1300-V2 & C; World War II - W8000-V3 & 4)
Milk Bottles & Collars - M6200-V2 & C
Mirrors - M6300-V2 & C
Mittens (See Gloves & Mittens - G5000-V2)
Mobiles - M6400-V2 & 4
Model Kits - M6500-V2 & C
Money Clips (See Jewelry (except Rings) - J2000-V2, 4 & C)
Mosaics (See Craft Sets - C9350-V1, 4 & C)
Motorcycle Road Race Sets (See Cars, Trucks & Airplanes - C3500-V1)
Mousegetars (See Musical Instruments - M9500-V2 & 4)
Movie Jecktors (See Projection Equipment - P7500-V3)
Movie Posters (See Posters—Movie - P6200-V3 & C)
Movie Stills - M7000-V2 & C
Movies (See Films, Slides & Viewers - F7500-V2, 4 & C)
Mugs - M8500-V2
Multiplane Set-Ups (See Animated Cels & Backgrounds - A7000-V1, 4 & C)
Music (See Sheet Music, Folios & Music Books - S3100-V3 & 4)
Music Boxes - M9000-V2 & 4
Musical Instruments - M9500-V2 & 4
Musical Toys - M9600-V2 (Also see Baby Needs (other than playthings) - B1000-V1; Roly-Polys - R7000-V3)
Napkin Rings & Holders - N1500-V2 (Also see Silver Cups, Plates, Bowls, Silverware & Flatware - S3500-V3 & C)
Napkins (See Table Linens & Napkins - T0200-V3)
National Porcelain Company - N2500-V2 & C
Necklaces (See Charms & Charm Bracelets - C6000-V1; Jewelry (except Rings) - J2000-V2, 4 & C)
Needlework (See Sewing, Needlework, Embroidery, Etc. - S2800-V3)
Nelson Books (See Books—Story - B5200-V1, 4 & C)
Newspaper Comic Strips - N3000-V2 & 4
Nightlights (See Lamps, Lampshades & Nightlights - L1000-V2, 4 & C)
Nodders - N6500-V2 & C
Noise Makers (See Cricket Noise Makers - C9750-V1 & 4; Party Supplies & Hats - P0600-V2)
Notebook Paper (See School Supplies - S2000-V3 & C)
Notepads (See School Supplies - S2000-V3 & C; Stationery & Note Paper - S6500-V3)
Numbers (See Alphabets & Numbers - A3900-V1; Blocks - B1800-V1; Books - B2500-V1 & C; Games—Educational - G2500-V2 & C)
Nurse Kits (See Playsets - P3810-V3 & C)
Nursery Items (See Baby Needs (other than playthings) - B1000-V1)
Oil Painting (See Paint Boxes & Sets - P0400-V2, 4 & C)
Olympics - O4000-V2
Original Comic Art - O5000-V2 & C
Ornaments (See Christmas Tree Ornaments & Decorations - C6400-V1)
Oswald the Lucky Rabbit - O8000-V4 & C

Outdoor Play Equipment (See Rocking Horses, Bounce, Spring Action & Other Play Equipment - R6000-V3, 4 & C)

Overalls (See Apparel - A8000-V1 & 4)

PAAS Dye (See Easter Egg Dye—Transfer & Decoration Sets - E1500-V2 & 4)

Pacifiers (See Baby Needs (other than playthings) - B1000-V1)

Pails (See Sand Box Toys, Sand Pails & Litho Metal Shovels - S1500-V3 & C; Toys—Wood - T8500-V3)

Paint Boxes & Sets - P0400-V2, 4 & C (Also see Crayon & Coloring Sets - C9400-V1, 4 & C)

Paint-By-Number Kits (See Craft Sets - C9350-V1, 4 & C; Paint Boxes & Sets - P0400-V2, 4 & C)

Painting Books (See Books—Coloring, Painting & Activity - B2775-V1, 4 & C)

Pajamas (See Apparel - A8000-V1 & 4)

Pants (See Apparel - A8000-V1 & 4)

Paper Dolls (See Dolls—Paper - D7800-V2, 4 & C)

Paperback Books (See Books—Paperback, Pocket Size - B3800-V1, 4 & C)

Paperweights (See Bookends - B1880-V1)

Party Games (See Games—Other - G3500-V2 & C)

Party Supplies & Hats - P0600-V2

Patches & Labels - P0800-V2 & 4

Patterns - P0900-V2

Pedal Cars (See Wheel Goods—Bicycles, Wagons, Scooters, Etc. - W6500-V3)

Pen Knives (See Knives, Pocket - K5000-V2, 4 & C)

Pencil Boxes (See Pens, Pencils & Pencil Boxes - P1300-V2 & C)

Pencil Coloring Sets (See Crayon & Coloring Sets - C9400-V1, 4 & C)

Pencil Sharpeners - P1000-V2 & C

Pencils (See Drawing Sets & Materials - D8500-V2, 4 & C; Pens, Pencils & Pencil Boxes - P1300-V2 & C)

Pendant Watches (See Watches - W4200-V3, 4 & C)

Pendants (See Charms & Charm Bracelets - C6000-V1; Jewelry (except Rings) - J2000-V2, 4 & C)

Pennants - P1200-V2 & 4

Penny Books (See Books—Big Little Books, Big Big Books, Better Little Books, Wee Little Books and Penny Books - B2600-V1, 4 & C)

Pens, Pencils & Pencil Boxes - P1300-V2 & C

Percolator Sets (See Cookware & Kitchen Sets - C9150-V1)

Perfume, Cosmetics & Toiletries - P1500-V2

Petticoats (See Apparel - A8000-V1 & 4)

Pewter Figures (See Figures—Pewter - F5000-V2)

Phonographs (See Radios, Phonographs & Tape Players - R1000-V3 & C)

Photo Albums (See Scrapbooks & Photo Albums - S2300-V3, 4 & C)

Pianos (See Musical Toys - M9600-V2)

Pic-Up Sticks (See Games—Skill - G3200-V2, 4 & C)

Picture Guns (See Projection Equipment - P7500-V3)

Picture Puzzles (See Puzzles & Puzzle Sets—Jigsaw, Tray, Wood & Others - P9000-V3 & 4)

Pie Bird - P1850-V4 & C

Pillows (See Sheets, Pillows, Bedspreads & Drapes - S3400-V3)

Pin-the-Tail (See Games—Other - G3500-V2 & C)

Pinback Buttons, Pins & Badges - P1900-V2, 3, 4 & C
Pinball Games (See Games—Skill - G3200-V2, 4 & C)
Pins (See Jewelry (except Rings) - J2000-V2, 4 & C; Pinback Buttons, Pins & Badges - P1900-V2, 3, 4 & C)
Pistol & Holster Sets (See Guns, Swords & Other Play Weapons - G9700-V2 & 4)
Pitchers - P3000-V3
Placemats - P3100-V3
Planters (See Flower Vases & Planters - F7900-V2 & 4; Leeds China Company - L2500-V2 & C)
Plaster Casting Sets (See Casting Sets & Figures - C5000-V1, 4 & C)
Plastic Containers (See Household Goods, Products & Misc. - H6000-V2 & 4)
Plastic Figures (See Disneykins - D4000-V1, 4 & C; Figures—Plastic - F5500-V2, 4 & C)
Plastic Molds (See Household Goods, Products & Misc. - H6000-V2 & 4)
Plastic Toys & Novelties Misc. - P3200-V3
Plates - Collectors - P3400-V3, 4 & C
Plates - Dinnerware (See Chinaware - C6100-V1, 4 & C; Dinnerware— Plastic - D3000-V1)
Plates - Silver (See Silver Cups, Plates, Bowls, Silverware & Flatware - S3500-V3 & C)
Platters (See Trays - T9200-V3)
Play Dough (See Clay & Play Dough Sets - C6575-V1)
Play Equipment - Outdoor (See Rocking Horses, Bounce, Spring Action & Other Play Equipment - R6000-V3, 4 & C)
Play Gyms - Indoor (See Furniture - F9700-V2)
Play Houses, Tents, Etc. - P3800-V3
Play Money (See Disney Dollars - D3575-V4 & C)
Playing Cards (See Games—Card - G2000-V2, 4 & C)
Playpens (See Baby Needs (other than playthings) - B1000-V1)
Playsets - P3810-V3 & C
Plush Stuffed Characters - P4000-V3
Pocket Knives (See Knives, Pocket - K5000-V2, 4 & C)
Pocket Watches (See Watches - W4200-V3, 4 & C)
Pocketbooks (See Purses & Handbags - P8500-V3)
Pool Toys (See Inflatables - I5000-V2)
Pop-Up Books (See Books—Pop-Up & Mechanical - B3900-V1, 4 & C)
Popcorn Popper & E-Z Pop Lids - P5500-V3
Porcelain Figures (See Figures—Porcelain Bisque - F6000-V2, 4 & C; National Porcelain Co. - N2500-V2 & C)
Postage Stamps (See Stamps—Postage - S6000-V3)
Postcards - P6000-V3 & 4
Posters - Character - P6100-V3
Posters - Movie - P6200-V3 & C
Posters - Other - P6500-V3 & 4
Potties - P6800-V3
Powder (See Soap & Bubble Bath - S5000-V3 & C)
Powder Horns (See Guns, Swords & Other Play Weapons - G9700-V2 & 4)
Premiums - Misc. - P6825-V3
Press Books - Film - P7100-V3
Printing Sets - P7250-V3, 4 & C

Prints - Art & Framed Pictures - P7300-V3, 4 & C
Programs - Movies, Special Shows & Events - P7400-V3
Projection Equipment - P7500-V3
Promotional Material (See Advertising Signs - A3000-V1 & 4; Fan Cards -
  F1000-V2 & C; Film Promotion Materials, Misc - F7450-V4; Merchandise
  Catalogs - M3900-V2, 4 & C; Posters—Movie - P6200-V3 & C; Press
  Books—Film - P7100-V3; Publicity Kits - P7600-V3)
Publications - P7550-V4
Publicity Kits - P7600-V3
Pull Toys - P7800-V3 & C (Also see Fisher-Price Toys - F7600-V2 & C)
Punch Out Books (See Books—Cut or Punch Out - B3100-V1, 4 & C)
Punching Bags (See Sporting Goods - S5600-V3)
Puppets & Marionettes - P8000-V3 & 4 (Also see Bread Cards & Premiums
  - B7100-V1 & 4)
Purses & Handbags - P8500-V3 (Also see Jewelry (except Rings) - J2000-
  V2, 4 & C)
Puzzle Games (See Games—Puzzle - G3000-V2, 4 & C)
Puzzles & Puzzle Sets - Jigsaw, Tray, Wood & Others - P9000-V3 & 4
  (Also see Sponge Toys - S5500-V3)
Radios, Phonographs & Tape Players - R1000-V3 & C
Raincoats (See Apparel - A8000-V1 & 4)
Random House Books (See Books—Pop-Up & Mechanical - B3900-V1, 4
  & C; Books—Story - B5200-V1, 4 & C)
Rattles (See Baby Rattles - B1200-V1)
Receiving Blankets (See Apparel - A8000-V1 & 4, Baby Needs (other than
  playthings) - B1000-V1)
Recipes - R2800-V3
Record Players (See Radios, Phonographs & Tape Players - R1000-V3 &
  C)
Records - Phonograph - R3000-V3, 4 & C
Reference Books (See Books—Reference - B4500-V1, 4 & C)
Ribbon (See Wrapping Paper, Ribbon & Tape - W8600-V3)
Ring Toss Games (See Games—Skill - G3200-V2, 4 & C)
Rings - R5000-V3, 4 & C
Roadsters (See Cars, Trucks & Airplanes - C3500-V1)
Robes (See Apparel - A8000-V1 & 4, Baby Needs (other than playthings) -
  B1000-V1)
Rockers (See Furniture - F9700-V2)
Rocking Horses, Bounce, Spring Action & Other Play Equipment -
  R6000-V3, 4 & C
Rods & Reels (See Fishing Tackle & Kits - F7750-V2)
Roller Skates (See Skates - S4000-V3)
Roly-Polys - R7000-V3
Rolykins (See Disneykins - D4000-V1, 4 & C)
Rub-On Transfers - R8700-V3 (Also see Decals - D2000-V1 & 4; Easter
  Egg Dye—Transfer & Decoration Sets - E1500-V2 & 4; Tattoos &
  Transfers - T1500-V3)
Rubber Figures (See Figures—Rubber - F7000-V2, 4 & C)
Rubber Pants (Baby Needs (other than playthings) - B1000-V1)
Rubber Stamp Kits (Printing Sets - P7250-V2 & 4)
Rugs, Tapestries & Mats - R9000-V3 & C
Rulers (See School Supplies - S2000-V3 & C)

Rutledge Books (See Books—Art & Animation - B2501-V1, 4 & C)

Saalfield Books (See Books—Coloring, Painting & Activity - B2775-V1, 4 & C)

Sailboats (See Boats - B1875-V1)

Salt & Pepper Shakers - S1000-V3 & C

Sand Box Toys, Sand Pails & Litho Metal Shovels - S1500-V3 & C (Also see Toys—Wood - T8500-V3)

Sandwich Bags (See Household Goods, Products & Misc. - H6000-V2 & 4)

Santa Bags (See Christmas—Misc. - C6510-V4)

Saxophones (See Musical Instruments - M9500-V2 & 4)

Scarves (See Apparel - A8000-V1 & 4)

Schmid (See Christmas Tree Ornaments & Decorations - C6400-V1; Figures—Pewter - F5000-V2; Music Boxes - M9000-V2 & 4; Plates—Collectors - P3400-V3, 4 & C)

School Supplies - S2000-V3 & C (Also see Pens, Pencils & Pencil Boxes - P1300-V2 & C; Stationery and Note Paper - S6500-V3)

Scissors - S2200-V3

Scooters (See Wheel Goods—Bicycles, Wagons, Scooters, Etc. - W6500-V3)

Scrapbooks & Photo Albums - S2300-V3, 4 & C

Scrub Boards (See Washing Machines & Washtubs - W4100-V3 & C)

Seeds & Bulbs - S2500-V3

Sewing, Needlework, Embroidery, Etc. - S2800-V3

Shampoo (See Household Goods, Products & Misc. - H6000-V2 & 4; Soap & Bubble Bath - S5000-V3 & C)

Sharpeners (See Pencil Sharpeners - P1000-V2 & C)Evan K. Shaw Co. - S3000-V3, 4 & C (Also see American Pottery Company - A5000-V1, 4 & C; Cookie Jars - C9000-V1, 4 & C)

Shawls (See Apparel - A8000-V1 & 4)

Sheet Music, Folios & Music Books - S3100-V3 & 4

Sheets, Pillows, Bedspreads & Drapes - S3400-V3

Shelves (See Furniture - F9700-V2)

Shirt Boards (See Household Goods, Products & Misc. - H6000-V2 & 4)

Shirts (See Apparel - A8000-V1 & 4)

Shoe Polish (See Household Goods, Products & Misc. - H6000-V2 & 4)

Shoe Shine Kits (See Household Goods, Products & Misc. - H6000-V2 & 4)

Shoelace Locks (See Baby Needs (other than playthings) - B1000-V1)

Shoes (See Footwear—Slippers, Socks, Shoes, Etc. - F8600-V2 & 4)

Shopping Bags - S3450-V4 (Also see Household Goods, Products & Misc. - H6000-V2 & 4)

Shorts (See Apparel - A8000-V1 & 4)

Shovels (See Sand Box Toys, Sand Pails & Litho Metal Shovels - S1500-V3 & C)

Show 'N Tell (See Films, Slides & Viewers - F7500-V2, 4 & C)

Shower Curtains (See Curtains & Draperies - C9800-V1)

Shower Heads (See Household Goods, Products & Misc. - H6000-V2 & 4)

Shrink Art (See Craft Sets - C9350-V1, 4 & C)

Signs (See Advertising Signs - A3000-V1 & 4)

Silver Cups, Plates, Bowls, Silverware & Flatware - S3500-V3 & C

Simon & Schuster Books (See Books—Art & Animation - B2501-V1, 4 & C; Books—Golden Books—Little, Big, Giant and Tiny - B3400-V1, 4 & C; Books—Reference - B4500-V1, 4 & C; Books—Story - B5200-V1, 4 & C)

Skates - S4000-V3

Skirts (See Apparel - A8000-V1 & 4)

Slates (See Blackboards & Slates - B1780-V1)

Sleds - S4200-V3

Sleeping Bags (See Apparel - A8000-V1 & 4; Baby Needs (other than playthings) - B1000-V1; Sporting Goods - S5600-V3)

Slide Whistles (See Musical Instruments - M9500-V2 & 4)

Slides (See Films, Slides & Viewers - F7500-V2, 4 & C)

Slippers (See Footwear—Slippers, Socks, Shoes, Etc. - F8600-V2 & 4)

Slips (See Apparel - A8000-V1 & 4)

Slotties (See Figures—Cardboard - F2500-V2 & C)

Smocks (See Apparel - A8000-V1 & 4)

Snowsuits (See Apparel - A8000-V1 & 4; Baby Needs (other than playthings) - B1000-V1)

Soap & Bubble Bath - S5000-V3 & C

Soap Holders (See Household Goods, Products & Misc. - H6000-V2 & 4)

Socks (See Footwear—Slippers, Socks, Shoes, Etc. - F8600-V2 & 4)

Song Books (See Sheet Music, Folios & Music Books - S3100-V3 & 4)

Sparklers - S5200-V3

Spinning Tops (See Tops - T6500-V3 & C)

Sponge Toys - S5500-V3

Spoons - Silver (See Silver Cups, Plates, Bowls, Silverware & Flatware - S3500-V3 & C)

Sporting Goods - S5600-V3

Sprinkling Cans (See Sand Box Toys, Sand Pails & Litho Metal Shovels - S1500-V3 & C)

Stamp Pads (See Printing Sets - P7250-V3, 4 & C)

Stamps - Postage - S6000-V3 (Also see Books—Stamps & Sticker - B4700-V1, 4 & C)

Stamps - Poster - S6200-V3

Stationery & Note Paper - S6500-V3 (Also see School Supplies - S2000-V3 & C)

Steamboats (See Boats - B1875-V1)

Steiff Dolls (See Dolls - D6100-V1, 2, 4 & C)

Stencils (See Crayon & Coloring Sets - C9400-V1, 4 & C)

Step Stools (See Furniture - F9700-V2)

Stickers & Sticker Books - S7000-V3 & 4 (Also see Books—Stamps & Sticker - B4700-V1, 4 & C; Gum Cards, Gum Wrappers & Trading Cards - G9100-V2 & 4)

Stills - Movie (See Movie Stills - M7000-V2 & C)

Stock Certificates (See Awards & Certificates - A9500-V1 & 4)

Stockings, Christmas (See Christmas—Misc - C6510-V4)

Store Displays (See Advertising Signs - A3000-V1 & 4; Animated & Other Store Displays - A5500-V1 & 4)

Story Hour Books (See Books—Story - B5200-V1, 4 & C)

Stoves - S8500-V3 & C (Also see Cookware & Kitchen Sets - C9150-V1)

Straws & Pumps - S9000-V3

Streetcars (See Trains & Handcars - T9000-V3, 4 & C)

String Art (See Craft Sets - C9350-V1, 4 & C)

String Puppets (See Puppets & Marionettes - P8000-V3 & 4)

Strollers (See Baby Needs (other than playthings) - B1000-V1)

Stuffed Characters (See Plush Stuffed Characters - P4000-V3)

Sugar Molds (See Household Goods, Products & Misc. - H6000-V2 & 4)

Sunglasses (See Glasses—Eye & Sun - G4900-V2)

Sweater Clasps (See Jewelry (except Rings) - J2000-V2, 4 & C)

Sweatshirts (See Apparel - A8000-V1 & 4)

Sweepers - S9800-V3

Swimming Pools & Accessories - S9900-V3

Switch Plates (See Household Goods, Products & Misc. - H6000-V2 & 4)

Swords (See Guns, Swords & Other Play Weapons - G9700-V2 & 4)

T-Shirts (See Apparel - A8000-V1 & 4)

Table & Chairs (See Furniture - F9700-V2)

Table Lamps (See Lamps, Lampshades & Nightlights - L1000-V2, 4 & C)

Table Linens & Napkins - T0200-V3 (Also see Sheets, Pillows, Bedspreads & Drapes - S3400-V3)

Tablets (See School Supplies - S2000-V3 & C)

Tackle Boxes (See Fishing Tackle & Kits - F7750-V2)

Tall Books (See Books—Big Little Books, Big Big Books, Better Little Books, Wee Little Books and Penny Books - B2600-V1, 4 & C)

Tambourines (See Musical Instruments - M9500-V2 & 4)

Tape (See Wrapping Paper, Ribbon & Tape - W8600-V3)

Tape Players (See Radios, Phonographs & Tape Players - R1000-V3 & C)

Tapestries (See Rugs, Tapestries & Mats - R9000-V3 & C)

Target Sets (See Games—Skill - G3200-V2, 4 & C)

Tattoos & Transfers - T1500-V3 (Also see Easter Egg Dye—Transfer & Decoration Sets - E1500-V2 & 4; Rub-On Transfers - R8700-V3)

Tea Sets - T2000-V3 & C (Also see Chinaware - C6100-V1, 4 & C; Dinnerware—Plastic - D3000-V1)

Teethers (See Baby Needs (other than playthings) - B1000-V1)

Telephone Books (See Books—Others - B6200-V1, 4 & C)

Telephones - T2500-V3

Tell-A-Tale Books (See Books—Story - B5200-V1, 4 & C)

Tempo Books (See Books—Paperback, Pocket Size - B3800-V1, 4 & C)

Tents (See Play Houses, Tents, Etc. - P3800-V3)

Thermometers - T3000-V3

Tickets & Ticket Books (See America on Parade - A4000-V1; Disneyland - D5000-V1, 4 & C; EPCOT Center - E6000-V2 & 4)

Tiddly Winks (See Games—Skill - G3200-V2, 4 & C)

Tie Tacks & Bars (See Jewelry (except Rings) - J2000-V2, 4 & C)

Ties (See Apparel - A8000-V1 & 4)

Tiles - T3500-V3

Tin Boxes & Containers - T4000-V3

Tin Toys (See Cars, Trucks & Airplanes - C3500-V1; Construction Sets - C8700-V1 & 4; Cookware & Kitchen Sets - C9150-V1; Cricket Noise Makers - C9750-V1 & 4; Drums - D9000-V2; Figures—Celluloid - F3000-V2, 4 & C; Fishing Tacket Kits - F7750-V2; Friction Toys - F9000-V2 & 4; Sand Box Toys, Sand Pails & Litho Metal Shovels - S1500-V3 & C; Tea Sets - T2000-V3 & C; Tool Boxes & Sets - T6000-V3; Toys—Battery Operated Mechanical - T7900-V3 & C; Trains & Handcars - T9000-V3, 4 & C; Washing Machines & Washtubs - W4100-V3 & C; Wind-Up Toys - W7000-V3, 4 & C)

Tiny Movie Series Books (See Books—Golden Books—Little, Big, Giant and Tiny - B3400-V1, 4 & C)

Tiny Tales (See Books—Story - B5200-V1, 4 & C)

Tiny Tot Tales (See Books—Story - B5200-V1, 4 & C)

Toiletries (See Perfume, Cosmetics & Toiletries - P1500-V2)

Tokyo Disneyland - T5000-V3 & 4

Tool Boxes & Sets - T6000-V3

Toothbrush Holders - T6400-V3 & C

Toothbrushes & Toothpaste - T6100-V3 (Also see Baby Needs (other than playthings) - B1000-V1)

Toothpaste Dispensers (See Household Goods, Products & Misc. - H6000-V2 & 4)

Tops - T6500-V3 & C

Tote Bags (See Luggage, Briefcases, Tote Bags, Etc. - L8500-V2)

Towels - T6800-V3

Toy Chests - T6900-V3

Toys - Battery Operated Mechanical - T7900-V3 & C

Toys - Tin (See Cars, Trucks & Airplanes - C3500-V1; Construction Sets - C8700-V1 & 4; Cookware & Kitchen Sets - C9150-V1; Cricket Noise Makers - C9750-V1 & 4; Drums - D9000-V2; Figures—Celluloid - F3000-V2, 4 & C; Fishing Tackel Kits - F7750-V2; Friction Toys - F9000-V2 & 4; Sand Box Toys, Sand Pails & Litho Metal Shovels - S1500-V3 & C; Tea Sets - T2000-V3 & C; Tool Boxes & Sets - T6000-V3; Toys—Battery Operated Mechanical - T7900-V3 & C; Trains & Handcars - T9000-V3, 4 & C; Washing Machines & Washtubs - W4100-V3 & C; Wind-Up Toys - W7000-V3, 4 & C)

Toys - Wind Up (See Wind-Up Toys - W7000-V3, 4 & C)

Toys - Wood - T8500-V3 (Also see Blocks - B1800-V1)

Tractors (See Cars, Trucks & Airplanes - C3500-V1)

Trading Cards (See Gum Cards, Gum Wrappers & Trading Cards - G9100-V2 & 4)

Training Cups (See Baby Needs (other than playthings) - B1000-V1)

Training Films (See World War II - W8000-V3 & 4)

Trains & Handcars - T9000-V3, 4 & C

Transfers - Iron-On (See Decals - D2000-V1 & 4; Iron-On Appliques & Transfers - I6000-V2)

Trays - T9200-V3 & 4

Tricycles (See Wheel Goods—Bicycles, Wagons, Scooters, Etc. - W6500-V3)

Trousers (See Apparel - A8000-V1 & 4)

Tru-Vue (See Films, Slides & Viewers - F7500-V2, 4 & C)

Trucks (See Cars, Trucks & Airplanes - C3500-V1)

Tumblers (See Glasses—Drinking - G4000-V2 & C)

TV Antenna (See Household Goods, Products & Misc. - H6000-V2 & 4)

Umbrellas - U6000-V3 & 4

Underwear (See Apparel - A8000-V1 & 4)

Uniform Labels (See Patches & Labels - P0800-V2 & 4)

Utensils - Silver (See Silver Cups, Plates, Bowls, Silverware & Flatware - S3500-V3 & C)

Valentines - V1500-V3 & 4

Vases (See Chinaware - C6100-V1, 4 & C; Flower Vases & Planters - F7900-V2 & 4; Leeds China Company - L2500-V2 & C; Vernon Kilns Ceramics - V3000-V3, 4 & C)

Vernon Kilns Ceramics - V3000-V3, 4 & C

Vests (See Apparel - A8000-V1 & 4)

Viking Books (See Books—Art & Animation - B2501-V1, 4 & C)

Video Tapes & Discs - V3500-V3

View Master (See Films, Slides & Viewers - F7500-V2, 4 & C)

Wagons (See Wheel Goods—Bicycles, Wagons, Scooters, Etc. - W6500-V3)

Walkers (See Baby Needs (other than playthings) - B1000-V1)

Walking Toys - W0500-V3

Wall Clocks (See Clocks - C6600-V1, 4 & C)

Wall Decorations - W1000-V3 (Also see Tiles - T3500-V3)

Wall Hooks (See Household Goods, Products & Misc. - H6000-V2 & 4)

Wall Lamps (See Lamps, Lampshades & Nightlights - L1000-V2, 4 & C)

Wallets & Billfolds - W1500-V3

Wallpaper & Trim - W1600-V3

Walt Disney Company Annual Reports - W1700-V3

Walt Disney World - W1900-V3 & 4

War Bond Certificates (See Awards & Certificates - A9500-V1 & 4)

Warm Up Suits (See Apparel - A8000-V1 & 4)

Warming Dishes (See Baby Needs (other than playthings) - B1000-V1)

Washing Machines & Washtubs - W4100-V3 & C

Wastebaskets - W4150-V3

Watches - W4200-V3, 4 & C

Water Color Paint Books (See Books—Coloring, Painting & Activity - B2775-V1, 4 & C)

Water Color Paints (See Paint Boxes & Sets - P0400-V2, 4 & C)

Water Guns - W6300-V3

Watering Cans (See Sand Box Toys, Sand Pails & Litho Metal Shovels - S1500-V3 & C)

Weather Houses & Vanes - W6400-V3 & C

Wee Little Books (See Books—Big Little Books, Big Big Books, Better Little Books, Wee Little Books and Penny Books - B2600-V1, 4 & C)

Wheel Goods - Bicycles, Wagons, Scooters, Etc. - W6500-V3

Whistles - W7920-V4 (Also see Musical Instruments - M9500-V2)

Whitman (See Books—Big Little Books, Big Big Books, Better Little Books, Wee Little Books and Penny Books - B2600-V1, 4 & C; Books—Coloring, Painting & Activity - B2775-V1, 4 & C; Books—Cut or Punch Out - B3100-V1, 4 & C; Books—Dell Fast Action - B3290-V1 & C; Books—Linen Like - B3300-V1, 4 & C; Books—Paperback, Pocket Size - B3800-V1, 4 & C; Books—Story - B5200-V1, 4 & C; Books—Whitman Novels - B6150-V1 & C; Comic Books & Digests—Newsstand - C7000-V1, 4 & C; Dolls—Paper - D7800-V2, 4 & C; Games - G1000-V2 & C; Games—Card - G2000-V2, 4 & C)

Whitman Novels (See Books—Whitman Novels - B6150-V1 & C)

Wind Instruments (See Musical Instruments - M9500-V2 & 4)

Wind-Up Toys - W7000-V3, 4 & C

Wire Art (See Craft Sets - C9350-V1, 4 & C)

Wonder-Lab (See Playsets - P3810-V3 & C)

Wonderful World of Disney Magazine (See Books & Magazines—Sponsored - B4000-V1, 4 & C)

Wood Burning Kits (See Craft Sets - C9350-V1, 4 & C)

Wood Figures (See Figures—Wood - F7200-V2 & C)

Wood Puzzles (See Puzzles & Puzzle Sets—Jigsaw, Tray, Wood & Others - P9000-V3 & V4)

World Globes (See Globe of the World - G4980-V2 & C)

World War II - W8000-V3 & 4

Wrapping Paper, Ribbon & Tape - W8600-V3

Wristwatches (See Watches - W4200-V3, 4 & C)

Writing Paper (See School Supplies - S2000-V3 & C; Stationery & Note Paper - S6500-V3)

Xylophones (See Musical Instruments - M9500-V2 & 4)

Yard Goods (See Fabric - F0500-V2)

Yarn Holders (See Lamps, Lampshades & Nightlights - L1000-V2, 4 & C)

Yo-Yo's - Y5000-V3

Zorro - Z5000-V3, 4 & C